THE
PROJECT
MANAGEMENT
QUESTION AND
ANSWER
BOOK

THE
PROJECT
MANAGEMENT
QUESTION AND
ANSWER
BOOK

Michael W. Newell, PMP

Marina N. Grashina, PMP

AMACOM
American Management Association
New York • Atlanta • Brussels • Chicago • Mexico City • San Francisco
Shanghai • Tokyo • Toronto • Washington, D.C.

This publication is designed to provide accurate and authoritative
information in regard to the subject matter covered. It is sold with the
understanding that the publisher is not engaged in rendering legal,
accounting, or other professional service. If legal advice or other expert
assistance is required, the services of a competent professional person
should be sought.

"PMI" and the PMI logo are service marks and trademarks registered
in the United States and other nations; "PMP" and the PMP logo
are certification marks registered in the United States and other
nations; "PMBOK", "PM Network", and "PMI Today" are
trademarks registered in the United States and other nations; and
"Project Management Journal" and "Building professionalism in
project management" are trademarks of the Project Management
Institute, Inc.

Library of Congress Cataloging-in-Publication Data

Newell, Michael W., 1945–
        The project management question and answer book / Michael W. Newell,
Marina N. Grashina.
        p.   cm.
    Includes index.
    ISBN-10: 0-8144-7164-1 (pbk.)
    ISBN-13: 978-0-8144-7164-7 (pbk.)
    1. Project management.   I. Grashina, Marina N., 1970–   II. Title.

HD69.P75N493   2003
658.4'04—dc21

                                                                2003009525

Printing number

10   9   8   7   6   5   4   3   2

CONTENTS

THE PROJECT MANAGEMENT QUESTION AND ANSWER BOOK

1

Introduction

What is a project?

"A project is a temporary endeavor undertaken to provide a unique product or service." This is the definition from the 2000 edition of *The Guide to the Project Management Body of Knowledge* (PMBOK®) published by the Project Management Institute (PMI®).

Projects are different from production work because all projects have a beginning and an end. Production work is generally ongoing for long periods of time and does not have a definite starting and stopping point; many production operations take place during the course of producing goods or services. Since projects provide at least a somewhat unique product or service, they must have a beginning and an end. Production work and project work both consume resources and produce products or services. They both cost money and require planning to be done successfully.

Projects can be literally any size. A project can be designed to do something quite small, such as painting the front door on a house. Projects can also be quite large and involve thousands of people and millions of dollars. Projects can take place at any and all levels of an organization and may take place completely within a small part of the organization or include nearly all of a very large organization. The amount of time can vary from a few hours or days to several years.

Tell me more . . .

One of the reasons for the popularity of project management is the great flexibility of projects. Projects and project management can be applied to any size project, in any industry, for any product or service. This is because the methodology for managing projects is flexible and adaptable to nearly anything we might want to do. All projects will have some kind of initiating phase, planning phase, execution phase, and closeout phase. In very large or complicated projects it will take quite a bit more time to go through these phases. The phases are the same for small projects, but they will be done much more easily and quickly.

We could describe something as simple as going to the store to buy a newspaper. We begin by making the decision that we want to buy a newspaper. The decision will be based on some cost-benefit evaluation such as the answer to the question, "Will the pleasure that I get from having this newspaper be worth the cost and effort of getting it?" If the answer to this question is yes, then we have started the project and gone through the initiation phase.

Next we must do the planning of the project. To get the newspaper, we will have to decide whether we will walk to the newspaper stand or drive our car. We will have to get some money to pay for the newspaper. Will we borrow the money from one of our children's piggy banks or get it from our wallet? If we are taking the car, we will have to determine if it has gasoline in the tank and so on.

During the execution phase, we will follow the plan, going to our daughter's bedroom and getting a dollar from her piggy bank, driving the car to the newsstand, buying the newspaper, and returning home. We even have a control system. As we pass landmarks on the way to and from the newsstand, we observe where we are and take corrective actions.

Closeout of the project occurs when we put the change from the dollar we took from our daughter's piggy bank into the piggy bank and tell our spouse that we have returned with the newspaper.

We said that projects were temporary endeavors to provide a unique product or service. We should probably look into this statement a little more closely.

Temporary. All projects are going to have a beginning and an end. The end of the project is when the project's objectives have been reached or it has become clear that the project will never reach its objectives in a practical way or that the need for the project no longer exists.

We once worked on a project to computerize a chain of fast-food stores. At the time there were no personal computers and all of the computers available were magnetic core memory and worked with about one or two thousand bits of memory. This was a pretty long time ago. The project ended suddenly when Digital Equipment Corporation produced the PDP6, a breadbox-size minicomputer that was hundreds of times better, cheaper, and faster than anything else on the market. Suddenly our project was completely obsolete and immediately terminated.

The fact that all projects are temporary does not mean that the products and services they produce are temporary. There are quite a large number of bridges and buildings that have been built by projects that have been around long after the project teams have been disbanded. In fact, the concept of "life cycle cost"—a concern for costs that occur long after the project is completed and delivered to the stakeholders—is becoming important lately.

"Temporary" should not imply that projects are short. Projects can go on for many years to reach their objectives. Large civil engineering projects such as the tunnel under the English Channel or the Apollo program to put an astronaut on the moon took many years to complete.

Unique. Projects involve doing something that is unique or at least somewhat unique. If we were doing the same thing over and over again, most of the things done to complete a project would not need to be done. It would not be necessary to justify or conceptualize the nonunique endeavor, and we would not have to plan it. We could simply do what we had done in the past. You might say that we should always be trying to improve what we did in the past and that would make it unique. You would be correct. That would make it unique and require justification and planning, and that part of it might be a project.

We also might say that all projects are not completely unique from one another and this is true as well. Companies are in certain kinds of businesses because they are good at what they do. Companies that build bridges are good at building bridges, or they would not last long in the bridge-building business. Other companies are good at selling food, building computers, and so on. They all do projects that are similar to the other projects they do. Although the projects they do are similar, they are each unique from one another. Bridges have different spans and different load-carrying capacities, are built on different soils, and use modern materials—yet all suspension bridges use cables and piers.

Why do organizations do projects?

This seems to be a simple question. You might say, "My organization does projects because it is in the business of doing projects." This is to an extent correct. A "temporary endeavor undertaken to provide a unique product or service" is a good definition of what is a normal business unit for many organizations that are working, for instance, in informational technology or construction. This way of organizing a company's business allows us to manage resources reasonably and, which is more important, to keep constant focus on the client for the product, which largely increases the ability for a company to be successful.

Tell me more . . .

It is true that many organizations are either using or moving toward using a managed-by-project approach to managing company business. But even those companies whose major field of activity is manufacturing and production will face a strong need for project-oriented activities from time to time. These times occur mainly during times of change in a company. This might include a wide variety of cases, from introducing a product line to installing a new internal personnel training program. Companies need projects to be able to develop, to be flexible in answering the market, to carry out organizational structure change, to grow in size, and to conquer new markets.

All of this has given project management a new and more strategically oriented perspective. Indeed, both making a strategic decision and implementing it can be described in the framework of project management. This is a major reason why project management is becoming more widely recognized and used throughout the world.

This also has two other major consequences. The first is that many of the practices of general management, especially those related to human resources management and communications, are becoming more and more important in project management. The second is that what had initially developed as a unification of rather technically or mathematically oriented tools and techniques focused on budget and schedule control is now gaining more and more "humanitarian" features. The use of project management, first in governmental projects and then as a tool for a company's internal change, has caused the development of new approaches and tools of more qualitative character. It is hard to develop profit forecasts for implementing new management training in a company or, worse, carrying out a major program of civil service reform. We can use figures here, but to a great extent that will mean falsification of data. Instead, project management starts by using many qualitative approaches and evaluations such as project success criteria.

We will spend some time later in this book discussing the actual process of strategic change and the application of project management tools and techniques to such projects. For now, it is important to point out that project management is slowly getting outside of the scope of a technical discipline that was developed to help choose between cost, time, and quality of a project. Project management is becoming more important strategically for the company as well as for general social and economic development.

What is the project life cycle?

Once again we turn to the Project Management Institute's *Guide to the Project Management Body of Knowledge* for a definition of project management. It defines project management as "the application of knowledge, skills, tools, and techniques to project activities to meet project requirements." In the project management triangle we are concerned with the management of the project's time, cost, and scope. These concerns lead us to manage the project's quality, risk, communications, integration, schedule, performance, stakeholder needs, desires, requirements, and expectations.

It is interesting to note that when PMI changed the PMBOK to its latest version, it changed this definition from ". . . meet or exceed project requirements" to ". . . meet requirements." This is a bit of a departure from the approach of giving the customer a little something extra. In the past it was considered good practice to give the customer a little more than was asked for. The customer was thought to be pleased at getting something for nothing. Today we realize that these little extras frequently come with a price. The little extra software routine we added may have maintenance problems that the customer will have to pay for later. This is not to say that improvements and cost savings should not be brought up to the customer and discussed. It does mean, however, that we should not give customers anything extra without discussing it with them.

Any project will be managed by the five project management processes of initiating, planning, executing, controlling, and closing. These processes will be used in every phase of the project. In the beginning phases of the project we may be closing out a phase while in the next phase of the project we may just be beginning the initiation process of that phase.

Tell me more . . .

As projects grow in size, it becomes more important that they be considered in phases where each phase of the project will have a certain number of deliverables that will be a result of completing that phase. Deliverables are tangible, verifiable products of the project. These deliverables will be passed on to one of the stakeholders. A stakeholder is anyone who has something to gain or lose as a result of the completion of this project or phase. The end of a phase of a project may have a review where a decision to continue or not continue with the project is made.

The project life cycle, illustrated in Figure 1-1, begins with the project charter and ends when all of the deliverables of the project have been delivered. This includes closeout and cleanup of the project because these too are deliverables. Referring to the figure, it can be seen that projects will generally start out with a relatively small cost per day and a relatively small staff. As the project progresses, the rate of spending increases and the number of persons involved with the project increases until some peak point in spending occurs. After this peak point, the project spending decreases as more work is completed on the project and fewer people are needed. Eventually the project comes to an end, spending stops, and all of the deliverables have been delivered. As the project progresses from the beginning to the end, the total risk associated with the project decreases.

The project life cycle comprises the stages of a project from beginning to end. There are five phases that can overlap somewhat but generally take place in chronological order. They are, in order, initiating, planning, executing, controlling, and closeout. The project life cycle begins when the project first comes into existence. This usually occurs with the creation and approval of the project charter. The project ends when all of the deliverables of the project have been delivered or disposed of and all of the final paperwork, including the lessons learned document, has been completed.

In general these are the different phases in the project life cycle. Since we all live in a world of freedom, companies may choose to give

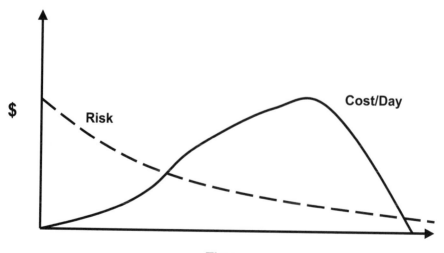

FIGURE 1-1: PROJECT LIFE CYCLE

these phases different names. If we were to consider the life cycle for the defense industry, we might have phases like concept and technology development, system development and demonstration, production, development, and support. In the construction industry we might see life cycles such as feasibility, planning and design, construction, turnover, and start-up. It is important to recognize that the life cycle for a project can be described many different ways, but we should recognize that whatever the phases are called by a particular company or industry, they will be chronological in order and the expenditures that take place in the early and late phases will be relatively less than in the middle of the project. For our discussions we will use a generic description of the phases of the life cycle: initiation, planning, execution, control, and closeout.

The probability that the project will not be completed is highest at the beginning. This means that there are many possible problems that could occur that would keep the project from being completed. As time goes by, it becomes impossible for many of these problems to occur, so the overall level of risk will decrease as the project goes on and eventually become very small toward the end of the project.

The project life cycle should not be confused with the project management processes. There are many different project phases for different projects, and the names and terms that are used in one industry can be different from those used in other industries. The project management processes—initiation, planning, execution, control, and closeout—take place in each of the project phases, and the phases of the project must use all of the project management processes. For example, in a project done in the aerospace industry we night have a project phase called "deployment." In the deployment phase of the project we would have to initiate the phase, plan it, execute it, control it, and close it out.

Some care must be used in managing the conclusion of projects. One of the outcomes of a successful project is that a strong relationship is formed between the stakeholders and the project team. Once the project is complete and the team is disbanded, it is difficult for the stakeholders to give up this relationship. If problems occur after project delivery, the stakeholder will of course contact the same person who gave such good service during the project even though he or she is now working on another project. It is important that some sort of hand-off of the stakeholders to a maintenance team be established, or project team members will become more and more involved in maintaining completed projects that they have worked on.

In many projects it may be necessary for a fixed price contract to be signed with a customer before the project initiation has been completed. This may be necessary to get the customer's business if other competitive companies are willing to do it. When this happens, it creates a risk for the project. In evaluating this risk, the probability impact and the resulting severity can be evaluated and factored into the contract even though the deliverables and perhaps even the customer's needs may not be known. By evaluating the risk associated with this contract, additional funding may be set aside and the quoted price to the customer may be adjusted.

One of the important things about the project life cycle is the rate of expenditure of funds for the project. In the beginning of the project there are relatively few people working on the project and the daily rate of expenditure is low. As the project progresses into the planning phase, the rate of expenditures increases. As project execution and control phases begin, the rate of expenditures increases still more until it reaches a maximum point where the most money per day is being spent. Once this point is passed, the rate of spending decreases. During the closeout phase the project spending decreases to zero as the project is closed.

One of the dangers in project management is that some projects never seem to close. In a good, well-managed project, the project team and the project manager establish good relations with the stakeholders. The stakeholders become familiar with the project team and are comfortable discussing problems and ideas with them. This relationship can be harmful after project completion unless a transition to an ongoing maintenance or service team is made. Stakeholders continue to contact the former project team with questions and discussions even though the project team member is now working on another project. This takes time and focus from the new project. It is important that a smooth transition be made between the project team members and the new support organization that will assist the stakeholders in the future.

What is the project management triangle or the triple constraint?

The project management triangle (Figure 1-2) is often used to illustrate that project management success is measured by the project team's ability to manage the project or part of the project so that the expected results are produced while managing time and cost.

The triple constraint is depicted as a triangle with cost, scope, and schedule as the sides of the triangle. It could be said that they contain customer satisfaction that could be considered figuratively to be the interior of the triangle since the customer should always be concerned about scope, time, and cost as well. Thus, in order to create customer satisfaction, we must perform all of the scope that was promised for the budget that we promised and deliver it when it was promised.

Tell me more . . .

The success of the project depends on the project team's ability to control the available resources of the project in terms of time, cost, and perfor-

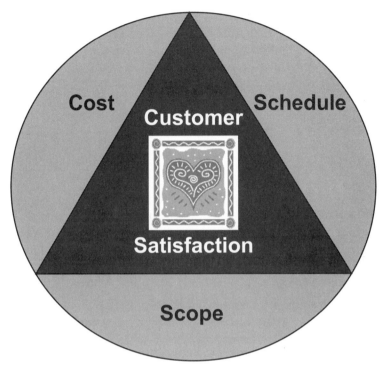

FIGURE 1-2: PROJECT MANAGEMENT TRIANGLE: THE "TRIPLE CONSTRAINT"

mance. The resources that most projects need to control are money, manpower, equipment, facilities, materials, and information.

In organizations using project management, the projects begin and end, and the project team members come and go. The resources in an organization like this must be someone's responsibility when they are not assigned to a project. These persons are the functional managers. The resources really have two managers: the project managers to whom they report when they are assigned to a project and the functional managers to whom they report when they are not assigned to a project.

The problem this creates for the project manager is that none of the people on the project team are assigned permanently to the project manager or the project. If members of the project team are dissatisfied about the progress of the project, there is a good chance they can leave the project and take another assignment. In a sense, nothing is going to get done on the project without the cooperation of the functional managers. If things go wrong on the project and the project manager needs additional resources, it will be the functional manager who juggles schedules for the resources to get the work done.

Project managers must be made responsible for the cost, schedule, and performance of the project. Many times the project manager is much more motivated to achieve high performance at the expense of cost and schedule. This is why it is important that the project manager set his or her own schedules and budgets.

This balance of the legs of a triangle is important to remember. In other words, if we or the customer want to change one of the legs, there will likely be an effect on the others. If the customer wants to shorten the schedule, we are likely to have an increase in cost or a reduction in the deliverables or both. If we add work to the project, called "scope creep," we are likely to have to increase the cost or revise the schedule or both. If the sponsor of the project wants to reduce the cost of the project, we will probably have to reduce the deliverables.

Today the customer and the stakeholders want all three and put the burden of meeting these constraints on the project manager. It then becomes the responsibility of the project manager and the project team to balance the trade-offs.

What are the project baselines?

A project has three baselines that will be used for performance and progress measurement. They are the scope baseline, the time or schedule baseline, and the cost baseline.

The *scope baseline* is the sum of the deliverables of the project. It represents all the work that must be done to complete the project. Any deliverables that are not included in the scope baseline will not be delivered to any of the stakeholders.

The *time baseline* is the schedule of all the work that will be done to produce the scope baseline. Each item of work in the schedule is an item of work that is required to produce an output that either contributes to the delivery of a deliverable or that is an input required by another scheduled task in the project. Scheduled tasks that do not contribute to the delivery of a deliverable or an input to another task should not be part of the project schedule.

The *cost baseline* is the budget of the project. A budget is the time-phased cost of all the work in the project schedule. The cost baseline does not include the contingency budget or the management reserve. The cost baseline is also called the performance baseline. Cost and schedule baselines will be discussed in the sections on cost and time management.

Tell me more . . .

Because projects are developed over time, the level of detail that is available at any point in time is changing. The establishment of all of the three project baselines is a significant point in the project and determines the end of the planning process.

In most projects the scope baseline can be established first. This is not always the case, as the total cost of the project, the budget, and even the schedule may be predetermined and the scope defined based on the time and money available. Generally, however, it is better to establish the scope of the project first and then, after the stakeholders have agreed to the scope, establish the cost and schedule.

The scope baseline is the baseline from which all changes must be made. The current scope baseline begins with the original scope baseline; all changes that are approved add or subtract from the original scope baseline. After the changes are made, a new baseline is created, which becomes the current baseline. The performance measurement system and the progress measurement system will measure performance and progress against the current baseline. The cost and schedule baselines will probably need to be adjusted each time the scope baseline is changed.

We may choose to establish the scope baseline early or late in the project. Early establishment of the scope baseline has the advantage of giving us a means of tracking changes early in the project since once the baseline is established, all changes to it must be tracked by means of an approved change notification. This is helpful for several reasons. Sometimes changes are requested over and over and are turned down as many times. Having good records of the changes requested and rejected allows these types of changes to be dealt with quickly and easily. Establishing the scope baseline early helps in showing how the project scope has grown since the early part of the project.

However, establishing the scope baseline too early in the project may prove to be costly. When the project is at an early stage in the conceptualization phase and very little of the project is defined, the cost of developing the project definition and recording all the development through the change process is unwieldy and unnecessary.

Once the scope baseline has been established, cost estimates can be made for the work and material costs that are associated with the project. It should be made clear to the stakeholders that the baselines are inclusive of the entire project. Work that is not identified in the scope baseline is not scheduled or budgeted and will not be done. Stakeholders should never assume that an item that is not specifically included in the baselines will be completed.

Who are the project stakeholders?

A stakeholder is anyone who has something to gain or lose as a result of this project. It includes all the people who have something to gain or lose by either the doing of the project or the results delivered by the project. The broadest interpretation of the stakeholder is used. This means that people we might not think of as being stakeholders in the project probably are stakeholders. All of the people on the project team are stakeholders. Suppliers to the project, outside contractors, our client, our management, and literally anyone else who has something to gain or lose is a stakeholder.

It is important for the project team to recognize all of the stakeholders. Unless we identify all the stakeholders, it will not be possible to fill their requirements, and the scope of the project will be understated. Generally the stakeholders who are not recognized will make their presence known toward the end of the project when they see that their needs have not been incorporated. These then become new requirements that have been neither funded nor scheduled.

Tell me more . . .

If we use the broadest definition of the term *stakeholder*, we will include everyone who gains or loses as a result of the project. Some of the stakeholders will be minor and will have only a small amount of involvement in the project. All of the legitimate stakeholders must be recognized and their requirements, if they have been funded and approved, incorporated into the project.

Although some of the stakeholders will play a minor role in the project, others will have a much more significant part in the project's management. These can be considered the key stakeholders. They include the project manager, the user or customer, the management of our own organization, and the sponsor.

The customer may sometimes be called the user. Customers or users are given many different names. The equivalent project manager on the customer's side is the person the project manager must satisfy when the deliverables are delivered. The people in the customer's organization who will actually use the deliverables of the project must also be considered. While the customers may not always be right, the project team must consider their needs to complete the project successfully.

The management of our own organization, as well as the other departments of the company, must also be considered. The management of our own organization may have strategic goals that this project is going to assist in accomplishing. For example, the project may be to design a new entry into the bicycle market. The project team needs to understand the company's strategic plan so that the bicycle can be designed to reach the needs of the buying customer and be consistent with the company's product line as seen in the future. The quality of the project needs to be considered as well. It may be the company's strategy to offer very cheap products at very low prices, or it may be its strategy to offer long-lasting high-priced bicycles.

The sponsor is the person or organization that pays the bills. It is the source of funding for the project. Without a sponsor, the project will not be done.

An important thing to consider is that the stakeholders of a project can be negative as well as positive. The project of moving a zoo outside of the city center can be considered as positive by all project stakeholders including the majority of population of the city except for those who work there and will now have to drive an hour extra every day to get to work. Negative stakeholders, especially in the case of a project having some social impacts, can become a very important force that needs to be considered if we want a project to succeed or even be initiated.

That also brings us to the fact that some of our stakeholders can be completely outside the scope of the project but still influence it. The trend in project management is to pay more attention and recognize more of the factors outside of the project and even outside of the company that may influence project success. This is surely important for government organizations, but it is becoming more important to private sector companies, especially those working under government contracts.

There will be many, many stakeholders in any project. It may be difficult to manage all of the needs and expectations of the stakeholders, and all of the needs and expectations of the stakeholders may not be compatible with those of the other stakeholders. Earlier we discussed a small project such as going to the newspaper stand to buy a newspaper and returning home. Let's imagine that before we left home to get the newspaper, we asked our spouse and our children if there was anything they needed from the store. Now instead of a quick trip to the newspaper stand to get the newspaper we find ourselves picking up the dry cleaning; buying a loose-leaf notebook, a liter of milk, a pound of butter, and a fashion magazine; putting gasoline in the car—oh yes, and buying the newspaper. In a construction project, the sponsor may want cost to be kept at a minimum, the user may want the most modern and beautiful building, and the engineers may want the most technologically perfect building possible.

2

Scope

What is the project charter?

The project charter is the first document that exists in the project. It causes the project to come into existence. The project charter names the project and briefly describes it. It names the project manager and causes a cost account to be opened to capture the cost of the project. Once these essential things have been done, work on the project can proceed. The project charter should be written by the project manager, but it must be issued under the signature of someone above the project manager who has the authority to make project assignments.

Tell me more . . .

The essential parts of the project charter are the naming of the project and the project manager and the creation of one or more cost accounts for the project. The signing and issuance of the project charter must be done by someone in authority who is able to assign project managers to projects.

Unless a project charter is written, there is no formal creation of the project, and there is no formal recognition that the project manager is the project manager for this project. The early creation of a unique cost account for the project is essential because without it, the cost of the project in the early stages could be lost or misapplied to other projects or functions in the company.

Since it is not possible for a project manager to assign himself to his own project, a person of authority must make the assignment instead. The project manager of the new project probably knows more about the project than anyone else. (Of course, this is not very much at this stage.) The project manager therefore writes the project charter, and a superior signs and issues the project charter.

In addition to the essential parts of the project charter, other items can be included. A description of the project along with goals and objectives and an explanation of how the project will fit into the strategic plans of the company can be included. Some companies also include a project justification.

Although it is good to give additional information in the project charter, there is a risk involved in doing so. Lengthy descriptions inevitably lead to claims about what the project is expected to do when it is completed. Not much is known yet about the project; therefore, claims about the savings or functionality of the completed project create a forum for debate among the managers and encourage questions that are difficult or impossible to answer at this point. This can cause unnecessary delays in the start of the project and may create quite a lot of unnecessary work for the project manager.

Since the project does not start until the project charter is approved and the cost account for the project is assigned, any delay in getting the project charter approved means that the cost of work that is done on the project is lost. We do not recommend including anything but the barest essentials necessary to get the project charter approved. A project manager who feels that it is necessary to fill several pages with project descriptions and speculation on the project that will result at completion may be deluged with questions that will take time and money to answer. Much money can be spent answering questions about the project, and this money will be unaccounted for if there is no project charter and cost account to capture the money spent.

Much of the same thing can be said about including project justifications in the project charter. It takes time and effort to create a project charter. This is true whether it is early in the project and very rough justifications are being made, or whether a definitive justification is being made. If the project justification is included in the charter, it means that the work of doing the justification was done without the project charter. Since the cost account cannot be created until the project charter is approved, the cost of the project justification must have been collected in some other cost account and now must either be reversed or lost as part of the project cost.

What is a deliverable in the project?

All projects accomplish something. The "something" that they accomplish can be either a good or a service and is usually a combination of both. The individual items of goods or services that are accomplished are called the project deliverables.

Tell me more . . .

It is reasonable to say that all projects must accomplish something, although those of us who have been involved in some projects may not have felt that way at the time. If projects do not accomplish something, we have no reason for doing them. The items that we call the project accomplishments are generally referred to as the project deliverables.

There are internal and external deliverables. The internal deliverables are those that are delivered to the other operating parts of the project. The external deliverables are those that are delivered to some stakeholder outside of the project team. Internal deliverables are the outputs of the project tasks that serve as inputs to other project tasks. The external deliverables serve as inputs to making the stakeholder's deliverables complete.

The external deliverables must be clearly and completely defined to each of the project stakeholders, who must understand that the list of deliverables they agree to comprises the items that will be delivered as a result of the project's completion. They must realize that they will receive all of these deliverables but that they will not receive any other deliverables. Making this clear to the stakeholders will go a long way in controlling changes in the project, especially changes that the stakeholders do not wish to pay for.

What is a project justification?

Although some projects are done by direct order, most of the projects that we will be involved with will have a justification. The most credible justification is one where the identified benefits of doing the project are greater than the cost of doing the project. It is important to understand that there are many ways of describing the cost-benefit ratio for a project in order to justify it. Using monetary value is just one approach that does not have to be forced over all projects. Many of you have been faced with the problem of making a justification to company top management to carry out corporate training for your department staff or of the importance of introducing a new product line to your company's production cycle. These are good examples of internal company projects that would be justified with more qualitative results, such as increasing motivation and productivity, the ability to enter newly grown markets, or other results where monetary numbers could be difficult to develop or fore-cast. In this case one thing that should not be done is falsifying data by developing figures that have no real value. Instead, develop tangible qualitative results with measurable indicators to monitor and link these results to some business opportunity for your company or some problem the project might help to attack.

Doing that, it is important to remember that we are describing a problem or an opportunity and NOT a solution. In other words, we can explain a project justification as a description of what will happen if the project is carried out and what will happen if the project is not carried out.

For example, our company decides to decorate its office space with modern art. This project could cost $100,000. The benefit the company would receive by doing this is pretty intangible, but it is reasonable to say that customers coming through our lobby will be impressed, we hope, by the artwork and might be more favorably disposed toward buy-ing something from us. If we try to justify our project that way, our boss will probably think there are cheaper ways of impressing the customer.

However, there is another aspect: If our lobby is a complete eyesore, we may impress some of our customers unfavorably. There is probably evidence that we have indeed lost some business. This may serve as a good initial justification for a project even without any figures about our potential profits.

Of course, justifications using intangibles are generally more diffi-cult to get approved, especially if project funds are scarce and require more talent on the part of the project manager in developing really per-suasive descriptions of the disadvantage the company will suffer if the project is not carried out.

On the other hand, there are many cases when the monetary bene-fits for the project CAN actually be measured. In that case, it is of course important that such justification be made for the project. In most compa-nies there is no lack of favorable projects; there is usually just not enough money or resources to do them. Monetary justification allows us to rank the possible projects with the most favorable projects at the top and the least favorable ones at the bottom. The company can then go down the list doing as many projects as the company's funds allow.

Let us digress a bit. A discussion about where companies get their money is in order. Obviously when a customer comes to us and offers to pay us to do a project, the benefits for us are the amount of money the customer pays us to do the project and some intangibles like providing experience so we can get more work like this in the future. Even when the customer is paying, we do not receive all of the money until all of the work is done. The company doing the project must supply the funds necessary to do at least part of the project. Where does the company get this money?

The money to do projects probably does not come out of the company's cash on hand. The company probably borrows the money from a lending institution or sells some stock to investors. All the money obtained for projects has a cost associated with it. This is the money the company has to pay the lenders and investors for the use of their money.

Another important factor involved here is when the money for the project is spent and received. Since we are paying for the use of the money, the longer we use it, the more it costs us. If the customer can be made to agree to advanced payment or progress payments, we will need to borrow less money for shorter periods of time, and money will be saved on the project. The justification for the project should take these things into consideration.

Tell me more . . .

There are many different justification techniques that can be used. Some of these require very little effort and produce results that are mere approximations of the justification. These are appropriate early in the project when we want to have a justification that will allow us to move to the next early step. Although the justification will consider all of the benefits and costs that are associated with the project throughout its useful life, early in the project we will be committing funds only to move the project to its next step or phase. At this point in the project, or at points in the future, we can decide to discontinue work on the project. It does not make sense to do a costly collection of estimates into the future when we are talking about committing another $5,000 to move the project to the end of the next phase.

The break-even chart in Figure 2-1 is one of the simplest justification methods that can be used for projects. Generally this type of justification is used early in the project conceptualization and is very much a rough justification technique. The break-even chart is merely a plot of the total expected cost of two alternatives over time. It can be used to compare two or more alternatives. The break-even point is the point at which one alternative begins to have a total cost less than the other alternative. Although there can be an algebraic solution to the break-even point, the graphic solution is adequate (in the days before computers, that's all there was).

The break-even chart is made on a set of X and Y axes. The Y axis is total cost, and the X axis is time. The scale should be chosen so that the break-even point occurs somewhere in the middle of the chart.

New alternatives will usually have a fixed cost associated with them. Once this cost or investment is made in the project, it will not have

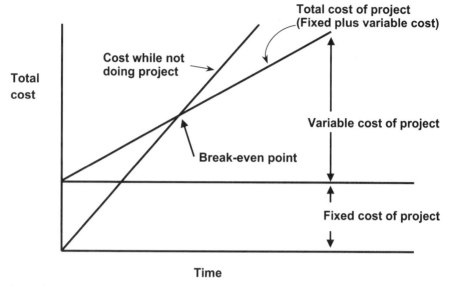

FIGURE 2-1: BREAK-EVEN CHART

to be made again during the project's life. This is called the fixed cost of the project. The variable cost of the project is the ongoing cost that continues to occur as we use the project throughout its useful life.

An example of this would be a company's considering the purchase of a new machine to replace an existing one that is used to manufacture its products. The new machine is faster than the old machine, has fewer maintenance costs associated with it, and produces less scrap and re-work. Suppose it would cost $500,000 to purchase the new machine, have it shipped to the site, set up, and started up with its initial tooling. This cost will not occur again so we can say that the fixed cost of the project is $500,000. There is no fixed cost associated with the old machine since it was purchased some time ago and is in place and operating.

The alternatives will also have a variable cost associated with them. The variable cost is the ongoing cost that occurs over time. In our example this is the cost of operating the machine over time, manufacturing parts, and doing the work that it was bought to do. In the example given, we are comparing a new machine to the existing process we now have in operation. When comparing the variable cost of the machines, it is important that the parameters of the comparison be the same for both alternatives. If the old machine is expected to produce 400,000 parts per year, the new machine should be expected to produce the same amount. The variable cost of the machine is the material cost, labor cost, maintenance cost, and all other costs that are significant.

If we were considering buying a new machine, we would expect the variable cost to be less than the variable cost of the machine it will be replacing. The slope of the variable cost line will be lower than that of the variable cost line of the old machine. The new machine's variable cost line starts at some point on the Y axis equal to the fixed cost of obtaining it. The variable cost line of the existing machine starts at zero on the Y axis.

At some point the total cost lines—the sum of the variable cost plus the fixed cost—must cross. This point is called the break-even point. It is the point at which the money saved in the variable or operating cost of the new machine compared to the old machine is equal to the investment in the new machine. That is, it is the point where the total cost of the two alternatives is equal. The sooner this occurs, the better the justification for the new machine. The difference between the two total cost lines after the break-even point is frequently referred to as profit. This is not correct. It is really the amount of profitability that the new machine contributes to the company in terms of total reduced cost. Profitability depends on the difference between total cash inflows (revenues) and total cash out-flows.

As we said in the beginning of this discussion, this is a rough justi-fication method. There are many assumptions made. No effort should be made to improve on the technique by creating more detail and better estimates over time. If a more reliable technique is needed, another justi-fication technique should be used instead.

The assumptions made generally include a static workload over time, constant maintenance cost over time, no additional wear and tear on the alternatives, and no changes in labor rates or material costs.

Figure 2-2 shows an illustration of the payback point. In this exam-ple we have made a $1,000,000 investment and have a cash inflow of

An investment of $1,000,000 receives
$750,000 per year for 3 years

YR	Flow	Net Flow	
0	-1,000,000	-1,000,000	
1	750,000	-250,000	←——— Payback
2	750,000	500,000	
3	750,000	1,250,000	

Payback period is   1 1/3 years

FIGURE 2-2: EXAMPLE: PAYBACK POINT

$750,000 each year following. When the net cash flows total zero, we have reached the payback point. That is the point where the cash inflows have offset the cash outflows.

The payback period justification method is another rough justification method. Before computers were readily available to project managers, this method was often used as the only justification method and was sufficient to justify many projects. The payback period is similar to the break-even point except that we are comparing the total cash outflows to the total cash inflows. In this method all of the relevant cash flows need to be considered. In most projects there is at first an outflow of money before the revenues, the inflows of money, can occur. The payback period is the amount of time that goes by before the total cash inflows are equal to the total cash outflows. The payback method does not require us to compare two or more alternatives. With this method we need to know only the cash flows associated with this project.

Suppose, as another example, that we are justifying the purchase of a machine that has a total cash outflow of $500,000. Let us say that the purchase of the new machine saves us $125,000 per year over the existing machine that we are using. This would be due to higher maintenance cost, since the older machine is slower and causes more scrap and re-work. If the cost savings of the new machine allow us to lower the cost of the product and this, in turn, allows us to have a greater market share, we should include those cash flows as well. Let us say that the cash flows are summarized in Table 2-1.

Notice that in Table 2-1 the cumulative cash flows go from negative to positive somewhere between the end of year four and the end of year five. We could even interpolate and say that the payback period occurred 5 percent into the next year with the first positive cash flow. This would be four years and about two weeks.

The payback period method has the advantage of resulting in a quantitative result that allows the ranking of this project with other projects according to their payback point. The other advantage of the payback method is that it allows for the independent estimation of the cash flows in and out for each time period. In the break-even method we assumed that costs would continue as they had before.

The major problem with the payback period and break-even point methods is that neither of them incorporates anything that happens after their respective justification points. If there were a sharp upturn in the cost of the new machine after the break-even point given in the example, or if there were smaller cash inflows in the payback point example, they would have no effect on either the break-even point or the payback point. This is rather short-sighted, and these two methods encourage projects that have high early returns on their investments. In other words they encourage us to invest in cheap equipment or projects. This may be false

Year	Cash outflows	Cash inflows	Net cash flows
0	500,000	0	-500,000
1	20,000	200,000	-320,000
2	20,000	125,000	-215,000
3	20,000	125,000	-110,000
4	20,000	125,000	-5,000
5	20,000	125,000	+100,000
6	20,000	125,000	+205,000
7	20,000	125,000	+310,000
8	20,000	125,000	+415,000

TABLE 2-1

economy. If we actually continue to use the equipment or the results of the project longer, we may find that spending less in the beginning will have the effect of making us spend much more later in the project's life. To solve this problem, we must use a more sophisticated justification method.

The internal rate of return on investment method of project justification considers nearly all of the things that are relevant to the project. It also adjusts the values of the money according to the time value of money. The time value of money is explained in Chapter 4, and we will not do it again here. This type of justification was rarely done in business until the advent of computers and then it was seldom done because it was difficult to explain to some managers, particularly managers who had been brought up using simpler methods of project justification. The main advantage of this justification method is that it is a model that is a very close approximation to the actual money flows that the real project will have and very closely represents the real benefits to the company.

Figure 2-3 shows the calculation that will be performed in determining the internal rate of return on investment (IRR). The equation shown is a summation. That is, the calculation shown is made for each time period relevant to the project. The results of each calculation will be the present value of the cash flow for each time period, positive or negative.

$$\sum_{n=0}^{5} \frac{FV_n}{(1+r)^n} = 0$$

FIGURE 2-3: INTERNAL RATE OF RETURN CALCULATION

The cash flows are then added together to get the total cash flow present value. The value of r is varied until the present value of the total cash flow over all the time periods is equal to zero.

Why would we want to do this? If we think about the present value of money at a given point in time, the present value of the money would be increasingly less than the future value of the money as the interest rates became higher. The higher the interest rate, the lower the present value of the money would be. In the equation, since the value of r is in the denominator, the greater the value of r, the less will be the present value of any money. As the value of n increases, the value of r will have a greater effect on the present value of future cash flows.

Eventually we will reach a point where the value of r decreases the present value of the future cash flows enough that the total of the cash flows comes very close to zero. The value of r when the present value of all the future cash flows reaches zero is called the internal rate of return on investment.

This calculation is quite simple for any computer to calculate and is usually included on financial pocket calculators as well. Computing to find the value of r that makes the total cash flow equal zero is solved by iteration.

The example in Figure 2-4 shows a project that has an initial investment of $1,000,000. One year later the cash flow is +$300,000, one year after that the cash flow is +$400,000, and so on as shown over five years. The calculation will have to be made six times for $n = 0, 1, 2, 3, 4, 5$. The calculation for $n = 0$ is simple since the value of $(1 + r)^n$ will always be 1 regardless of the value of r. In other words, the value of the negative cash flow in year zero adjusted to present value is simply the same value.

The calculation of $n = 4$; $r = 0.3$ and $FV = +$400,000$ is shown in Figure 2-5.

The table in Figure 2-6 shows the present value of the cash flows for year zero through five for various values of r. Notice that as various values of r are tried, the net cash flow comes closer to zero. Ultimately the last calculation produces a value of $r = 25.7\%$. This is the IRR for this project.

What is the requirements process?

There are many ways to develop the deliverables of a project. It is important that a procedure be established for each project that will ensure that

What is the IRR of a project that has an investment of $1,000,000, including shipping and installation, and start-up and cash flows at the ends of the years as follows:

1	$300,000
2	$400,000
3	$500,000
4	$400,000
5	$300,000

FIGURE 2-4: EXAMPLE: INTERNAL RATE OF RETURN

all of the necessary deliverables of the project are found and that all unnecessary requirements are eliminated from the list of deliverables.

$$\sum_{n=0}^{5} \frac{FV_n}{(1+r)^n} = 0$$

Calculation for $n = 4$ and $r = 30\%$ and $FV = 400$

$$\frac{400}{(1+0.3)^4} = 140.05$$

FIGURE 2-5: INTERNAL RATE OF RETURN

CALCULATION

All of the stakeholders of the project must be considered in the development of the deliverables list. The deliverables of the project can come from many different sources. The client or customer and the user will usually have the bulk of the specified deliverables, but special care must be taken to avoid overlooking deliverables because of the other stakeholders.

The requirements process should identify at least 95 percent of the deliverables that will be required for the project. This will vary with the

Years	Flows	r = 10%	50%	30%	20%	25%	26%	25.50%	25.70%
n		0.100	0.500	0.300	0.200	0.250	0.260	0.255	0.257
0	-1000	-1000.00	-1000.00	-1000.00	-1000.00	-1000.00	-1000.00	-1000.00	-1000.00
1	300	272.73	200.00	230.77	250.00	240.00	238.10	239.04	238.66
2	400	330.58	177.78	236.69	277.78	256.00	251.95	253.96	253.16
3	500	375.66	148.15	227.58	289.35	256.00	249.95	252.95	251.75
4	400	273.21	79.01	140.05	192.90	163.84	158.70	161.24	160.22
5	300	186.28	39.51	80.80	120.56	98.30	94.46	96.36	95.60
Total	900	438.445	-355.556	-84.1115	130.5941	14.144	-6.83432	3.566321	-0.61496

Cash flows are shown in $1,000

FIGURE 2-6: EXAMPLE SOLUTION: EIGHT ITERATIONS

project. Projects that have a great deal of uncertainty associated with them, such as research and development projects, have more poorly defined deliverables. All projects have a certain amount of uncertainty associated with them. Depending on the uncertainty, it will be necessary to discover and define some of the deliverables as the project develops. This is called progressive elaboration.

Tell me more . . .

One of the greatest reasons for failed projects is poorly defined project deliverables. If the project deliverables are poorly defined at the beginning of the project, the budget and schedule will be understated. The resources for the project will be understated as well. While this simply makes the project a smaller project than it really is, the missing deliverables will be discovered at some point, and they will have to be provided. Now we are getting into the execution part of the project, and we have to add new requirements and find the budget and resources to do them.

There are many ways to arrive at the required deliverables list. Figure 2-7 suggests a process that has many of the characteristics of a good deliverables definition process.

We begin by listing the needs and desires of the stakeholders. This is not too difficult, although it will take some time and will be a lengthy list. At this point we allow anything that anyone wants to become part of the "wishes and desires" list. Many of these items will be quickly eliminated from the project. For the proper care and feeding of the stakeholders, it is good to allow this kind of list to be created. It ensures that everyone has had a chance to state his or her favorite requirement.

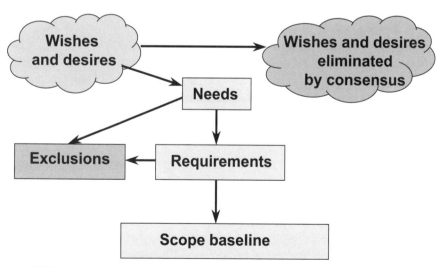

FIGURE 2-7: REQUIREMENTS PROCESS

Next we review the wishes and desires. We eliminate any of the items on the wishes and desires list that can be agreed to unanimously. If there is an objection, the item should remain on the list for the time being until further investigation can be made. The group reviewing the lists can be all of the stakeholders on a small project. On larger projects, review committees of specific stakeholders can be organized to review groups of items that are related. The result of this meeting or this series of meetings is the list of "needs."

The items that are on the list of needs now are investigated. Some items will require individual justifications while others will require minimal investigation. Regardless of the investigation that takes place, items that are excluded are documented as to why they have been excluded from the project. At this stage in the process, the items excluded as well as the items not excluded will have their descriptions elaborated to reduce any misunderstanding. The items that remain are the potential deliverables for the project. We will call them the "requirements."

The requirements are not the final deliverables of the project. For many reasons some of the requirements may be eliminated before the scope baseline is established. Until we establish the scope baseline, there is no requirement to process a change request through the change management process to add or delete requirements.

What is a scope statement?

The scope statement is the defining statement of the project. It is the document that defines the project and is the basis for making decisions about the project. The scope statement is a dynamic document in that in the beginning it contains the information available, and as the project progresses, it is changed and added to. It is the primary document used for understanding the project and its nature. The scope statement includes the goal statement, the project justification, the products that the project will produce, the deliverables, and the success criteria of the project. The scope statement should also include the things that the project will *not* do. These statements should include exclusions from the project deliverables and any identified constraints and assumptions that have been made.

Tell me more . . .

The goal statement is a short statement of what this project is about. Goal statements are not strictly required but help to give a short description that people can use to recognize the project where the name of the project would not be sufficient. The goal statement should be written by the project manager but must be approved by the manager above her. Goal statements can also be included in the project charter that was discussed elsewhere. If a goal statement is included in the project charter, there is the danger that the project charter approval and the official start of the project will be delayed while people struggle over the wording of the goal statement. For this reason we think it is a good idea to include it in the early documents of the project like the scope statement rather than in the project charter.

The project manager has some control of the overall direction of the project with the goal statement. For example, a company wanted to develop a computerized system that would control the fire and burglar alarms in a building. The system would automatically call for help if the alarms were breached or if the sensors detected heat, light, or smoke where it should not be.

One project manager wrote a goal statement that said, "The goal of this project is to install a fully operational automated alarm management system in the XYZ Company's facility by January 2004." Another project manager said, "The goal of this project is to make a prototype automated alarm management system that can be brought to the consumer electronics trade show in October 2004."

Notice that the work that has to be done in either of these projects is quite different. The two goal statements indicate completely different ways of introducing the new product. In the first statement the project manager feels that the best approach is to build a complete prototype system that will be a showcase for customers to see. In the second statement the project manager feels that the best approach is to breadboard a model of the system that can be shown to a large number of customers. As these goal statements are reviewed by the stakeholders, they will be refined and the project will move forward.

To show how short goal statements can be, we will give one more example of a short goal statement for a gigantic project. To launch the Apollo Project, then president of the United States John F. Kennedy said, "I believe this nation should commit itself to the goal of sending a man to the moon before the end of the decade and returning him safely to Earth." This statement launched a project that lasted for more than ten years and cost well over $50 billion.

The project deliverables were discussed above. They are the specific items that will be delivered as a result of doing this project. The detail of the deliverables should be such that there will be no disagreement as to whether or not the deliverable was actually delivered. Disagreements with the stakeholders about the description and nature of the deliverables should be settled at this time rather than when the deliverable is actually delivered. The stakeholders need to understand that any item that is not on the list of deliverables will not be delivered.

The project success criteria are the tangible objects by which the project will be judged in order for it to be considered successful. We can consider the success criteria for both product and project. The fundamental success criteria of any project are those related to the items specified in the project management triangle—cost, schedule, and scope—but may include other tangible and specific measures as well. It is important that we are as precise as possible in describing our success criteria according to our performance against budget, schedule, and scope. We need to choose measures that would be easy to verify in order to clearly demonstrate our project success. For instance, using "Being on Schedule" as a criterion is a bad thing to do because it does not give us actual figures to measure. Also, does that mean that being late *or* early is bad for project success, or is it just being late that is bad? Is it missing a schedule by ten months or by ten hours that is bad?

The product success criteria, unlike the project success criteria, may have to be measured long after our project is over, but it is still important in the long run from the business point of view. In learning how we will manage our projects for the best customer relations development, our overall company development, and our own project portfolio management improvement, product success criteria may and will involve things that are outside of the scope of the project. This criterion must be considered if reaching customer satisfaction is one of the important goals in our projects. Product success criteria must be described with the same precision as project success. Do not say, "We want to increase productivity of our employees by having them attend certain technical skill improving training courses." Instead, say something like, "One of the product success criteria for a training project will be for us to increase the productivity of our software development department 15 percent within the two months after training is completed." We should also have the actual method of measurement in hand to demonstrate the change in productivity.

Just as we need to identify all the stakeholders for our project, we also need to understand how the stakeholders will measure our product and our project success. In many cases, this will give us important insights into how to manage our project better. For example, if we understand that the product success criterion our customer will use in a training project is the ability of IT managers to manage their projects in a unified way, then we need to make sure that our client understands her responsibility to ensure all of the managers' presence in class along with providing other measures to make what was learned applicable to their practical activities. If we understand that the real project success criterion for our client is for us to not overrun our budget by more than 20 percent, we could then be more conservative with the need for taking risks in the project.

The final comment to be made in this section is that there is an important need to keep success criteria from different areas balanced. In measuring project success, we have to make sure that we have thought about schedule success criteria as well as budget and scope. With product success criteria, we have to make sure we did not leave out important stakeholders whose satisfaction will have a large impact on overall project success.

What is a work breakdown structure (WBS)?

Once we have identified all of the things that we are supposed to produce in the project, it is necessary to develop the specific items of work that must be done to complete all of the work. The work breakdown structure takes the project and divides it into smaller pieces. These can be called subprojects. The subprojects can be broken down into smaller pieces. This process of breaking down the project can continue until the project is broken into small, more manageable pieces.

The work breakdown structure allows us to approach the formidable task of finding all of the work that is necessary for completion of the project. This is done by taking the formidable project and dividing it into small projects that can be looked at one by one, allowing the project to be attacked one piece at a time. When the work breakdown structure is not used, it is very likely that many of the tasks will be missed. Since this is the place in the project where the work is defined, we find the work breakdown structure useful in determining much of the information we will require in our project plans.

To make work breakdown structures even easier, they are not restricted to only dealing with work. Many work breakdown structures start out as product breakdown structures. That is, the first few levels of the WBS are the breakdown of the products of the project from major products into smaller subproducts. For large projects this frequently makes the construction of the WBS much easier. If, for example, you were to consider the construction of the U.S. space shuttle, you would first see a product breakdown followed by a work breakdown.

Some of the major components of the space shuttle program were construction of the launch facility, construction of the space shuttle vehicle, construction of the solid rocket boosters, construction of the external fuel tank, modification of the world tracking stations, modification of the astronaut training facility, development of new space suits, and development and construction of the robot arm assembly.

The space shuttle program had several layers of product breakdown before the WBS considered actual work packages, tasks, and activities. In huge projects like this, the individual products are so large in themselves that there might be little interaction between team members working on widely separated branches of the project. People working on the external fuel tank had relatively little contact with the people working on the tracking stations around the world.

The work breakdown structure is a simple, easy-to-read, graphical representation of the project that is very useful for communicating to the stakeholders of the project.

The work breakdown structure provides us with the basis for performing the bottoms-up cost and schedule estimate for the project as well. Since the WBS represents all of the work that must be done to complete the project, we can estimate the cost and duration for each of these small pieces of work and roll the estimate up to the project level for the total cost and duration estimate.

Tell me more . . .

The work breakdown structure is one of the most useful tools in project management. It is easy to use and simple to understand. Essentially, the project is first taken as a whole and broken down into a small group of subprojects. These subprojects can each be broken down into sub-subprojects. These can be broken down further until very small pieces of the project can be described.

This breaking down of the project has some major advantages. The main advantage is that it allows us to concentrate our efforts on small parts of the project one piece at a time. If we were to try to determine at once all of the work necessary to complete a project, we would probably do a good job in some areas and a not very good job in other areas. By breaking the project into successively smaller subprojects, we can organize groups of people to concentrate on finding the work associated with one, and only one, part of the project at a time and do a thorough job, with only the appropriate people for that part of the project.

The WBS is one of the tools in project management that allows us to manage any size project. A very large project can be broken down through many levels of the WBS until an element of a manageable size is achieved. In a smaller project, the same manageable element can be achieved with fewer levels of breakdown. In this way even the largest project can be broken down into a small manageable subproject (see Figure 2-8).

So, the top level of any WBS is the project that we are concerned with. The levels between the top and bottom of the WBS are elements of breakdown. The larger the project, the more levels of intermediate breakdown we have. Eventually we come to the bottom of the WBS. This is the smallest level of detail that the project manager will have to manage. *The Guide to the Project Management Body of Knowledge* is a little bit confusing in this area. It says that the WBS should continue only to the work package level since this is the lowest level to which the project manager will have to manage. It goes on to say that the work packages can be broken down into activities and the activities can be further broken down into tasks.

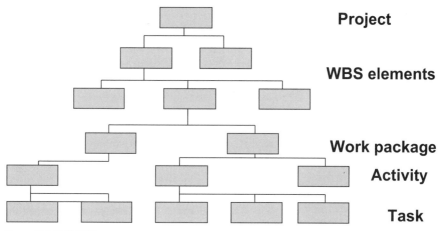

FIGURE 2-8: PMI WBS DEFINITIONS

Most project managers will construct a WBS that is appropriate to their project. Even if a very large project is being managed, the entire WBS will actually contain all the work associated with the project, and the project manager will be responsible for it all. In very large projects there will be intermediate managers. They may even be called work package managers. These intermediate managers may have their own responsibilities, but the project manager they report to is still responsible for their work as he is responsible for all aspects of the project. So, in our way of thinking, the WBS contains all of the work involved in the project. If the project is large and the project manager wants to display the WBS only down to the work package level, that is fine. The complete WBS, however, goes down to the level of detail that can be assigned to an individual person. In this way the project manager and the intermediate managers can each construct their part of the WBS, and the pieces will fit together into an overall project WBS. This will, in turn, support the planning process for the project in a consistent way.

The work breakdown structure also has the capability of including the non-task-related work. This is the work that is considered to be "level of effort" work. The best example of this is the project manager. There are other cases, especially when projects become large, where other level of effort persons are involved. Level of effort work is the work that must be done in the project, but it is work that is not connected to any one task in particular. Level of effort work is work that affects many of the activities of the project. For example, a person that is responsible for operating the copy machine used by everyone in the project is a level of effort person. Administrative assistants and anyone else who does work that contributes to the project but does not work on any specific task is a level of effort person. A major attempt should be made to avoid calling work level of effort when it should really be assigned to a particular task. Level of effort work is budgeted but is difficult to measure in terms of performance. Level of effort people and their work can be shown in the WBS at the level at which they do their work.

The WBS must be a flexible tool that can be used with as little restriction as possible so that it will be used with ease and comfort. Since each project is unique, the requirements of the project will change each time, and the WBS must be able to be used in all circumstances.

You may have noticed that we have been careful so far to avoid some of the usual words that are associated with the work breakdown structure. This is because there is some disagreement about what exactly should go into the WBS. As recently as April 2000, PMI published "Work Breakdown Structure Practice Standard Project—WBS vs. Activities" by Cindy Berg, PMP, and Kim Colenso, PMP, in the PM Network.

This paper addressed the disagreement between project managers as to whether it was appropriate for the WBS to contain the project activities. One opinion is that it is not appropriate for the WBS to contain the project activities because the level of planning in the WBS is only to the deliverable level and does not go to the level of the individual assignment. It is therefore inappropriate for the WBS to contain the project activities. The opposite view is that the WBS *should* contain the project activities. This is appropriate because the lowest level of the WBS contains elements that in fact produce the deliverables of the project. In this opinion, the process of creating the deliverables leads us to the definition of the work that is required to produce them.

We think that the paper correctly states that it is really up to the project manager to construct the WBS in a way that is appropriate for the project. All projects are different, and the WBS is a tool that should be used in a manner that is appropriate for each project encountered. It would be inappropriate for PMI to place restrictions on their options. The WBS is a project management tool that can be used in different ways, depending upon the needs of the project manager. Therefore, there should not be arbitrary limits set on how the WBS should be created.

How do I do a work breakdown structure?

Doing a work breakdown structure is one of the simplest things that you will do as a project manager, yet it is one of the things that many project managers and their staff do not do well. Part of the reason must be that it is so simple that many managers do not think that something so simple will be of use to them. In reality, the WBS is simple, but it is also one of the most useful tools in project management.

To do a WBS, you start at the top, which is the project level. The project is then broken down into subprojects. As we discussed, we could be doing a product breakdown at this point. Usually a project is first broken down into four to seven subprojects or products. Once the first level of the breakdown for the project has been completed, a different group of people on the project team can be used to break each one of the subprojects into sub-subprojects. In this way the proper expertise can be used for each area of the project.

The work of breaking each project and subproject down further and further continues until the level of breakdown is achieved at which an individual can be assigned to be responsible for the work of the defined sub-sub-sub . . . . . project. At this point we have what is usually called a task or an activity. There is plenty of flexibility in doing this, as there should be since each project and each project manager is unique and we do not want to burden the process with unnecessary rules and restrictions.

Tell me more . . .

While the WBS process is easy and simple to do, there are some difficulties. Most of these are problems created by forcing unnecessary rules onto the process. Some people get frustrated working hard to try to make the WBS come out according to some preconceived notion about what it should look like. Others reach high levels of frustration trying to conform to norms or standards that are imposed from outside the project. Generally these kinds of standards inhibit the process much more than they help it. The WBS should be unique to each project, and the flow from top to bottom should feel natural to those who are creating it.

As a guideline but not a rule, each level of the WBS should break the previous element into four to seven new elements. If a project seems to want an element to be broken down into more or fewer elements, then that is what should be done. Generally the guideline is a good one, however. If we consider a project that is broken down to four levels, we can see that there is a considerable disassembly of the project. Level one is the project; level two has as many as 7 subprojects; level three has 49, and level four has 343. This is probably more breakdown than most projects need.

The second guideline is that the elements of the WBS should be relatively the same size. This means that elements at the same level of breakdown should be close to having the same amount of budget as the others of the same level. This is just to help people understand what they are looking at when they look at the WBS. In the graphic for the WBS, each element is represented by a box of the same size. People will naturally think that each box represents a similar amount of work.

If elements on the same level represent large differences in budget, some of the stakeholders may think that they are similar in magnitude and give each of the elements the same attention. This can create problems for the project manager when she is trying to focus the attention of the stakeholders on some critical part of the project, and the stakeholders want to focus on another element in the WBS. In large projects there will be several levels of breakdown, and there will be several elements on each level.

The breakdown process can be accomplished by different groups of people. These groups have different cumulative skills and can meet at different times to accomplish the breaking down of their individual elements. Thus when we are breaking down the software development part of the project, we can have the programmers involved, and when we are breaking down the mechanical design part of the project, we can have the mechanical designers work on that part. This allows us to have the appropriate people work on defining all of the tasks that are necessary to complete the project. The meetings we hold to do this should take place in less than two hours and should have fewer than ten people attending.

The breakdown process continues until the level of detail is reached at which a single person can be assigned to complete that small piece of project work. It is important that the breakdown process continue to this point because the individual work assignments or tasks that are identified at this level become the fundamental building block for schedule development and detailed budget estimates. This is not to say that the individual person in charge of a task is not allowed to further break down their individual tasks if it is convenient. Reporting the WBS can include all of the minutest detail, or it may suppress some of the detail according to the communications needs of the project.

In the two examples in Figures 2-9 and 2-10, we see the work breakdown structure for building a house. In Figure 2-9 we have divided the work of building the house by discipline. The work is divided into skill areas: masonry, carpentry, plumbing, and electrical. All the work of building the house is forced to fall into one of these four disciplines, or we must add another element at that level. This approach makes things simple for dividing up the work. If we want to discuss the masonry work for the project, we gather the masonry workers. If we want to talk about the electrical work, we gather the electricians and so on. This makes it unnecessary for the electricians to go to a meeting where masonry work will be discussed. The project organization can even fit into the WBS, but this is not a necessary thing.

In Figure 2-10 the project is broken down by phase. Phases are points in time at which a significant part of the project is complete. In the example, we have divided our house project into three phases: foundation, rough construction, and finish construction. All of the work of building the house from the very beginning to the end of the foundation

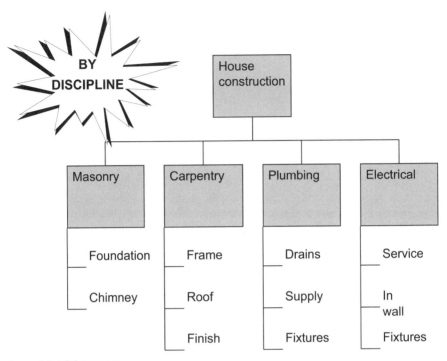

FIGURE 2-9: WBS EXAMPLES

phase is included in this phase. This would be clearing the land, getting permits to build, excavating, building forms, and pouring concrete for the foundation. We begin the second phase as soon as the first phase is complete. This phase is completed when the walls, roof, doors, and windows are in place, and the house can be secured. The third phase begins at this point and continues to the end of the project.

Notice that in a phased WBS, one phase ends when the next begins. This is helpful in placing decisions to continue with the project. In a research project the end of a phase might include justification and approval to move on to the next phase. The difficulty with this arrangement is that if you need to call a meeting for phase one, you will probably include all of the people of all of the disciplines involved in the whole project.

While this is only an example showing two ways of doing the work breakdown structure, by discipline and by phase, there are many other ways that the breakdown can occur. The method of breaking down can even be changed from level to level within the WBS. It might be convenient to start with a product breakdown structure in the first level or two of the WBS. Each of the subproducts in the result might be broken down by phase and then, further down the WBS we might ultimately shift to skills breakdown. The point is that the WBS should be done in a smooth

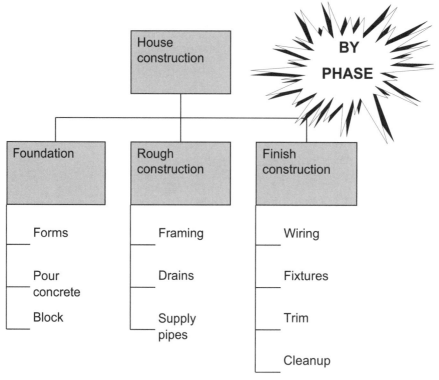

FIGURE 2-10: WBS EXAMPLES

and natural way, and it should be relatively simple to accomplish. If the WBS is difficult, the process will be difficult and hard to understand.

To complete the WBS we need to test the accuracy of the lowest level of breakdown. This level should contain all of the work necessary to complete the project. Each of these lowest level elements or tasks has a single individual who is responsible for it. From the budget standpoint, each element at this level has a budget designed so that the total budget for all of the elements at this level equals the total operating budget for the project. It is also true that if all of the budget for each of the elements at each level were added together, we would get the total operating budget for the project.

How do I test the work breakdown structure?

From the systems engineering and systems management way of thinking, we can say that each task in the WBS is a process that converts inputs to outputs. In the WBS we have identified the tasks that must be completed in order for us to complete the project. Is this really good enough, or can we do a better job?

The answer is "Yes, we can do a better job." By applying a little systems management methodology, we can vastly improve the level of accuracy of our work breakdown structure. The technique here is to look at the inputs and the outputs of each of the processes or tasks in the WBS. Each input for each task must come from somewhere, and each of the outputs generated as a result of doing each task must be needed by some other part of the project. By ensuring that each input is coming from somewhere in the project and each output is needed by some other part of the project, we can raise the accuracy of the WBS considerably.

Tell me more . . .

Although the WBS is an excellent way to find all of the work that needs to be done to complete the project, we can improve this ability considerably by looking at each of the already identified tasks as a process that converts inputs into outputs.

In order for a task to be accomplished it must have the necessary inputs. This is the same thing as saying that before we can make an aluminum die casting, we have to have the metal, the mold, the design, and the metallurgical specification. When we have all of that, we can process the inputs into outputs, the finished casting (see Figure 2-11).

The problem is much the same in managing project work breakdown structures. Before we can complete a task in the project, we must have certain inputs from other parts of the project or from somewhere or someone outside of the project. Once we have the necessary inputs, we can process them by doing the work of the task and produce outputs that are the results or products of that task. The outputs of the task must be needed by some other part of the project, or they must contribute to the delivery of a deliverable.

Suppose part of the deliverables of a project is the production of an aluminum die cast heat sink for an electronic assembly (see Figure 2-12). Before we can produce the die casting we will need to have a design for the heat sink, a metallurgical specification and a design for the mold that will produce it. Before we can design the casting we will have to know

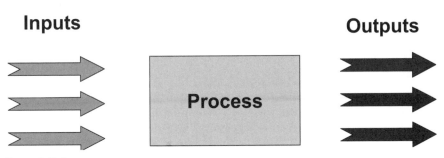

Inputs   **Outputs**

Process

FIGURE 2-11: SYSTEMS APPROACH

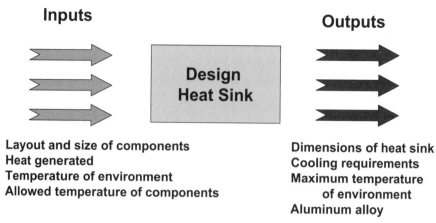

Inputs

Outputs

**Design
Heat Sink**

Layout and size of components
Heat generated
Temperature of environment
Allowed temperature of components

Dimensions of heat sink
Cooling requirements
Maximum temperature
    of environment
Aluminum alloy

FIGURE 2-12: SYSTEMS APPROACH: DESIGN A HEAT SINK

the size and layout of the components that will be mounted on it. We will also have to know the amount of heat that will be generated by each component, the temperature of the environment, and the maximum allowable temperature that each component will be allowed to reach.

When we have completed the design task, certain outputs will be produced. Among them might be the dimensions of the heat sink, cooling requirements, maximum allowable temperature, and the aluminum alloy to use, to name a few.

When we use this approach to creating the WBS and testing it, we end up having at least two people look at the definition of each task. One person on the project team is looking at the inputs that are necessary for them to do their work and determining the outputs that will be the products of their work. At the same time another person is doing the same thing for their task. In this case they are trying to find another task manager who is looking for the inputs that they will be producing as outputs and they are looking for another task manager who will supply them with the inputs that they need. One task's output is another task's input. In this way each input and each output is looked at from the creation and the consuming standpoint.

Every input to a task must come from somewhere and every output from a task must go somewhere. Inputs must come from somewhere within the project or must come from somewhere external to the project. All outputs must be the input to some other task in the project or must contribute to the production of a deliverable.

If a task requires an input and the input cannot be found, it may be necessary to create a new task or at least assign this input as the output of one of the project tasks, or even purchase the input from an outside source.

If the output of a task cannot locate another task that requires it as an input or if it does not contribute to the completion of a deliverable, then the question must be asked, "Is this output necessary?" It might be possible to eliminate this work from the project. So, as an additional benefit we have the opportunity to eliminate from the project unnecessary features or work that someone feels should be done but that is not required by the project.

What is scope change control?

Any project that has ever been done has probably had scope changes. It is only reasonable that as a project develops, learning takes place and the environment of the project changes. These changes can result in scope changes on the project. Since they are nearly inevitable, it is best to prepare to deal with changes rather than be surprised when they occur and try to resist them.

One of the things you will need in order to control the changes is a clear definition of the project deliverables. Unless the deliverables are clear when the scope baseline of the project is established, it is difficult to know when a change is requested whether it is or is not part of the already established project scope. Many conflicts can be avoided by having a clear scope baseline that all of the stakeholders have agreed to.

Since changes to the project scope are inevitable, we should have a means of changing the scope in such a way that the changes can be managed successfully into the project without causing havoc. This is what we mean by scope change control.

Tell me more . . .

Any project that has ever been completed has probably had changes to its scope. Many times you hear managers say, "Changes are killing us!" What the manager really means is that our inability to control changes is what is killing us. In reality, properly controlled and managed changes can be a great benefit to the company. The reason for this is that we are paid for changes if they are managed correctly.

Changes are the result of many things. They can be caused by an external event such as the change of a government regulation, a change in technology, a change in the marketplace, an error or omission in the original scope of the project, and an addition to the value to the project.

The basis for a good change management system starts with the establishment of the scope baseline. The time at which the scope baseline is established depends on the amount of tracking that is desired for changes. Once the scope baseline is established, it is necessary to process an approved change to change the baseline. The scope baseline can be established early in the project. This will provide a tracking system for changes to the project scope from the beginning. The trouble is that establishing the scope baseline too early in the project will make it necessary to generate a lot of change orders before the project requirements are finalized. The advantage is that there will be a record of the changes requested, accepted, and rejected starting early in the project. The cost and benefits of deciding when to establish the baseline must be considered.

A good scope change control system is one that makes sure that all of the stakeholders concerned with the change are made aware that it is being submitted, agreed upon, processed, disapproved or approved, and implemented. Change management must be careful to ensure that budgets, schedules, performance, and documentation are all changed to reflect the change.

Changes should be managed through a change management procedure, as shown in Figure 2-13. The procedure should require that some formal document be filled out collecting the important information, such as a full description of the requested change and places for the originator and contact information. Space should be provided to gather the information on researching and processing the change.

One of the most important things that the change control procedure will do for the project team is to determine who pays for the change. Any good change procedure should require an evaluation and investigation

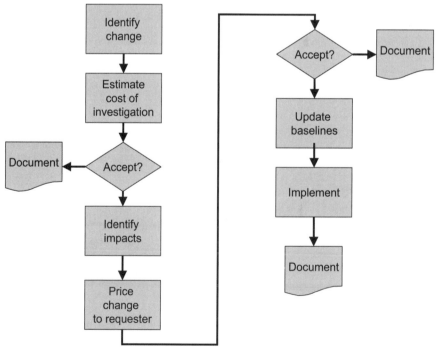

FIGURE 2-13: CHANGE MANAGEMENT PROCESS

phase. This will ensure that the change is carefully thought out and that all of the stakeholders affected have an opportunity to confer on it.

It is important that the investigation of the change be paid for by the stakeholder who originated the change. This is important for two reasons. The project budget and resources can be quickly used up investigating changes suggested by various stakeholders. This is especially true if there is no cost to the stakeholder requesting the change. The requesting stakeholder will be more reluctant to request changes if he must first obtain approval for the request and obtain funds for the investigation.

3

Project Estimating

What is a project estimate?

In order to run the project we must know how long things take, how much they will cost, and what kind of resources will be required. The only way we can get this data is by doing good estimates. Without good estimates we have no way of knowing where we are at any point in the project, and we have no way of predicting how much the project will cost or how long it will take to do it.

An estimate is the determination of a likely quantitative result. There are two major things that we estimate in a project; one is the cost of the project or the money that will have to be spent to produce it. The second is the time that the project will take to be completed. Whenever we are doing project estimates, we will not only be estimating the cost of doing the work but also the time that it will take to complete it.

Tell me more . . .

There are many pitfalls in producing a good estimate for a project. The deliverables may not all be identified, stakeholders change their minds, project team members may be optimistic or pessimistic, time may be limited, and so forth. If the project is poorly defined, there is not much of a possibility that the cost and schedule estimates are going to come out anywhere near what the actual cost and schedule time for the project will be. Optimistic schedules can cause problems in estimating as well. Stakeholders or management frequently shorten schedules without adding budget to the project. Generally we can look for increases in cost when schedules are shortened. An inaccurate work breakdown structure causes work tasks to be missed. When the individual estimates for the tasks are added up to make a bottom-up, definitive estimate for the project, missed work tasks cause underestimation. Understating risks underestimates our cost and schedule estimates as well. Risks that are not identified and identified risks that have the wrong value for their estimated probability or impact cause management reserves and contingency budgets to be misstated. Cost inflation and failure to include appropriate overheads cause erroneous estimates. It is important to recognize wage and price increases that will occur during the project and adjust estimates accordingly.

Whatever estimating method is used at the appropriate time in the schedule, a range of possible values for the estimate should be given. This range of values should be accompanied by an estimate of the probability that the actual cost will fall within the given range of values. An estimate of $1,000 does not mean nearly as much as the estimate $995 to $1,005 with a 95 percent probability that the actual cost will be in this range. Too many estimates are given in a single value. When the range of values is not known, much needed information is missing and bad decisions can easily be made.

Suppose that in the above example, we gave the manager the cost estimate of $1,000. Suppose that manager had to make a decision as to whether or not to market a new product for the company. If the marketing department says that they can sell the product at a profit with a price of $1,000, should the manager go ahead with the product?

All estimates really have a range of values. There is very little chance that an absolute estimate like our estimate of $1,000 will truly be the actual cost of the product. It will probably be different from that exact value by some amount. It is reasonable to say that all estimates should be given in terms of a range of values.

Suppose that our manager says that the estimate for the product is $1,000, and the sales department says that this will be profitable. The manager decides to go ahead with the product introduction.

Suppose we had told the manager that the product could be built for $995 to $1,005 and that we had a 95 percent probability that the true cost of making the product would fall in that range of values. The manager would probably decide to go ahead with the product and recommend that the selling price be $1,005.

If, on the other hand, we had given her an estimate of $900 to $1,100 and said that we have a 90 percent probability that the actual cost will fall within this range of values, the manager might feel that trying to sell the product at $1,100 could be a very small market penetration and decide not to introduce the new product.

Of course, what this really tells our manager is that the estimate needs to be studied more and the accuracy needs to be improved.

A bottom-up estimate is one in which the cost estimates are independently made for individual, small details of the project. These individual cost estimates are then added together or rolled up to make the cost estimates for the entire project. They can also be added up to create estimates for subprojects within the project. A top-down estimate is one in which the entire project is estimated as a whole, and this value is divided into the component subprojects of the project.

We can think of a bottom-up estimate in terms of the work breakdown structure. If we were to estimate the cost of each task at the bottom of the work breakdown structure independently and add the individual estimates together, we would have a bottom-up estimate for the project.

Bottom-up estimates for the project are inherently more accurate than top-down estimates. This is intuitively true. It is mathematically true as well. When a large number of small details are individually estimated and added together, there is a chance that the individual detailed estimates will be either high or low. That is, some of the individual details will be underestimated, and some will be overestimated. When we add them together, some of the overestimates will cancel out some of the underestimates. The result is that the total project estimate's accuracy will improve simply by creating more detailed estimates. Of course, since small details are less likely to have forgotten details within them, overall estimates will improve considerably more.

Top-down project estimates are appropriate when we are doing estimates early in the project or at times when relatively inaccurate estimates are acceptable. These estimates are called rough order of magnitude or budget estimates. When it comes time to commit serious money to the project, bottom-up estimates, often referred to as definitive estimates, should be used.

Parametric and analogous estimating methods are used as types of top-down estimates. With the analogous estimating technique we identify another project or subproject that will be used as the basis of the estimate, and we scale it up or down to match the project or subproject we are trying to estimate. If the actual cost of the basis project was collected accurately and if there is a great deal of similarity between the basis project and the project being estimated, these estimates can be quite accurate. For example, a contractor is estimating a project to build fifteen houses. In the past the contractor has built projects with up to ten houses. He could estimate the cost of the new project by scaling up the ten-house project by 1.5.

Parametric estimates are based on some parametric relationship between cost and the parameter that can be measured for the project. In a parametric estimate we use some measurable parameter that changes in the same way that cost does. We then find an adjusting factor that will relate the parameter to the cost of the item being estimated. For example, suppose we wanted to estimate the cost of driving to California. If we know from past experience that gasoline, tires, oil, and wear and tear on the car cost $0.35 per mile and if the distance to California is 2,000 miles, we could estimate the cost of driving to California at $700. Building contractors frequently quote the cost of building residential houses as being $70 per square foot. A 5,000-square-foot house could thus be estimated at $350,000.

Generally speaking, order of magnitude estimates have an accuracy of about -25 percent to $+75$ percent; budget estimates have an accuracy of about -10 percent to $+25$ percent, and definitive estimates have an accuracy of about -5 percent to $+10$ percent. You may ask why the range of values here is lopsided. This is simply realistic. If we estimate the cost of something to be $50 it would be impossible for us to be more than $50 overestimated but it is quite possible for us to be $50 or even more underestimated.

What terms are used in estimating?

The terms used in estimating are related to the use of project management software. Because of the defaults used in project management software, we have been using these terms in our estimates.

> *Effort:* The hours of labor to do work. Effort is usually expressed as man-hours or people-hours but could be expressed as man-days, man-months, or man-years.

Effort = Number of equivalent full-time people × Duration

If a task contains four hundred people-hours of effort and there are ten people working on it then it will take forty hours of duration to complete it. If five people are working on the same task, it will have a duration of eighty hours. If the five people working on this task are working on a part-time basis and available 50 percent of the time the duration will be 160 hours.

> *Duration:* Number of time intervals to do work. Duration is usually expressed in working days but could be expressed in any time interval that is convenient. Project management software has been used in a number of nontraditional schedule and resource management applications. One application used project management soft-

ware to schedule jobs through the central processor of a computer, and the durations were measured in microseconds.

Level of Effort Work: Work done directly for a project but not for a specific activity. One of the things that we want to do in managing our projects is to be able to account for all the things that cost money and take time. This creates a problem for people who work on the project but do not have specific task assignments. Probably the best example of a level of effort person is the project manager. The project manager is managing the entire project but no one task specifically. Since the project manager works on many tasks simultaneously, it is not practical for him to report time against the specific tasks. Time is just charged against the project. Others who provide project level services can also be level of effort workers. The number of people who report to the project as level of effort workers should be kept at a minimum since they may be doing work for specific tasks while not accruing actual cost against a specific task. People who are shared between two or more projects may also be level of effort workers.

Work Time: Calendar time available for work. This term is used to describe the work schedule a person is working. This factor is necessary for project management software to properly allocate and show the availability of people and equipment. Work time is expressed as 09:00 to 05:00, Monday through Friday.

Elapsed Time: Time between start and finish regardless of working or not working. The elapsed time of a task in the project shows the start and finish dates of the task regardless of whether the task is being worked on. A task might start on January 1 and finish on January 10 and have a duration of only five days. The task might be scheduled to be worked on January 1, 2, 3, 9, and 10. January 4 and 5 are Saturday and Sunday, nonworking days, and January 6, 7, and 8 are days when the persons working on the task are transferred to another task. The elapsed time is still ten days.

Availability: The amount of time that a person is available to do work. This can be expressed as a percent of the person's full-time availability. A person may be available for 50 percent of his or her time.

What are estimating factors?

Productivity and utilization are the two factors we are concerned with when doing estimating for projects. Both of these factors are applicable to cost as well as schedule estimates. Productivity is a measure of how much faster or slower a particular resource is from the normal resource.

A person who is very good or very experienced at what they do will probably take less time and make fewer mistakes than a new person with little experience. Productivity factors allow us to adjust the cost or the duration of the task depending on the particular individual used.

Utilization is another adjustment factor to the cost estimate. Utilization is based on the idea that even though we pay someone for a full eight-hour day, the person seldom, if ever, actually works the full eight hours. Utilization is a way of adjusting the cost of a task to allow for the time that the person is being paid but not actually doing things that are productive.

Tell me more . . .

Productivity and utilization factors are important in deriving the total project cost and schedule estimates. Failure to use them could result in otherwise good estimates being off by as much as 40 percent or even more. Failure to manage them properly could result in demoralizing the entire project team.

Productivity is a measure of how productive one person is when compared to a normal person. The normal person is a hypothetical person who works at a pace that is not abnormally fast or abnormally slow. This is a concept we inherit from industrial engineers whose job it is to manage factory people. Since most factory workers perform the same task over and over again, the industrial engineer is very concerned with being as close as possible to the actual cost. The productivity factor is an adjustment to the time that it takes a person to do work when compared to a normal person. In the industrial environment it would not be fair to measure everyone's work in comparison to that of someone who is abnormally fast or slow.

Although the idea of productivity has its roots in factory operations, it is significant to project management as well. It is difficult to measure a person's productivity accurately in project work because the nature of projects is that the work is generally not very repetitious. However, it does make sense to adjust cost and schedules depending on who is actually going to do the work. Suppose we have a choice of using John or Mary on a particular task on our project. Mary is very senior and has a lot of experience doing this kind of work. John is new to the company and has never done this kind of work before. Mary receives a much higher salary than John. Mary will most likely get the work assignment completed in a minimum amount of time and make very few mistakes. John will probably take longer to complete the work and make more mistakes doing it.

As a project manager doing estimates, we will be faced with many conflicting problems in terms of the resources we can use. We would all like to have the best people on our projects for all the positions we have on the team. Unfortunately this is not always possible. The needs of other projects should also come into play and this is one of the important jobs that the functional manager in a matrix organization must face. His or her job is to see to it that the correct and appropriate resource is used in each assignment, and this is not always the one that the project manager feels is the best one for the project.

Let us say that Mary has a salary of $125,000 per year, and John has a salary of $40,000 per year. Mary estimates that the task will take her four weeks to complete if she works on it full-time. John does not have any idea how long it will take him to do the task, but with help he estimates that it will take him eight weeks. Checking the schedule we find that the task in mind has sixty-three days of total float and forty days of free float associated with it. Although John's productivity is half of Mary's, it is cost-effective to use John for this task.

When early project estimates are put together, we frequently do not know precisely who will be available to do the work when the work is actually scheduled to be done. This is where the normal person concept comes in. The amount of time that should be put into the estimate at this point should be the amount of time that a normal person will take to do the task and the cost of that time. As we become more definitive in our estimating and as the time to actually do the project work comes closer, we should make adjustments in our cost and schedule estimates to reflect the person who will actually be doing the work. At the point the person who will do the work is identified, the cost of that person to the project and the estimated time that the task will take should be recognized.

Utilization becomes important to project managers as well. Remember that utilization is the adjustment factor to correct for the fact that everyone is paid to work a certain number of hours in a day, say eight hours, but that no one actually works that many hours in a day. Everyone has interruptions, visits from an immediate boss, coffee breaks, telephone calls, calls of nature, meetings in the hall on the way to and from the calls of nature or the coffee machine, and many others.

Where utilization becomes a problem is in recognizing whether a person doing an estimate has or has not included a utilization factor in the estimate. If a utilization adjustment has been made to an estimate we receive and if we apply a utilization factor to it, we will be adding unnecessary cost to our estimate. On the other hand, if a utilization factor has not been applied to the estimate and if we do not add it, we will have underestimated the cost of doing the task. This utilization factor is of some importance when you consider that the amount of time that is lost in a typical eight-hour day is about 30 percent. This 30 percent is based on people who have very good timekeeping records. In most companies it is probably higher than this.

Generally you can standardize on a utilization factor for your project. This utilization factor will usually not change much from project to project and will generally be set by a company policy. The real problem comes when we are trying to determine whether or not someone on our project team has included the adjustment of utilization or not. The rule here is that when you are in doubt about an estimate, you need to make sure the person doing the estimate has thought about it and deliberately included it in the estimate or excluded it from the estimate. Most people who are not professional estimators will not include a utilization factor when they estimate the time that it will take to do a task in hours as in, "I think this task is going to take me fifteen hours to complete." This person probably means that if they can start working on this task and work without interruption, they will finish it fifteen working hours after they started. We should probably increase the estimate by 30 percent and use 19.5 hours for this task.

Another person submits an estimate of the time to do a different task as two weeks. This person probably means that if they start working on Monday, they will finish the task at close of business one week from the following Friday. In this case the person has probably included the utilization and interruptions.

Neither of these estimates is wrong. They are just different. As the project manager we must be sure we understand the estimate that is being submitted to us and make utilization adjustments accordingly. It is no wonder that we have so much trouble with estimating cost and time.

Now, about those morale issues (that's *morale* not *moral*). As a project manager we do not want to use productivity and utilization factors directly and individually. Usually we will not have much of a choice with utilization factors because they will generally be established by project or company policy. Productivity is another matter. It can be quite demoralizing for a project team member to see that the productivity level of the task he or she is working on has been set at 65 percent. Most people feel that their productivity level is more like 100 percent or even higher. This is because they view productivity as the amount of effort they are putting into the work. In other words, they are working as hard as they can. We do not want to publish that they are working at a 65 percent productivity level.

A much better way to incorporate productivity into our project is to allow the individual who is going to do the work make his own estimates. When the estimates are reviewed with the person, time can cooperatively be added or reduced to reflect what we observe to be that person's productivity compared to what he sees as his own productivity.

What is life cycle cost?

Life cycle cost is the cost that is associated with the project from the beginning of the project to the end of its useful life and beyond. It includes the cost of acquiring the project, operating it, and disposing of it at the end of its useful life. It may even include money spent after the project's useful life that is a result of the project's existence and effects.

Normally the cost of a project is considered only from the beginning of the project to its end. This is reasonable because the project team is formed to carry out the work of creating the project, deliver the deliverables, and do it within the schedule and cost goals of the project. This is really a narrow view because there are many costs that may occur for the stakeholders as the result of decisions made within the project but occurring after the project has been completed. Life cycle cost considers all these costs.

For example, the project team is able to reduce cost by limiting the number of design reviews. The result of this may be that the design is compromised. The compromised, nonoptimal design may cost the stakeholders many times the money saved by limiting the design reviews. The cost of this will not necessarily occur until the project is delivered and the project team disbanded. Life cycle cost would include this cost.

Life cycle cost is quite important in the justification of projects. The total cost of a project should be considered over the entire life of the project and not just within a fixed period of time.

Tell me more . . .

The cost and benefits of the project must be considered over the life of the project. By this we mean that we must consider all of the effects of the project from beginning to end. If we were building a nuclear power plant and we were to consider only the cost of building the plant and operating it for the twenty-five or so years it would be in operation, we would be very naive. There is tremendous cost associated with decommissioning a nuclear power plant and cleaning up the area where it was in operation and disposing of the radioactive materials that are left. Today we have a legacy of nuclear power plants where this was not done very well. In the 1960s and 1970s many nuclear plants were built with little regard for what would have to be done when they were worn out. Little consideration was given to the disposal of spent nuclear waste, and we still have no workable plan for disposing of it. Many of these facilities probably would not have been constructed if the full cost had been recognized at the beginning of the project.

When project decisions are made, we must consider the effect of these decisions outside the direct area of the project. When cheaper materials are used for a project, it will usually result in a shorter useful life or a product that is more fragile and has higher maintenance costs. Sometimes the application and the desires of the stakeholders are that the cheaper product be made regardless of the future maintenance cost and the shorter useful life. This can be a valid decision.

The important obligation of the project manager and the project team is that the customer and the stakeholders be made aware of these options and that informed decisions are made with the realization that money saved today may cost more in the long run. This again points out the importance of doing a good project justification.

In project justifications, the period of time that should be considered in justifying the project must be long enough to include the recognition of the life cycle costs until they reach a steady state or go to zero. By doing this in our project justifications we assure that all of the costs of the project are considered. If the client wants the project done at a minimum cost, the justification will show the increases that are going to occur after the project is delivered.

For example, suppose we could do a project two different ways. If we do the project the first way, we will spend the money to make the project robust and long-lasting, which will result in minimum maintenance costs. If we do the project the second way, we will minimize costs by using the minimum amount and strength of material and design the project for minimum cost and sacrifice future maintenance costs. Suppose the first method of doing the project could deliver the project for $2,000,000 and the future maintenance costs were estimated at $100,000 per year for the fifteen years of the project's useful life. The second method could deliver the project for $1,500,000 and the estimated maintenance cost would be $200,000 per year.

As can be seen in this very simplified example, the life cycle cost of the project is much lower if the cost is not minimized in delivering the project.

What is statistical cost estimating?

Statistical cost estimating is a method of using statistics to determine the range of values of a cost estimate and the probability that the actual cost will occur between the two values in the range. This is the same technique that is discussed in the PERT method that is discussed in Chapter 5 under "What is the PERT method?" The PERT technique is used to estimate the project duration. Here it is applied to estimating cost. The calculations are exactly the same here as they are in the PERT technique.

**Expected value of cost = (Optimistic +
(4 × Most Likely) + Pessimistic) / 6
Standard deviation = (Pessimistic − Optimistic) / 6**

Most of the time in cost estimating we are satisfied with an estimated range of values that has a 95 percent probability of having the actual cost of the estimated item falling within the range. This is the range of values that is the expected value of cost plus two standard deviations and minus two standard deviations.

Tell me more . . .

In the PERT technique discussed in Chapter 5, we attempt to determine the probability of the project's being completed between a pair of dates. The range of dates is the expected completion date of the project plus or minus two standard deviations calculated using the equations above. While the dates are approximations based on using a normal distribution, a skewed probability distribution such as the beta distribution (see Figure 3-1) would be more correct, but the results are accurate enough for schedule estimates. These same assumptions are equally valid for cost estimating.

Note that because of statistical convergence, the more details that are included in the cost estimate, the more accurate the cost estimate becomes. This is simply because, mathematically, the more detail that is present in the estimate, the more accuracy there will be. In a detailed estimate we have individual estimates for each of the details. It is reasonable and statistically accurate to say that some of the estimates will be overestimates and others will be underestimates. When these estimates are added together, the overestimates and the underestimates will tend to cancel each other out. This, in turn, makes the overall cost summary more accurate.

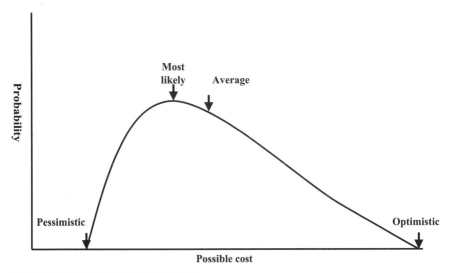

FIGURE 3-1: SKEWED PROBABILITY DISTRIBUTION

Suppose we have an estimate that we are doing for a new product. It is estimated that the most likely cost for the project will be $63,000. Based on this estimate, we have determined that the standard deviation of the estimate is $1,250. If we were interested in an estimate that had a range of values such that the actual cost would be more than the minimum and less than the maximum, it would be reasonable to use + or − two standard deviations from the most likely value. In this case it would be $63,000 +$2,500 and −$2,500 and the range of values would be $65,500 to $60,500. If this project were being bid competitively or if the product we were making had a very narrow price range, we would probably want to have more accurate estimates.

To do this and take advantage of the convergence of the standard deviation, we could break the product into five subassemblies as shown in Figure 3-2. Once the subassemblies were identified, we could estimate the cost of each by estimating the optimistic, pessimistic, and most likely values. We could then calculate the expected value of each subassembly and its standard deviation. To get the overall revised estimate of the cost of the whole product, we then sum the standard deviations by first squaring them, then adding them together, and then taking the square root of the total.

Now we still have an expected value of $63,000, but the standard deviation is $640. To get the 95 percent range of values as we did earlier,

An estimate is broken down into five subestimates (figures in thousands)

Group	Mean	Std Dev	(Std Dev)^2
1	$12	$.10	$.01
2	11	.15	.0225
3	5	.20	.04
4	20	.50	.25
5	15	.30	.09
	63		$\sqrt{.4125}$ = .64

Complete estimate has total cost of $63,000 with $640 std dev.

FIGURE 3-2: EXAMPLE: INCREASING DETAIL OF AN ESTIMATE

we take the $63,000 and + or − two standard deviations but now use $640 instead of $1,250. This gives us $63,000 + $1,280 − $1,280, or a range of values of $64,280 to $61,720. Simply decomposing the project into five components has had a significant increase in the accuracy of our estimate.

The interesting thing about estimating using this technique is that it tells you when you have done enough estimating work and what you must do to improve the estimate to where it will serve your current needs. Many times people spend too much work in producing an estimate that is too accurate for the purpose. This is a waste of effort.

By the use of this technique we begin our project with order of magnitude estimates that have a relatively low accuracy required (− 25 percent to + 75 percent). As we progress closer to making a commitment, we will want to increase the accuracy of our estimates to a 95 percent probability of having the actual cost come between the range of values that is estimated. To do this all that needs to be done is to look at the value of the largest subcomponent in the previous estimate and break that component down into sub-subcomponents and independently estimate the cost of each of those components. By doing this we will reduce the magnitude of the standard deviation of the total and thereby improve the overall accuracy of the total estimate. If the range of values and the probability of the actual cost being within them is good enough for this estimate, then we can stop work. If the range of values or the probability is not good enough, then we look for the next large component of cost and break it down into subgroups and recalculate our estimate. The standard deviation magnitude will become smaller and the range of values for a given probability will also become smaller.

What is the difference between estimated cost and price?

Estimating cost means developing the approximate cost of completing the entire project or part of it. It is the expected quantitative result. When we estimate the cost of doing a project, we are estimating the amount of money that it will take to complete the entire project.

In addition to the project completion cost, we may frequently include the life cycle cost as well. Normally the cost of the project includes only the amount of money that will be spent by the project team up until the time the completed project is turned over to the client and the stakeholders. Life cycle cost includes the cost of the project that continues after delivery of the project throughout the useful life of the project. Although the project team will be concerned with the cost of the project up until the time of delivery, many of the decisions it makes will affect life cycle cost and should be discussed with management and the stakeholders and shown in the project justification.

The selling price minus the cost of the project is equal to the profit of the project.

Selling price is the amount of money the organization will charge to deliver the project. This may be more or less than the cost of the project. The price of a project should be equal to the perceived value to the customer. The value to the customer is generally what money the project will generate for the customer and has little to do with what it costs to produce the project.

Tell me more . . .

Many companies undersell their projects. For example, a client comes to the company and asks that the company do a project for them. The description of the requirements of the project produces a cost estimate for the amount of money that must be spent to deliver the project. Many times the company has a history of making a certain percentage of profit on its projects. It uses this percentage to factor up the estimated cost of the project to develop the selling price. It may be that the customer is willing to pay much more to have the project completed. The reason the customer is willing to pay more is that the customer is going to use the project in a way that will generate revenue for the company. This anticipated revenue justifies the higher price for the project. This is the perceived value to the customer. In other words, if we can deliver a project for a cost of $25,000 that has a value to our customer of $100,000, should we charge them $100,000 or something slightly more or less than that?

What we should do is sell the customer the project at $100,000 and use the $75,000 profit to improve our business so that we will continue to be competitive when our competition offers our customer similar projects at lower prices in the future. In a free market economy this is what will surely happen. Competitors will see that we can make large profits in this type of business and will enter the market to compete with us at ever lowering prices.

Where a company can get into trouble is in not realizing this. Let us say that in the above example, we mistakenly estimated the cost of doing this same project at $50,000 and we sold it to our customer at a price of $100,000, making a nice profit of $50,000. If the estimate to complete the project were $50,000, it is likely that the actual project cost will be close to $50,000. In most companies there will be little for management to complain about if the project is completed for the budget that was set for it. The project team will usually not take corrective action if project tasks are being completed within the expected budget. Most companies work this way because they have other, more serious problems to worry about. They follow the adage, "If it ain't broke, don't fix it."

Remember that the correct cost for this project was $25,000 and our company is making the project for $50,000. Of course the company does not know that the project should really cost close to $25,000. It thinks that the estimate is correct at $50,000. Since the company is making a $50,000 profit, it will be very satisfied. Eventually the competition will start quoting similar projects to our customer at lower prices and the customer will accept them. This means that we will have to reduce our prices as well. If we think that we are operating at the least cost of $50,000, this price reduction will reduce our profits. This may still be acceptable until our point of minimum profit is reached. If competition forces us to reduce our price below $50,000, we will be losing money on this business.

Many times companies leave the business rather than find out that their cost has been $25,000 higher than it should have been for years. They tend to be resistant to change. They frequently cannot convince themselves that they can reduce the cost of what they have been doing so successfully for years. They will claim instead that the competition is "buying" the business and is doing the work for less than their actual cost. They will claim that their long-time customer is being lost for any reason other than the correct one. That reason is that they have been wasting money all these years and doing projects like this at far above what their true cost should be.

It is important then to have accurate cost estimates for what we are to produce because without good cost estimates, we will never know what the true cost should be. Having made good and realistic estimates we must then sell our projects for the perceived value that they have to the customer and the stakeholders.

What is the law of diminishing returns?

The law of diminishing returns says that each time we do something to receive a benefit, the benefit will be less and less. The best way to think of this is by a simple example. If we are with a small child on a hot summer day and we pass an ice cream stand and buy the child an ice cream cone, it will taste wonderful. A short time later we pass another ice cream stand and buy the child another ice cream cone. This time the cone does not taste as good as the first one. If we continue passing ice cream stands and buying ice cream cones for the child, we will find that the taste of the ice cream gets less and less wonderful with each ice cream cone. Eventually the child will become sick of eating ice cream cones (and may become sick as well) and will not want another one. This is the law of diminishing returns.

Tell me more . . .

In the world of business there are many applications of the law of diminishing returns. When we make reductions in the scheduled completion date of a project, we receive large reductions at first for relatively small amounts of time, effort, and money. As we continue to reduce the schedule, we will receive smaller reductions in schedule time for the same amount of spent time, effort, and money.

If we buy a piece of maintenance equipment, the benefits received from buying the first piece of equipment are a certain amount. If we are happy with that piece of equipment and buy another piece of the same equipment, the benefits received from the second piece of equipment are less than the benefits received from the first piece of equipment.

If we decide to get married, we receive many benefits from the marriage. If we decide to get married to a second spouse, the benefits received are considerably less than the benefits received from the first marriage. In this case the benefits might be considerably less since in most states bigamy is illegal and we could end up in jail with no spouse at all.

What is a cost improvement curve?

A cost improvement curve is based loosely on the idea of a learning curve. In some contracts, generally large ones, the client may require the vendor to reduce the price of items supplied later in the project to less than the delivery price of earlier items of the project. The application of cost improvement curves borrows heavily from the learning curve theory but is based on somewhat different concepts. In the cost improvement curve it is reasonable to think that even though there is little chance for real learning, the cost of delivering items that are produced later in the project should be less than the cost of producing similar items early in the project.

The rationale for this is that the vendor will learn how to deal better with the customer, the specifications of the project deliverables, and the quality requirements. Although the deliverables of the project are not the same, a certain amount of improvement can be gained with the delivery of each deliverable.

The improvement curve rationale is then put into the contract. The improvement curve specification specifies that the price will be a certain amount for the first quantity of deliverables and will be somewhat lower for the next quantity delivered, and so on. Frequently the price of subsequent items will show a fixed percentage of reduction in price for each doubling of the number of units delivered, which is the relationship with classical learning curves.

Tell me more . . .

Let us start with classical learning curves. The learning curve originated in the time of Frederick Taylor (1856–1915), many times called the father of industrial engineering and time study in industrial applications, and Henry Ford (1863–1947), the father of the assembly line. Taylor noticed that when workers were given a piece of work to do, the time that it took them to do the work decreased each time they repeated the piece of work.

After a considerable amount of study, Taylor found that the time that it took to do a piece of work decreased by a fixed percentage when the number of times the work was performed was doubled. This means that if it took four minutes to do a certain amount of work the first time, the second time the work was performed, it might take 85 percent of the first time or 3.40 minutes. The fourth time the same work was done, it would take 2.89 minutes, and the eighth time the work was done, it would take 2.46 minutes, and so on. Each time the number of times the work is performed doubles, the time it takes to do one piece of work becomes less by a smaller amount, since it is a fixed percentage of the last doubling of the work. The second time is less than the first, the fourth time is less than the second, the eighth is less than the fourth, and so on. Eventually, after enough doublings, the curve will flatten out and the reduction in time for additional doublings becomes relatively insignificant.

Henry Ford made great use of this information in developing the assembly line. If very short work operations are used, the amount of time that it takes to double the number of times to do the work becomes short as well. What this means is that if we were to design work so that the time interval to do the work is very short, people would come down the learning curve very quickly and reach the flat part of the curve. At this point they could be considered to be fully productive on their work assignment.

What Ford wanted was a way to incorporate new people into his factory with a minimum of training and experience. By making the work tasks very short, people would become proficient at them very quickly. This allowed him to dismiss people who were not working to his standards and replace them easily. Back in the days before unions, people were terminated without the slightest provocation, and it was important to be able to bring in a new person with very little experience or training to learn the job and do the job proficiently as quickly as possible.

Improvement curves (see Figure 3-3) are similar to learning curves in that the fixed percentage reduction of price is applied to each doubling of delivery of the product. The improvement curve is not really based on learning, as was the learning curve. Improvement curves are based on the idea that similar project deliverables will cost more early in the project than they will later in the project.

This is rational since the vendor of a multideliverable type of large project will learn how to deal with the customer's requirements as subse-

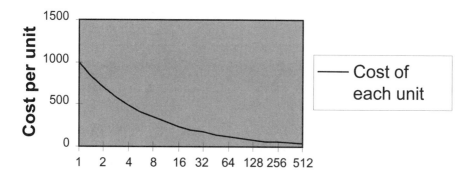

Number of units

FIGURE 3-3: 70% IMPROVEMENT CURVE

quent deliverables are delivered. There will be a certain amount of value engineering that will take place as well, and the vendor's vendors will have improvements as well.

The improvement curve is then a consistent way of recognizing that improvements do occur over time and that they will be significantly larger earlier in the project than they will be later in the project.

An example of the application of improvement curves: An aerospace contractor had a contract to produce a part that had a cost of $1,000 the first time it was made. Because it was the first time the part was made, it could be expected that subsequent parts would be made at a lower cost. It was agreed that a 70 percent improvement curve would be applied.

The cost of parts delivered subsequent to the original unit would be progressively less. These contractually agreed to reductions in cost are shown in the improvement curve plotted in Figure 3-3.

4

Cost Management

What is the cost baseline?

The cost baseline is the basis for the earned value reporting system. It is the budget for the estimated cost of the project spread over the time periods of the project. As we noted in Chapter 1, in managing a project we are concerned about three baselines: the schedule baseline, the cost baseline, and the scope baseline. These three baselines comprise the goals of any project and deliver to the stakeholders what was asked for, in the time predicted, and for the money that was estimated.

The cost baseline is the part of the project concerned with the amount of money that the project is predicted to cost and when that money will be used. The three baselines are closely related, and changes to one of them will result in changes to the others. If a change is made in the project scope baseline, either by adding or removing some of the work that is required, the schedule baseline and the cost baseline will probably have to be changed as well. It is foolish for managers to change the project scope without considering the effect on budgets or schedules, yet it is done to project managers all the time.

Tell me more . . .

In order to develop the cost of the project and complete our project plans, it is necessary to do a bottom-up, definitive, detailed cost estimate for all the activities of the project. The cost of all of the planned activities spread over time is the operational budget, sometimes called the performance budget.

Some care must be exercised when planning the cost baseline. Since this is the basis for our performance measurement system, we must be careful that the budget is shown on the cost baseline at the same point in time where we expect the actual cost to occur. This can be quite a problem. Suppose we show the budgeted expenditure for an item we are purchasing to be on a particular date, say April 15. To the project management planners this is the date that the project team completes the work that will make the purchase take place. In other words, the project team decides what it needs to purchase and issues a purchase requisition to the purchasing department to actually buy it. The actual expenditure, the time when the money is actually spent, the time when the company actually issues a check to the company supplying the parts to the project team, might be several months later. Because of the time delay, the actual cost will be below the budgeted cost for several months. This will, of course, have the effect of making the performance reports look better than they are. If there are many delays in the reporting of actual cost in the project, the entire project may look much better than it really is. Of course, sooner or later the actual costs are shown. Then the project performance suddenly falls.

The cost baseline is not enough money to get the project done. In addition to all the work that has been identified, we will have some other work to do that was not planned. This unplanned work is the result of risks we took. Some of the risks in the project were identified and planned for while others come as a complete surprise. We will discuss risk management in Chapter 8. Risks are just project work activities that have a probability associated with them. The probability is a measure of the likelihood that they will or will not have to be done in the course of the project. The risks that have been identified must have an estimated cost associated with them as well as a probability. Multiplied together, the result is the expected value of the risk. For example, suppose that there is a risk of 5 percent that the paint on our project will not adhere properly and we will have to strip it off and repaint. If the cost of the repair is $1,000, it would not make much sense to budget $1,000 into the project for this risk. If we did this, all of our projects would be greatly overbudgeted. While it will indeed cost $1,000 to make the repair, it is only necessary to budget the expected value, 5 percent of $1,000 or $100. If the project is painted acceptably the first time, we will have an extra $100 in our project risk budget; if it is not, we will spend the $100 and $900 more.

Since any project will have many risks, some of them will result in extra cost and work, and others will not. If our estimates for probability and impact were correct, at the end of the project the budget for these risks should end up to be equal to the total expected value of all of the risks that actually took place in the project.

This takes care of the identified risks, but what about the risks that came as a surprise and were not anticipated? These risks, the unidentified risks of the project, must be budgeted as well. Unfortunately, the budget for these risks is going to be a bit of a guess. We can only rely on our past experience with other similar projects to come up with this estimate. These budgets for unknown and unidentified risks are generally estimated very roughly as some percentage of the total project. The percentage should be quite small, however.

Where the budget for unknown risks is higher than a very small percentage of the project cost, there is a chance that the risk identification process was poorly done and that many of the risks that could have been identified were not. In this case the budget for the unknown risks is frequently inflated as a way of compensating for this lack of identification. A much better solution would be to spend more time identifying the risks that can be identified, evaluating them properly, and setting aside a small amount of budget for the unknown risks.

Why do we have two separate reserves to take care of the risks?

There are two kinds of reserves set up to budget for risks: the contingency reserve and the management reserve. The contingency reserve contains the money to do the risks that were identified. The management reserve contains the money to do the risks that were not identified. These two reserves are separated in order to have more control over how they are spent. Use of the two reserves usually requires one additional level of management approval. The normal operating budget of the project is controlled by the individual responsible for the work; the contingency budget is controlled by the person to whom that responsible individual reports. The management reserve requires one more level of approval, the person to whom the responsible person's supervisor reports.

In normal-size projects this puts the contingency reserve under the approval of the project manager and the management reserve under the approval of the project manager's supervisor. It should be noted that someone outside the project approves the spending of funds from the management reserve in this case.

Tell me more . . .

Our budget philosophy in project management is to allow the responsible members of the project team to manage their own activities. This means that where budgets are concerned, each person on the project team should have the budgeted cost of work scheduled, the BCWS, allocated to the activity she is responsible for. The BCWS budget can be spent by the responsible person without having to get additional approvals. The Project Management Institute has redesignated the BCWS to be called the planned value or PV. It remains to be seen whether the rest of the world will adopt this designation.

There is some danger in assigning the contingency reserve and management reserve to the same individual, however. If this is done, the reserves are tempting pockets of money that might be used to cover poor performance instead of risks that come to be.

For this reason the contingency reserve must have the approval of a manager one level above the individual responsible for the activity where the risk has occurred. This is for risks that have already been identified. When this approval takes place, money is removed from the contingency reserve and added to the operating budget, the BCWS for the activities affected by the risk. When a previously identified risk occurs, the preplanned money to take care of this risk is removed from the contingency budget and allocated to the normal operating budget. The BCWS is adjusted for the amount of money that is added to the project operating budget, and the BCWS is adjusted for the points in time when the new expenditures will occur. The budget at completion, the BAC, will also change.

The management reserve is also tempting. Since the management reserve is money available to take care of risks that have not even been identified, it is tempting for the manager to use this money improperly. Therefore, another level of authority is required for approval for using funds in the management reserve. When this approval takes place, the funds are removed from the management reserve and added to the operating budget, the BCWS for the activities affected by this risk.

Notice that since the risks are all probabilistic in nature, they are not included in the project operating budget and are not included in the BCWS for each activity. Therefore, the operating cost accounts for the project, and the budget at completion for the project does not include the reserves either.

To summarize, the operating budget or the cost baseline is equal to the budgeted cost of work scheduled and does not include the management reserve or the contingency reserve. When risks occur in the project, funds are removed from the appropriate reserve and added to the cost baseline. The total expected expenditures for the project are therefore the sum of the operating budget plus the contingency budget plus the management reserve. The amount of money that is contained in the contingency budget is the sum of the expected values of the identified risks in the project. The amount of money in the management reserve is a percentage of the project or the contingency reserve. The value of the management reserve should be quite small since money in the management reserve is relatively uncontrolled. The amount of funds put into the management reserve is a function of the amount of risk in the project. Very risky projects tend to have larger management reserves than less risky projects.

Why am I concerned with cost budgeting?

Cost budgeting or setting the cost baseline for a project is very important since it forms the foundation for the measurement of performance in the project. Ultimately our performance measurement system is going to measure the actual costs of the project in terms of time and quantity and compare that to the planned expenditures in terms of time and quantity. Any error we have in the amount of budget set aside for a particular activity in our project or the timing of that expenditure will result in over- or understating the performance of that part of the project team. If one of the tasks in the project is budgeted for $2,000 when it should have been budgeted for $1,500, the performance on this overbudgeted task will be unjustifiably high. Worse, the actual cost of the task could actually be $2,000 because work tends to fill the time allowed and spend the amount for which it was budgeted. Most managers will not take corrective action when tasks are being done within their predicted budget.

Setting of budgets also has an effect on the business itself. All companies have financial managers who must concern themselves with the timing of the expenditures of the company and making sure that there are funds available to pay the bills. Budgeting too much for a project means that excessive funds that are not required will be on hand. Not budgeting enough for the project means that funds will have to be found for the project on short notice.

Tell me more . . .

Placement of the budget in terms of the amount of money that will be spent on the individual tasks of the project as well as the timing of those expenditures is necessary for any performance measurement system to work. It is also important in helping the company manage its cash reserves so that enough, but not too much, money is available when it is required to pay bills that become due.

Any performance measurement system will be a measure of the comparison of the expected result to the actual result. In the case of projects, we are usually interested in the measurement of performance in terms of the amount of money that is being spent and the time in which it is spent. The earned value reporting system is excellent for measuring project performance but requires careful placement of the project plan in terms of quantity and timing of the planned expenditures. If the planned expenditures are not in close synchronization with the actual expenditures in terms of quantity and timing, the project will indicate a level of performance that is higher or lower than is actually the case. Suppose we have a project with a sizable amount of internal labor being used to complete many of the project tasks. We plan the expenditures for this work according to the project schedule. The project schedule shows when the work is taking place. Each person working on project tasks reports the work by task worked on and by the number of hours spent on each task. We will assume that we are doing this on a weekly basis. So, for example, Saralee works on four different tasks during the week. She works twenty hours on task one; ten hours on task two; four hours on task three, and six hours on task four. The time card she reports this on is sent into the payroll system in the accounting department and processed through the computer system. Corrections are made in the payroll system, and a report comes to the project manager one week later. At that point the time is shown as actual cost, but it is a week later than the time when the work was actually done. In addition, if the project manager finds a mistake on the report, it will take another week for the report to be corrected.

Figure 4-1 shows the overall effect of timing on cash flows. The timing of planned and actual cash flows must be the same or project status and performance reports can be misleading.

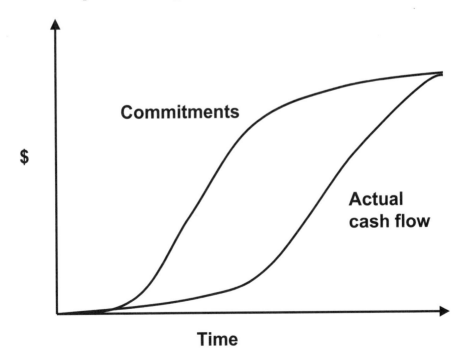

FIGURE 4-1: COMMITMENTS AND ACTUAL CASH FLOW

This problem can become worse if there have been errors in reporting from other projects or functional areas. What we mean by this is that one department or project team accidentally charges time to one of your project tasks. If you catch it at all, it is in a report that you see one week later. If you find the error and make the correction, it will be another week before the report shows it correctly. If the change requires approval of the person who made the mistake in the first place, it may take another week for the change to be made. All this makes the timing late for the actual cost to be recognized. Meanwhile the work has been done, and the completed work has been credited to the project, but the actual cost is less than it should be, and the performance is unjustifiably high for that task.

Material cost is a problem as well. Frequently the task of ordering material for a project is considered complete when the project team has finished the work.

Figure 4-2 shows that there is quite a lot of time involved between the time when the project team finishes the work of writing the requisition for materials for the project and the time when the actual cost of the expenditure is recognized. It is most convenient for the project team to recognize the completion of the work when the work of the project team is complete, but it is more accurate if the cost is recognized at the time the invoice is paid. In terms of the timing of the completion of the task, it is better to show the task as being completed when the person doing the work has completed the work.

As far as the quantity of money spent on the material is concerned, it may be better to show the expenditure when the actual invoice is paid. Final payment for items purchased usually includes the cost of inbound shipping and any other price adjustments. The shipping cost is usually not included in the original requisition but is included in the final cost of the purchase.

FIGURE 4-2: TIMING THE BUDGET

It is extremely important that the timing and quantity of the planned expenditures and the timing and quantity of the actual expenditures be synchronized. It is less important that they be recognized at the precise time they occur than it is that planned and actual costs be recognized at the same time. It does not matter very much if the planned and actual expenditure on any material is shown early in the project or late in the project. It does matter that the planned and actual costs be shown at the same time. If actual costs are shown later than they were planned, the project will be shown as healthy when it could be in trouble. If actual costs are shown before the planned costs, the project will appear to be in trouble when it is not.

Suppose we have a project that requires the purchase of a piece of equipment to be used exclusively for this project. This equipment has an estimated cost of $50,000. The completion of the equipment investigation and the issue of the requisition are scheduled for April 1. It takes the vendor two months to deliver the equipment. The payment for the equipment is made one month after delivery. Suppose our earned value reporting system recognizes the equipment in the plan when the project team generates the purchase requisition, but the actual cost is not recognized until the invoice is paid. Table 4-1 is an excerpt from the project's earned value reporting system.

In this example, because of the error in timing for reporting the $50,000 expenditure, all of the cost performance index (CPI) calculations during the month of April, May, and June (through June 23) show the project having a CPI greater than 1.00. This indicates that the earned value (EV) of the total project is greater than the actual cost (AC) for the project. In reality the project's CPI should be 1.00 for the entire time.

$$CPI = EV / AC$$

Financial managers for our company also depend on the accuracy of our estimates and the timing of our budgets. Money costs money whether we borrow it or get it from our investors. The cost of money is generally expressed in terms of the interest rate, which is just a way of stating the amount of money it costs to use money. When we use someone else's money, we have to pay them for the use of it.

The challenge to the financial manager is to have enough money on hand to pay all the bills as they come due but not have a surplus of funds that the company is paying to have on hand but does not need. In the example above, if the project plan called for the acquisition of the $50,000 piece of equipment on April 1 and the invoice was not paid until July 1, we were holding the money unnecessarily for three months. The cost to hold the money is approximately $1,250, assuming a 10 percent annual interest rate.

$$50,000 \times \tfrac{1}{4} \text{ yrs} \times 10\,\% \text{ interest} = \$1,250$$

While $1,250 might not seem like a lot of money in a single pur-
chase on a single project, if these types of errors are occurring on many
projects, the cost of holding surplus funds unnecessarily adds significantly to the cost of the projects. I would not like to pay this money out
of my salary. Of course the problems associated with not having enough
funds to pay the bills when they become due is worse. On-time payment
discounts can be lost, and interest rates to obtain money on the short
term are higher.

Financial managers often learn not to trust project estimates and
schedules if the project managers have a history of not making their expenditures happen when they plan them. An untrusting financial manager may anticipate budget overruns by having too much cash on hand.
This raises the cost of the money needed for the project if the project
follows its plan.

The lesson then is that we must have accurate predictions of when
these expenditures will be made so that our financial planners can be

Date (Week ending)	Planned value (PV)	Actual cost (AC)	Earned value (EV)	Cost performance index (CPI)
April 1	300,000	250,000	300,000	1.20
April 8	400,000	350,000	400,000	1.14
April 15	500,000	450,000	500,000	1.11
April 22	600,000	550,000	600,000	1.09
April 29	700,000	650,000	700,000	1.08
May 5	800,000	750,000	800,000	1.06
May 12	900,000	850,000	900,000	1.06
May 19	1,000,000	950,000	1,000,000	1.05
May 26	1,100,000	1,050,000	1,100,000	1.05
June 2	1,200,000	1,150,000	1,200,000	1.04
June 9	1,300,000	1,250,000	1,300,000	1.04
June 16	1,400,000	1,350,000	1,400,000	1.04
June 23	1,500,000	1,450,000	1,500,000	1.03
June 30	1,600,000	1,600,000	1,600,000	1.00
July 7	1,700,000	1,700,000	1,700,000	1.00
July 14	1,800,000	1,800,000	1,800,000	1.00
July 21	1,900,000	1,900,000	1,900,000	1.00

TABLE 4-1

sure to have the money on hand when the bills are due. To do this we must carefully budget our projects in terms of the amount of money and the date when it will be spent.

What is the time value of money?

The time value of money refers to the fact that money we receive in the future is worth less to us than money we receive today. If you loaned us $100 today and we paid you back the $100 two years from now, it would not be fair to you because we have had the use of your money for two years and paid nothing to use it. If we borrowed your car for two years, you would expect us to compensate you for its use.

The correct thing for us to have done would have been to have paid you some amount of money for the use of your money for two years. Professional lenders, banks and others, do this all the time. The amount that they charge for the use of their money is called interest, and it is calculated from what is called the interest rate.

Besides knowing how much banks and other lenders will charge us for the use of their money, we also need to know the value of money we will receive in the future, the future value, when it is compared to money we receive today, the present value. For convenience we make the adjustment using the same interest rate.

Tell me more . . .

It is very important for project managers to understand the time value of money. Projects of almost any size have cash flows that occur in the future. Generally, the timing of these cash flows is far enough in the future that an adjustment of these cash flows to their present values is important enough to be considered.

The concept in this adjustment forms the same basis for the payment of compound interest for money that is loaned. When we lend money to someone for a period of time, we expect him to pay for the use of that money. Compound interest is just the amount of money we have at the end of a given period of time if we do not use any of the money or the interest it earns. After the first amount of interest is paid, we will earn additional interest on the interest as well as the money we started with.

We should not only be paid for the use of our money, but we should also be paid for the risk that we are taking by lending the money. There is a possibility that the person to whom we are lending the money will never pay us back. The most conservative estimate of the interest rate, the risk-free investment, is usually equivalent to the U.S. Government Treasury bill rate of interest. The U.S. Government is considered a risk-free investment since it can almost always be expected to pay its bills and is not expected to go out of business any time soon.

When we put a sum of money into a bank account, there is an interest rate associated with the account. The interest is usually called the annual interest rate. This is the amount of interest that will be paid if the money is left in the account for one year. The interest is usually compounded, which means that the interest earned is left in the account so that the next time the interest is calculated, the interest that was paid last time earns interest as well.

For example, if we had $100 that was put into a 10 percent annual interest account, it would yield $110 the first year it was left there. The

$$FV_n = PV(1+r)^n$$

FIGURE 4-3: COMPOUND INTEREST: CALCULATING THE FUTURE VALUE OF MONEY

second year the interest would be calculated on the $110, so at the end of two years we would have $121 and so on. The formula in Figure 4-3 calculates the future value of money if a sum of money, the present value, earns compound interest at an interest rate r for n periods. It should be noted that the value of n and r must be compatible. If the time periods are measured in years, then r must be in terms of the annual interest rate. If the value of n is in months, days, weeks, or any other time period, the interest rate r must be in terms of interest per month, day, week, and so on. Most bank interest rates are given in annual interest rates, but the interest is paid more often, monthly, quarterly, weekly, or even daily.

Suppose we put $10 in a bank account that pays 10 percent annual interest monthly. What amount of interest would we earn at the end of two years? Since the interest is paid each month, we must calculate it each month. If the interest is 10 percent per year, one month of interest is 10/12 percent. In the first month our $10 would earn $0.083. The second month we would calculate the interest on $10.083 instead, and we would earn $0.084 for a total of $10.167, and so on for the next twenty-two periods. We would earn $22.29 in interest.

If we take the equation for the future value of money and solve it

$$PV = \frac{FV_n}{(1+r)^n}$$

FIGURE 4-4: DISCOUNTING: CALCULATING THE PRESENT VALUE OF MONEY

for the present value of money, we will be able to calculate the present value of money that we will receive in the future (see Figure 4-4). This is a little more abstract. What it says is that if I receive money in the future, the value of that money to me today is going to be somewhat less. Suppose I am to receive a $10,000 payment from a customer two years from now and the interest rate that is being used to borrow money is 10 percent. The future value is $10,000, *r* is 10 percent and the value of *n* is 2 (see Figure 4-5).

$$PV = \frac{10,000}{(1+0.10)^2}$$

$$PV = \frac{10,000}{1.21} = 8,264$$

FIGURE 4-5: *DISCOUNTING: CALCULATING THE PRESENT VALUE OF MONEY*

Let us make one more example. Suppose we have a project that will require an investment of $1,000,000. The project has estimated cash inflows of $750,000 per year for the next three years. If we calculate the present value for these cash flows, we end up with the numbers in Figure 4-6.

In this example we have a net cash flow at the end of the third year of $1,250,000. This is a pretty good return on our million-dollar investment. The net cash flow is the sum of the inflows and the outflows.

Suppose we adjust the cash flows to their present values, as shown in Figure 4-7.

The net cash flow adjusted for net present value is only $865,100. This value is substantially less than the $1,250,000 that we had without adjusting the future values for present values. It is important to note that this adjustment is very important for anticipating the cash flows that actually occur in projects.

These adjustments are very real. Since most companies depend on borrowed money or stockholder investments for their operating funds, it is correct to assume that they have to pay something for the use of these funds. When we make an investment in a project because we expect to receive some future returns on that investment, we should adjust the money being received in the future to something less because of the

An investment of $1,000,000 receives
$750,000 per year for 3 years

Year	Flow	Net Flow
0	-1,000,000	-1,000,000
1	750,000	-250,000
2	750,000	500,000
3	750,000	1,250,000

FIGURE 4-6: *EXAMPLE: SIMPLE CASH FLOW*

YEAR	FLOW	RATE	PV	NPV
0	-1,000,000	1.0	-1,000,000	-1,000,000
1	750,000	.9091	681,825	-318,175
2	750,000	.8264	619,800	301,625
3	750,000	.7513	563,475	865,100

Compare to $1,250,000

FIGURE 4-7: EXAMPLE: CASH FLOW ADJUSTED TO PRESENT VALUE

time that we do not have the money. Remember that any money received in the future will be worth less than money we receive today.

What is the fundamental accounting equation?

Project managers and project management methods are becoming more widely known, and project management successes are becoming more frequent. For this reason project managers are being given more responsibility in the businesses they work in. It has become more important that project managers treat their projects like small businesses and that they be responsible for more of the functions that were traditionally managed by others. This is because project managers are seen as being successful in what they do. Why not give them more responsibility? One of the areas where project managers need to take more responsibility is in the accounting for cost of their projects.

The fundamental accounting equation is the basis for any accounting system used in business today. These accounting systems are called double-entry accounting. This is somewhat different from the accounting system we use at home, which is single-entry accounting or cash accounting.

In a cash accounting system we make one entry for each transaction and worry about maintaining our cash balance in positive numbers. We subtract money that we spend, and we add money that we receive. As long as we maintain a positive balance, we have money in the bank and can continue to spend it. When our balance approaches zero, we have to stop spending.

In business we need to have a more accurate way of accounting for all the money and other assets and liabilities we have in our business. This brings us to the fundamental accounting equation:

Assets = Liabilities + Equity

Assets are the things of value that the company owns. These are things such as cash, equipment, property, land, accounts receivable, loans due from others, stock that is owned in other companies, and so forth. Liabilities are the things of value that the company owes to others. These are things like accounts payable, long-term loans, short-term loans, and so forth. Equity is the amount of value the company has after all of its liabilities are subtracted from its assets. The equity account is divided into stockholder equity and retained earnings. Retained earnings are monies that are held by the company to be used for anticipated expenditures. What is left after all of that is the stockholder's equity.

Each of these major areas is divided up into accounts. The various accounts are referred to as asset accounts or liability or owner's equity accounts. On the asset side we might have accounts such as cash, accounts receivable, inventory, buildings, and equipment. On the liability side we might have accounts such as accounts payable and long-term loans payable.

This equation is fundamental to all business accounting because the things called assets of the business must always be equal to the sum of the liabilities plus the owners' equity. Whenever any change is made in the business, it is called a transaction. Each transaction causes two entries to be made in the accounting system.

Tell me more . . .

The fundamental accounting equation is the basis for all accounting in business today. Any transaction that is made in the business must have two entries in the system to keep the books balanced. If, for example, one of our customers pays us $1,000 against its account, we would have one entry to reduce the accounts receivable by $1,000 and another to increase the cash account by $1,000. These are both asset accounts so to keep the accounts balanced, we have an increase of the cash account and a decrease of the accounts receivable, and the equation remains balanced.

Let us say that we have a customer who writes us a purchase order for a new project that has a purchase price of $1,000,000. Let us further say that the project's actual cost was $700,000 and that the money was divided as $400,000 material cost, $200,000 internal payroll cost, and $100,000 subcontract cost.

Let us start with the most pleasant part, the billing of the customer. When we send the invoice for the project to the customer, we make an entry in our own accounts receivable, an asset. The second entry cannot be a liability so it must increase equity by $1,000,000. Equity goes up, and assets go up. This is a good thing, but we are not done yet. We have to pay money to do the project.

We accumulate cost in the payroll due account as work is done. We do not pay all our employees at the end of each day, so this money accumulates until we write paychecks. We first make entries in payroll due that will eventually total $200,000. Each time we pay our employees for the work they do, we pay them from our cash account by writing them a check. When the employee works, the payroll due account must be increased. The second entry to balance the equation reduces the equity account. These are both on the right side of the accounting equation.

When the money is actually paid to the employees, a check is given to each employee for his or her pay. This money comes from the cash account, so it is reduced by the amount of the payroll check. The second entry is made to the payroll due account on the liability side of the equation, and it is reduced by the amount of the payroll check written. Once we have paid everyone, the payroll due account goes to zero.

When we buy material, the invoice is sent to us when the material is delivered. This causes an entry for the amount of the invoice to be made in the accounts payable account. This increases this account, and the second entry reduces the equity account. When the invoice is paid, it is paid from the cash account as were our payroll checks. The cash account is reduced by the amount of the check that is paid for the invoice due, and the accounts payable is reduced to show that the invoice was paid.

Subcontractor fees are paid like material cost. The hours that a subcontractor works are generally accumulated over a period of time, and the supplier submits an invoice for the amount due, which causes an entry in the accounts payable.

When this project is completed, all the accounts payable will be paid out of cash and the accounts payable will be reduced to zero for the project's suppliers. The invoice that went to our customer will eventually be paid, the accounts receivable relevant to the project will be reduced to zero, and the cash account will be increased by the amount of the invoice to the customer. Since we have $1,000,000 coming into our cash account, and we have only $700,000 being paid out to our suppliers and staff, we have to increase our equity account. This means that our company is making a profit.

Notice that whenever a transaction is made, there are two entries that keep the equation in balance. It is not necessary to have one entry on each side of the equal sign since both positive and negative entries can be made. If a positive entry is made on the asset side, another entry, a negative entry, must be made on the asset side or a positive entry must be made on the liability-equity side of the equation. If a negative entry is made on the asset side of the equation, a positive entry must be made on the asset side, or a negative entry must be made on the liability-equity side of the equation.

What are the financial measures ROS, ROA, and EVA?

There are several measures that are useful in measuring the health of a company. These measures are also useful in measuring the health of a project. The trend in project management is to have the project manager take on more and more responsibility for the projects she is managing. Project managers in the future will be more concerned with their projects from the standpoint of managing them as small businesses. It is therefore useful for them to have some financial knowledge. Return on sales (ROS), return on assets (ROA), and economic value added (EVA) are three simple measures that a project manager can use to help determine the financial health of a project that is in progress or one that is being contemplated.

The return on sales is the ratio of net operating profit after taxes (NOPAT) compared to gross sales. The higher the ROS, the more favorable the project.

The return on assets is the ratio of net operating profit after taxes (NOPAT) compared to the gross assets needed by the project. The higher the ROA, the more favorable the project.

The economic value added is a measure of the amount of increase in the company's assets after subtracting the cost of the capital used on the project.

Tell me more . . .

The return on sales is a relatively easy calculation to make. It is simply the net operating profit after taxes divided by the gross sales. The gross sales is the total amount of revenue that the project generates. That is the total amount of money flowing into the company as a result of doing this project. The gross sales minus all of the cost and expenses associated with the project gives us the net operating profit before taxes. Net operating profit before taxes minus the taxes paid relative to the project gives us the net operating profit after taxes (see Figure 4-8). For example,

Net Operating Profit Before Taxes = $3,000,000 − $2,500,000 = $500,000
Taxes = $250,000
Net Operating Profit After Taxes (NOPAT) = $250,000
Return on Sales = $250,000 / $3,000,000 = 8.3%

In this example, a company does a project for a client. The client pays the company $3,000,000 to do the project. This is the gross sales of

Gross sales (Revenue)
<u>   **Less cost of goods sold (Cost)**</u>
Gross profit
<u>   **Less operating expenses (Expenses)**</u>
Operating profit
Less other expenses
<u>**Plus other income**</u>
Net operating profit before taxes
<u>**Less taxes**</u>
Net profit after taxes (NOPAT)

FIGURE 4-8: INCOME STATEMENT

the project. The company has $2,500,000 of cost and expense associated with the project, and the company's tax rate is 50 percent.

The return on sales is a measure of the amount of profit that a dollar of sales generates. Projects that return higher profits per sales dollar are generally more favorable to the company than projects that have a lower profit per dollar of sales. The return on sales ratio tells us that some projects are relatively more profitable than others. If it is our wish to generate more profits, we should look for those projects that have higher ROS's.

ROS is not the only financial measurement we should be interested in. Some projects use more of our assets than others. Projects that generate profits and use relatively lesser amounts of our assets than others are generally more favorable than those that have relatively lesser returns and use more of our assets. Projects that use large amounts of our assets make those assets unavailable for other projects and the profits those projects can generate.

The return on assets is the ratio of the net operating profit after taxes to the assets that are used by the project. The net operating profit after taxes is calculated just as it was in the ROS calculation. The assets that are used by the project are represented by the share of the company's assets that are needed by the project. Much of the assets used by a project is the cash the company must use while completing the project. The share of the assets the company uses is included in this calculation of the assets used as well. In the above example, let us say that the assets this project uses are equal to $4,000,000.

$$\text{NOPAT} = \$500,000$$
$$\text{Assets used by the project} = \$4,000,000$$
$$\text{Return on Assets} = \$500,000 \, / \, \$4,000,000$$
$$\text{ROA} = 12.5\,\%$$

The economic value added calculation compares the cost of maintaining the assets with the net operating profit after taxes. The rationale behind this calculation is that the profit generated by doing a project should be greater that the cost of the assets the project uses. Capital or assets cost money to own. Whether we owe the money to some lending institution or whether our stockholders have generated the investment money that paid for them, they still cost money.

If the money necessary to acquire assets was generated by borrowing the money from a lending institution or some other lending person or agency, we must pay for the use of the money lent. This is called interest. If the money came from people investing in our business, they expect to have some return on their investment. This is usually in the form of dividends to the stockholder. Most companies obtain assets by a combination of these means.

The first thing we need to do is estimate the percentage of the company assets that are acquired by loans. These are the short- and long-term liabilities. The difference between the total assets of the company and the total long- and short-term liabilities of the company is equal to the amount of the company assets financed by our investors and stockholders. Let us say that in our continuing example the percentage of the company's assets that is financed through loans is 30 percent. The amount financed through investment and stockholders is therefore 70 percent. We can also find the average annual interest rate on our loans. Let us say that this is 9 percent. We can also calculate the money that we have to return to our investors each year. Let us say that this figure is 14 percent. The length of time that the project uses these assets is six months.

We can now calculate the weighted average cost of our assets in Table 4-2.

The economic value added calculation compares the cost of the

	Percentage of total capital assets	Annual percentage cost	Total
Loans	30%	9%	.0270
Stock	70%	14%	.0980
		Average cost of assets	.1250 or 12.5%

TABLE 4-2

assets for the time they are used by the project to the NOPAT generated by the project.

EVA = NOPAT − (Assets Used × Average Cost of Assets × Months / 12)
$$EVA = \$500,000 - (\$4,000,000 \times .125 \times 0.5)$$
$$EVA = \$500,000 - \$250,000$$
$$EVA = \$250,000$$

Of course, the higher the EVA, the more favorable the project will be. All companies will be happier if they are getting the most profit out of their investment. There is a problem with managing to this ratio, however. If projects are being measured according to their EVA, one way the project manager can have a good EVA is by reducing the amount of capital the project uses. This may mean using less equipment than is necessary for an efficient operation, which might, in turn, increase cost and expenses rather than decreasing them. You can always tell when a project manager is taking this calculation too seriously: He has a project team that is using out-of-date computers and is working on old desks and is always borrowing equipment from other projects.

What is depreciation?

Depreciation is important to project managers because it has an effect on the overall justification of a project, equipment, and other capital assets that are used on projects and the profitability of projects to the company. Depreciation can make a difference between a project that is justified and one that is not. It can also influence the choice of equipment that is needed for a particular project.

Depreciation is an accounting method of deferring the expense of capital asset items so that the cost of an item is spread out over the useful life of the item rather than taking the full cost of the item in the year in which it is purchased.

There are two methods of depreciation: straight-line depreciation and accelerated depreciation. Straight-line depreciation spreads the cost of the asset evenly over its useful life while accelerated depreciation takes more of the cost of the asset earlier in its life rather than later.

Tell me more . . .

If we did not have depreciation methods to account for capital assets, it would be very difficult to make any sense out of a company's financial statements. Without depreciation methods, if a company purchased a large capital asset, it would have to recognize the cost of the asset in the year that it was purchased. Even though the asset had a life of several years, all of the cost associated with acquiring the asset would be recognized in the year it was purchased.

This recognition of all of the cost of the asset in the first year it is purchased would cause a company's financial statements to be irregular from year to year. Investors, seeing a reduction in profits, would not be able to tell whether the company had suffered a loss in business, which is bad, or simply purchased capital assets, which is generally good. For this reason we have depreciation.

Depreciation simply says that if we buy a capital asset that has a life of some years, we should distribute the cost of the asset over the years that are equal to its useful life rather than recognizing all of the cost in the first year of its life. This will also have an effect on the taxes the company pays.

For example, say a company purchased a machine for $100,000 and the machine had a useful life of ten years. Furthermore, the machine had a scrap value of $3,000. If we did not depreciate the machine, we would have to show an expense of $100,000 in the first year. This is an expense that occurs only once in ten years so once every ten years, the company's profits would be unusually low. For the other nine years there would be no machine expense, and the company would show an unusually high profit. A better way of accounting for this machine is to distribute the expense of the machine over the ten years of its life.

To use any of the depreciation methods, we need to know three things about the asset: the useful life of the asset, the original cost of the asset including delivery, installation, and start-up costs, and the scrap value of the asset at the end of its useful life. The depreciation expense is the amount of expense that is recorded each year during the life of the asset. This expense is the amount by which before-tax profit is reduced.

Perhaps a little accounting is in order to explain what is going on here. When a capital asset is purchased, the company pays for the asset with cash. The transaction reduces the company's cash assets by the amount of the purchase and increases the company's equipment assets by the same amount. There is no change in the company's total assets; there has been a trade between the two accounts. Each year the depreciation amount for the year is calculated, and the depreciation expense reduces the net profit before taxes by the same amount. At the same time, the asset account for the equipment is reduced by the same amount.

For the following examples we will use the same asset. The asset has a purchased cost of $39,000. The purchased cost of the asset includes shipping, installation, and start-up. Installation and start-up include the initial tooling that the equipment needs to make it function. It has a useful life of eight years and a scrap value of $3,000.

Straight-line depreciation

Straight-line depreciation is the simplest method of depreciation. We start with the purchase price of the asset. From this we subtract the scrap value and divide the remaining value by the number of years of useful life.

In Figure 4-9 it can be seen that the depreciation taken each year is the same, $4,500. Each year the accumulated depreciation increases by $4,500, and the book value of the equipment is reduced by the same $4,500. The $4,500 of depreciation is taken each year until the scrap value is reached. From this point on, if the asset is still owned by the company, depreciation expense is no longer taken. If the asset were sold before the end of its useful life, the difference between the selling price and the remaining depreciation would be taken as depreciation expense in that year.

Suppose the asset were sold at the end of year four for $20,000. At the end of year four, the remaining book value is $21,000. We would take the $1,000 of depreciation expense and clear the asset from our books. If the same asset were sold for $25,000, we would show a profit of $4,000. A depreciation expense of $21,000 would be taken, $25,000 would be added to the cash account, and $4,000 would be added to the equity account as profit on the machine.

Accelerated depreciation is used because it effectively reduces taxes on the company. Although the total amount of depreciation expense taken is the same as it is in straight-line depreciation, with the accelerated depreciation method, the depreciation taken in the earlier years is significantly greater than it is in the later years. Since larger amounts of depreciation mean that the depreciation expense is larger, the net profit before taxes is going to be smaller. The taxes are figured on the net profit before taxes, so the taxes will be lower as well. Now the total amount of tax the company pays over the years is going to be the same regardless of the depreciation method, but some of the taxes will be deferred to a

Year	Depreciation	Accum. dep.	Book value
1	4,500	4,500	34,500
2	4,500	9,000	30,000
3	4,500	13,500	25,500
4	4,500	18,000	21,000
5	4,500	22,500	16,500
6	4,500	27,000	12,000
7	4,500	31,500	7,500
8	4,500	36,000	3,000

Annual depreciation is 36,000/8 = 4,500

FIGURE 4-9: STRAIGHT-LINE DEPRECIATION

later time. Since the money we pay someone (the IRS in this example) later in time has less value, we will profit from accelerated depreciation.

This may all seem a bit strange, but it is a win-win situation all around. Companies like to accelerate their depreciation because it reduces their taxes in the early years of the equipment's life. The government likes this too because it encourages the company to sell the equipment before the end of its useful life and buy a new piece of equipment. The new piece of equipment not only makes the company more profitable and pays the government more taxes, it also makes profit for the equipment manufacturer, who in turn pays taxes on that money to the government as well.

Sum of the years' digits

This is an accelerated depreciation method (see Figure 4-10). The depreciation for each year is calculated by first taking the digit of each year of the equipment's useful life and adding them together.

In our example the equipment has a useful life of eight years, so we add $1+2+3+4+5+6+7+8 = 36$. The first year we take $8/36$ of the allowable depreciation; in the second year we take $7/36$ of the allowable depreciation; in the third year we take $6/36$ of the allowable depreciation, and so on. Adding the numerator of the fractions we get $36/36$. That is, we have taken all of the allowable depreciation.

Notice that in the sum of the years' digits depreciation method, we are still taking $36,000 depreciation just as we did using the straight-line method. Notice too that we still have $3,000 of scrap value. The only difference is that we have taken larger amounts of depreciation in the earlier years than we did in the later years.

Year	Factor	Deprec.	Accum.	Book value
1	8/36	8,000	8,000	31,000
2	7/36	7,000	15,000	24,000
3	6/36	6,000	21,000	18,000
4	5/36	5,000	26,000	13,000
5	4/36	4,000	30,000	9,000
6	3/36	3,000	33,000	6,000
7	2/36	2,000	35,000	4,000
8	1/36	1,000	36,000	3,000

Sum of years' digits = 1+2+3+4+5+6+7+8 = 36

FIGURE 4-10: SUM OF THE YEARS' DIGITS

Double declining balances

This is another accelerated depreciation method. The first thing we do in this method is calculate the percentage of depreciation that would apply if we were using straight-line depreciation. In our example of straight-line depreciation we were taking straight-line depreciation over a period of eight years. That would be 12.5 percent each year. So, the double declining balances percentage is 25 percent. The depreciation expense for each year is taken by multiplying the remaining book value of the asset by 25 percent.

As can be seen in Figure 4-11, we start with a remaining book value of $39,000. This can be thought of as the remaining book value at the end of year zero, the time we purchased the asset. Multiplying $39,000 by 25 percent gives us the first year's depreciation of $9,750. This $9,750 is subtracted from $39,000 to give us $29,250, which is the book value at the end of year one. $29,250 is multiplied by 25 percent to get the next year's depreciation expense of $7,310.

Year	Deprec.	Accum.	Book value
1	9,750	9,750	29,250
2	7,310	17,060	21,940
3	5,490	22,550	16,450
4	4,110	26,660	12,340
5	3,090	29,750	9,250
6	2,310	32,060	6,940
7	1,970	33,800	4,970
8	1,970	35,100	3,000

FIGURE 4-11: DOUBLE DECLINING BALANCES

The calculation is continued until the last two years of the asset's life. For the last two years the scrap value is subtracted from the remaining book value and the difference is divided by two and used as the depreciation expense for both years.

The calculations for depreciation may seem a bit strange for engineers who are used to having things depend on natural laws of physics and other logical causes. Some accounting rules—including depreciation methods—are not subject to the laws of nature but are subject to "generally accepted accounting practices." These are the rules of accounting that are agreed to by committees of qualified accountants. As long as everyone follows the same rules and the calculations for things like depreciation are carried out consistently, businesspeople, the IRS, and investors can all be confident that everyone is performing the same calculations in the same way.

5

Time Management

What is a network diagram?

Network diagrams are used in many ways, from engineering to computer programming to management. In project management the network diagram is usually associated with the scheduling function. The network diagram for a schedule shows the logical relationships between the activities of the schedule for a project.

The activities are taken two at a time. The relationship between them is such that one activity is the independent activity and the other is the dependent activity. Typically, for example, this relationship shows that the independent activity must finish before the dependent activity is allowed to start.

The network diagram clearly delineates the sequence of activities that the project must follow to reach its end. Once all the relationships between the activities are shown on the diagram, the actual schedule dates can be calculated.

Tell me more . . .

There are two kinds of network diagrams, the "activity on arrow" network diagram and the "activity on node" network diagram. The "activity on node" network diagram is also called a "predecessor-successor" network diagram, and a "precedence" network diagram.

"Activity on arrow" network diagrams, as the name implies, have arrows representing the activities; any special information can be annotated to the arrows. The arrows terminate in events that are depicted as circles at the beginning and end of the arrows. Since the activities are depicted by the arrows, the arrow length can be varied in proportion with the duration of the activity.

"Activity on arrow" diagrams, as seen in Figure 5-1, were used for many years in project management schedules before the advent of personal computers. In the "good old days" there were entire rooms full of draftsmen keeping these diagrams up to date with paper and pencils. As personal computers became more popular and powerful this type of diagram fell into misuse in favor of the "activity on node" diagram. Today this method of diagramming is rarely used in project management.

The usual method for diagramming the "activity on arrow" diagram is to place the activities on a piece of paper with the tail of the activity arrow over the date of the activity's start and the head of the arrow over the date of the activity's planned completion. At the head and the tail of the activity arrow, circles are drawn to show the beginning and ending events associated with the activity. A time scale is not always used for this diagram. This reduces the need for many of the "dummy" activities but loses the ability to graphically depict the durations, start dates, and finish dates of the schedule.

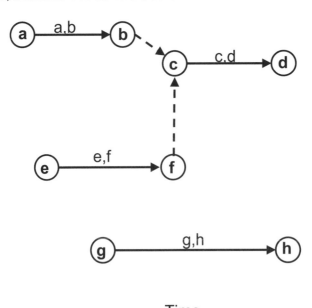

FIGURE 5-1: ACTIVITY ON ARROW DIAGRAM

The activity number consists of the beginning event letter and the ending event letter separated by a comma. Activity "a,b" is an arrow with event "a" and "b" at each end. By tradition lowercase letters are used for the events and activity numbering scheme.

If an activity is dependent on another independent activity, the tail of the dependent activity is connected to the head of the independent activity.

In the event that the independent activity has more than one activity depending on it, a dummy activity, indicated as a dotted or dashed arrow, with zero duration, can be shown.

"Activity on node" network diagrams, as seen in Figure 5-2, have the activity information written in small boxes that are the nodes of the diagram. Arrows connect the boxes to show the logical relationships between pairs of the activities. It is important to note here that in network diagramming, circles connected by arrows always represent "activity on arrow" diagramming, and boxes connected by arrows always represent "activity on node" diagrams.

In this type of diagram the activity numbers are usually sequential and numeric. The number of the independent activity is called the predecessor and the number of the dependent activity is called the successor. Each activity has a unique number.

The arrows in this diagram show only the logical relationship between the activities. The most common of these is the "finish-start" relationship, which is the default and is generally not shown explicitly in the diagram. It is so commonly used that if there is no name given to the relationship, it is assumed to be "finish-start." In a "finish-start" relationship between two activities, the independent activity must finish before the dependent activity is allowed to have its start scheduled.

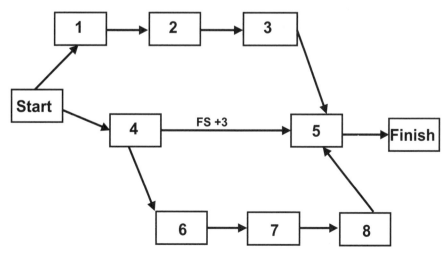

FIGURE 5-2: ACTIVITY ON NODE DIAGRAM

There are several other relationships possible: "Start-start" and "finish-finish" are useful in diagramming to show the other possible ways in which activities can be related. In the "start-start" relationship the independent activity must start before the dependent activity is allowed to start. In the "finish-finish" relationship the independent activity must finish before the dependent activity is allowed to finish. A couple of examples are in order. If we were writing a book, the editing process could start as soon as some of the book had been written, but the editing process could not be finished until the writing of the book was complete. If we were making Thanksgiving dinner for the family, we could have a "start-start" relationship between putting the plates on the table and placing the silverware. We can't tell where the silverware goes until at least some of the plates are placed on the table. We could have a "finish-finish" relationship between cooking the turkey and cooking the sweet potatoes. The potatoes and the turkey should come out of the oven at the same time so they can be served hot.

The "start-finish" relationship is seldom used but is available in most project management software packages. This kind of relationship is unusual and is normally represented in some other logical way. It is difficult to find examples of this kind of relationship. We leave it up to the readers to find examples. If you can think of one, please send us the example by e-mail at mnewell@psmconsult.com.

In addition to the logical relationships between pairs of activities in the diagram, there are offsets in the relationships as well. These offsets are called "leads" and "lags." A lead is shown as a negative number added to the relationship and a lag is shown as a positive number added to the relationship. When these are used, the relationship is shown explicitly, and the lead or lag is shown added to it or subtracted from it as in the relationship between activity 4 and activity 5 in Figure 5-2.

Depending on your preference, a network diagram can be shown with or without two special activities to show the start and finish of the project. If these are used they are generally shown as milestones in that they both have a duration of zero. They are helpful if there are several different project activities that have no predecessors at the beginning of the project or if there are several activities at the end of the project that have no successors. The activities at the beginning of the project are then made to have the start activity as the predecessor for each of them, and the activities at the end of the project are made to have the finish activity as their successor. In this way it is easy to find the start and finish of the project.

What are the early start, early finish, late start, and late finish dates of a project schedule?

The early start, early finish, late start, and late finish dates of a project schedule are the primary dates that are calculated in any project schedule. The early start dates of the project schedule are the earliest that any activity in the schedule can be scheduled to start given the logic and constraints of the schedule. The early finish of an activity in the schedule is the earliest that the activity can be scheduled to be completed given the logic and constraints of the schedule. The late start of an activity is the latest that a project activity can be scheduled to be started without having to reschedule the calculated early finish of the project. The late finish of an activity is the latest that a project activity can be finished without having to reschedule the late finish of the project. The late finish of the project is the late finish of the last activity to be completed in the project.

The schedule that is made up of the early start and early finish of each activity in the schedule is called the early schedule. The schedule that is made up of the late start and late finish of each activity in the schedule is called the late schedule.

Tell me more . . .

The early start of the project is declared first. Unless we have at least one date that tells where the project begins or ends, it will be possible to know the schedule only relative to other activities. Normally we want to know the project schedule relevant to real calendar days over a specific period of time. All activities that have no predecessors must have a declared start date. In most of the project management software available today, this information is entered as the project start date and is used for any activity not having a predecessor. Most software also allows the calculation of a schedule using a declared project finish date as well. For our discussion let us say that we will be declaring the date that we will start the project.

Once we have declared the beginning of the project, we can say that the early start of each of the activities without at least one predecessor will have an early start equal to the declared project start date.

By convention and agreement between schedulers, it is assumed on project schedules that work always begins in the beginning of the work period that the activity starts in and always ends at the end of the work period that the activity ends in. This means that if an activity is scheduled in days on a one-shift basis, which is the true for most project work, the activity is scheduled to start in the morning of the day it is scheduled to start and finish in the afternoon of the day it is finished. This means that an activity that has a one-day duration would start in the morning on Monday, January 15, and finish in the afternoon on Monday, January 15. An activity having a two-day duration starts on January 15 and finishes on January 16. This creates some confusion since many people would expect that the difference between the early start and the early finish of an activity should be equal to its duration, and this is not the case. The early finish of an activity is the early start of the activity plus the duration minus one.

$$EF = ES + duration - 1$$

In the case of the early schedule, the early start of the successors of any activity is the beginning of the next time period after the completion of the preceding activity. If an activity finishes on January 25 and is the predecessor to another activity, the successor activity will be scheduled to start on January 26.

Notice that in the early schedule if a successor activity has more than one predecessor, the early start of the successor activity is calculated as the time period following the latest of all of the predecessor early finishes.

The early finish date of these activities is calculated by taking the early finish date of the activity and adding the duration to it. When this is done, some care must be taken to ensure that the duration is added to the early start date and that the weekends, holidays, and other nonworking days are also added to calculate the early finish date.

The late finish date must have a way of getting started as well. In the case of project schedules, the late finish of the project is set equal to the early finish of the latest early finish date of any activity in the project. Every activity in the project schedule that has no successor is given this date as its late finish. If we had five activities that had no other activities logically following them (no successors), each of them would have a late finish equal to the early finish of the last activity to be completed on the early schedule.

To get the late start of each activity, we must subtract the duration from the late finish of the activity. Again, as with the calculation of the early schedule care must be taken not to include weekends, holidays, or other nonworking days. As with the calculation of the early schedule, we must be careful to adjust the scheduled late start date because of the convention that all activities will start on the morning of the day on which they start and finish on the afternoon of the date on which they finish. This means that an activity that has a late finish date of January 20 and a duration of three days has a late start date of January 18.

$$LS = LF - duration + 1$$

In the case of the late schedule, the late finish of the predecessor of an activity is the end of the last time period before the succeeding activity is scheduled to start. If an activity is scheduled to have its late start on February 7, all of its predecessors must be completed not later than

February 6 in order to allow it to start as scheduled. Notice that in the late schedule, if a successor activity has more than one predecessor, the late finish of each of the predecessor activities is calculated as the time period before the late start of the successor's late start. This just says that no activity can finish later than the date necessary to support the late start of its successor.

How do I make a project schedule?

In its simplest form the calculation of the schedule is a matter of establishing a start date for the project and adding the durations of the activities in the schedule, being careful not to include the activities that are scheduled to be done in parallel with other activities. The schedule consists of determining the start and finish dates for each of the activities and can be calculated with or without considering the influences of resources or the lack of them. The scheduling of each activity must consider the logic of the schedule. That is, the scheduling of each activity depends on the activities that it depends on for its schedule. These logical relationships are best seen in the "precedence diagram."

Tell me more . . .

The initial schedule is calculated based on the logic of the schedule and does not consider the constraints that result from the resources available to work on the project. Probably the easiest way to learn to calculate a schedule is to do one. We will walk you through the calculation of the project schedule the same way computer software does it and explain things as we go along.

Referring to Figure 5-3, we will calculate the early start and early finish dates for the schedule and then go on to calculate the late start and late finish dates as well. These are normally the dates that are calculated. What they show is the earliest dates that a particular activity can be started and finished and the latest that a particular activity can be finished. The pair of early schedule dates is referred to as the early schedule and the pair of late dates is referred to as the late schedule.

These two schedules are useful because they tell us something about the flexibility of our schedules. Activities that have no difference between the early schedule and the late schedule do not have any flexibility. If an activity has the same dates for its early schedule as it has for its late schedule, it means that the activity cannot be delayed even one day without causing the project completion date to be delayed. If there is a difference between the early schedule and the late schedule, there is some flexibility, which means that this particular activity could be delayed as much as the late schedule without affecting the finish date of the project.

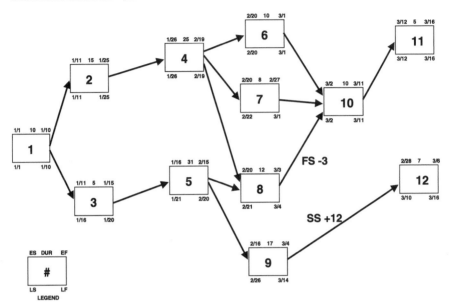

ES 1/1
EF 3/16
LS 1/1
LF 3/16
CRITICAL PATH
PROJECT START DATE JANUARY 1, 2003

FIGURE 5-3: NETWORK DIAGRAM

The first thing that must be done in any project schedule is to declare a project start date (or finish date if that is mandated). If you do not do this when you are using project management software, the software will assign today's date as the project start date. This is usually not the date for the project to start. In the example we have determined that the project is to start on January 1, 2003.

Next we look for the activities that have no predecessor. These are the activities that do not have any arrowheads going to them. There can be more than one activity with this condition. Some people prefer to create an activity with zero duration called "start" and another one called "finish." When this is done, there is only one activity that is first and one activity that is last. Software for project management will not do this automatically. It is not necessary for proper schedule calculations since the computer will come up with the same schedule dates whether you use start and finish milestones or not. In our example this is activity 1.

The start of activity 1 is January 1, shown as 1/1. The duration of this activity is ten days, so the completion of the activity is scheduled for 1/10. This is the early start and early finish date for activity 1. You may wonder why you don't simply add ten days to January 1 and get a completion date of January 11. This is not the case when doing date calculations since it is assumed that the work will start in the morning of January 1 and finish on the afternoon of the day it finishes. The work is done on the first and last day of the activity schedule. The next activity, since it starts in the morning, will start on the next day. This is a generally accepted convention used by all schedulers, and it is the way your project management software will calculate dates.

Schedules can also be done by tracking time on the same basis as the hands of a clock. If an activity started at 1:00 P.M. and took two hours, it would finish at 3:00 P.M., and the next activity would be able to start immediately afterward at 3:00 P.M. plus a few microseconds. When schedules are calculated on calendar days, the schedule is generally using the former method. When schedules are done in hours, they are usually done with the latter method.

Activities 2 and 3 have a finish-start dependency with activity 1. This means that neither of them is permitted to start until activity 1 is completed. By our convention, activities 2 and 3 have early start dates of January 11, the morning after January 10. Adding the durations of activities 2 and 3 to their early start dates gives us early finish dates of January 25 and January 15 respectively.

Similarly, activities 4 and 5 have early start dates of January 26 and January 16. Adding the durations to the early start dates gives us the early finish dates of February 19 and February 15.

Activities 6 and 7 both depend on activity 4, so both of them have early start dates of February 20. Adding the duration of the activities gives us the early finish for each of March 1 and February 27. This is not a leap year so February has 28 days.

Activity 8 is a little different in that it is dependent on two activities, 4 and 5. Since activity 8 must not start until both 4 and 5 are finished, the earliest it can start is the morning after activity 4 is completed, and its early start date is February 20 and its early finish date is March 3.

Activity 9 can start immediately after activity 5. Its early start and finish dates are February 16 and March 4.

Activity 10 is interesting. It depends on activities 6, 7, and 8. As before, we must investigate all three of these activities before determining the early start date of activity 10. Activities 6 and 7 have normal finish-start relationships with activity 10. With respect to activity 6, activity 10 could start on March 2. With respect to activity 7, activity 10 could start on February 28.

With respect to activity 8, we have a different kind of relationship. This relationship is a finish-start relationship with a lead of three days. The lead subtracts three days from what zero lead or lag would have. In this case the zero lead or lag relationship would be a normal finish-start relationship and the early start date for activity 10 would be March 4.

Introducing the three-day lead means that activity 10 is allowed to start three days earlier than it would be allowed to start without the lead time. So, with respect to activity 8, activity 10 has an early start date of March 1.

Since activity 10 depends on all three relationships being completed, activity 6 determines the early start date of activity 10, and its early finish date is March 11.

Activity 11 depends on activity 10 and has an early start and finish date of March 12 and March 16.

Activity 12 depends on activity 9. The relationship between these two activities is a start-start with a lag of twelve days. In a start-start relationship the dependent activity is allowed to start as soon (on the same day) as the independent activity starts. This would be February 16, the same date as the start of activity 9. There is a lag of twelve days in the relationship so the early start date of activity 12 is February 28, and its early finish date is March 6.

The calculation of the early schedule is often called the forward pass since it moves forward in time to the end of the project. The project completion date is the latest early finish date in the schedule. In this case it is March 16, and activity 11 is the latest finishing activity in the early schedule. It should be noted that the latest early finish date in the project schedule determines the project completion date, not the early finish of the activities that have no successors. Leads and lags in schedules can cause activities that have successors to be scheduled to be later than activities that have no successors.

Since we have a forward pass, it seems only natural to expect there will be a backward pass as well. The backward pass is just what it sounds like. We will start at the end of the schedule and work back to the beginning, calculating the latest possible dates that activities can be scheduled without delaying the project completion date of March 16.

Activities 11 and 12 have no successors. Since they have no successors, both of them could be finished at the latest possible date. This would be the project completion date, March 16. The late finish for both of these activities is set to March 16. Durations of the activities are subtracted from the late finish dates to get the late start dates much as we added durations to the early start dates to get the early finish dates. Activities 11 and 12 have late start dates of March 12 and March 10.

The latest that activity 10 can finish in order to support a late start date of March 12 for activity 11 is March 11. Subtracting the duration gives a late start for activity 10 of March 2.

Activity 9 has a start-start relationship with a lag of twelve days with activity 12. The latest that activity 9 can start in order to support the late start of March 2 is twelve days earlier so activity 9 must have a late start date of February 26 and its late finish date is March 14. Notice that here we are not concerned with the finish date of activity 9 because the start of activity 12 depends on the start, not the finish, of activity 9.

Activity 8 has a finish-start relationship with activity 10 but there is a minus-three-day lead associated with the relationship as well. Since the latest that activity 10 can start is March 2, the late finish of activity 8 must be three days later than it normally would without the lead. This means activity 8 finishes on March 4. Subtracting the twelve-day duration, we get a late start of February 21.

Activities 6 and 7 must support a late start of March 2 in activity 10 so they must both have late finish dates not later than March 1. The late start dates for activity 6 and 7 are February 20 and February 22 respectively.

Activity 5 must support the late start dates for both activity 8 and activity 9. Since activity 8 has a late start of February 21 and activity 9 has a late start of February 26, activity 5 must have a late finish of February 20. Subtracting its duration gives it a late start of January 21.

Similarly activity 4 must support the late start dates of activities 6, 7, and 8, which are February 20, 22, and 21. Therefore activity 4 must have a late finish date of February 19, and its late start date must be January 26.

Activity 3 supports activity 5 and has late start and finish dates of January 16 and 20.

Activity 2 supports activity 4 and has late start and finish dates of January 11 and 25.

Activity 1 must finish to allow activity 2 and 3 to start on their late start dates of January 11 and 17, so it must have a late finish of January 10 and a late start of January 1. This is how the schedule is calculated in the computer software for project management. It makes sense to make this calculation before resources are introduced to the project schedule because there is a lot of work involved in entering the resources, and the schedule with resources will never get shorter than the schedule with no resources. If the logical schedule is too long to satisfy the stakeholders, the problem can be addressed in the logical schedule before resources are introduced. This will save considerable time and effort.

What is float or slack in a project schedule?

First of all, *float* and *slack* are two words that mean the same thing. It is perfectly fine to use either term in project management. Float is a measure of flexibility in the project schedule. There are two kinds of float, total float and free float. Total float is usually called float. (Sometimes it seems that we try to make things unnecessarily confusing.) Total float is the amount of time that an activity can be delayed without having to reschedule the project completion date. Free float is the amount of time an activity can be delayed without having to reschedule any other activity in the project.

Tell me more . . .

Total float is a measure of flexibility in the project schedule. It tells the project manager how many days an activity can be delayed before the project completion date must be delayed. This is valuable information. If there is trouble in the project, the project manager may divert resources from one activity to another. The obvious places to divert resources from are the activities that have considerably large amounts of float.

If, for example, an activity having fifteen days of total float has not yet started and the resources are needed to solve a problem in another area for five days, the resources can be diverted to the problem, and the start of the activity with fifteen days of total float can be delayed five days. By doing this the float will be reduced from fifteen days to ten days.

The calculation of total float is very simple. In the calculation of the schedule we calculated the early start, early finish, late start, and late finish dates. To calculate total float simply subtract the early start from the late start. You could also subtract the early finish from the late finish since both sets of dates are separated only by the duration of the activity.

The problem with using total float is that delaying an activity with total float only tells us that we will not have to reschedule the finish date of the project. It does not tell us how many other activities will have to be rescheduled in the project. To help us with this we need to know about free float.

Free float is the amount of time that an activity can be delayed without having to reschedule any other activity in the project. Free float is determined by comparing the early finish—if the relationship between the activities is a finish-start relationship—of the predecessor activity with the early start of the successor activity. (These are sometimes also called the independent activity and the dependent activity.) If there is a difference, it means that the predecessor activity can be rescheduled without having to reschedule the successor activity. If another kind of relationship exists between the two activities then the early start or finishes of each may need to be checked instead.

In Figure 5-4, activities 7 and 12 are the only activities with free float. Activity 12 has free float because it has no successor and must finish only before or at the end of the project, March 16, as determined by activity 11.

Activity 7 can be delayed up to two days without affecting its successor, activity 10. All the other activities that have float must reschedule at least one other activity in order to allow the delay and use the float.

One thing that should be noticed about total float is that when it is used up in one activity by a delay, the successor activities will lose some of their float as they are rescheduled. Notice activities 3, 5, 9, and 12. If

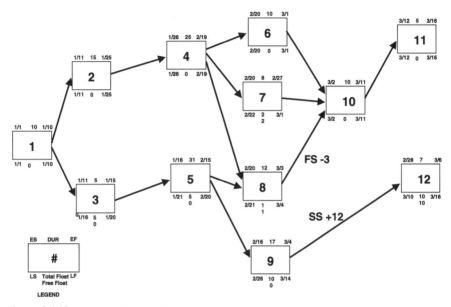

```
ES 1/1
EF 3/16
LS 1/1
LF 3/16
CRITICAL PATH
PROJECT START DATE JANUARY 1, 2003
```

FIGURE 5-4: NETWORK DIAGRAM WITH FLOAT

activity 3 is delayed two days, activities 5, 9, and 12 must have their early start and early finish dates rescheduled as well. This in turn reduces the total float of each by two days as well. Notice also that delaying an activity within its total float does not affect the late schedule dates; they remain the same.

The use of free float does not affect the other activities; the early start and early finish dates of the activity with free float are the only ones affected if we reschedule the activity within the amount of the free float. This means that an activity with five days of free float could be rescheduled to start or finish five days later without having to reschedule the project completion date or any other activity in the schedule.

What is a Gantt chart?

A Gantt chart, as seen in Figure 5-5, is used to show the project schedule in a graphic form.

It is probably the most used graphic report in project management and may be the most used of any of the reports used in project management. The Gantt chart is about 100 years old and was invented by Henry L. Gantt in 1917. Back then the charts were, of course, drawn by hand instead of computer. Today every project management software package

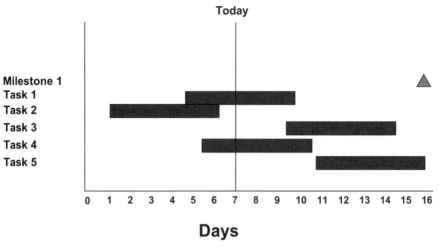

FIGURE 5-5: GANTT CHART

produces the Gantt chart. It is clearly the favorite graphic for displaying the project schedule.

In its simplest form the Gantt chart consists of a calendar as the horizontal axis and a list of tasks along the vertical axis. There are one or more lines allowed for each task. In the main part of the Gantt chart, each task is represented by a bar or rectangle. The bar or the activity bar is positioned with the left end over the date on the calendar axis when the activity starts. The right end of the activity bar is positioned over the date that the activity ends. Thus the length of the bar represents the elapsed time of the activity and also shows the approximate duration of the activity. Most representations of the Gantt chart show the activity bar through the nonworking days. This means that the length of the Gantt bar for an activity will be equal to the duration plus the nonworking days plus any scheduled interruptions of the activity.

Tell me more . . .

The Gantt chart is very helpful for representing the schedule. It makes it easy to see when an activity is scheduled to start and when it is scheduled to end, and it also shows which activities should be in progress on a given day. If a vertical line is drawn over the calendar date for today, it can be easily seen which activities are complete, which are ahead of schedule or behind schedule, or how soon activities are scheduled to begin or finish.

If a vertical line is drawn through a given day, the activities that are scheduled to be taking place simultaneously will have the line pass through them. In this way the need for simultaneous resources can clearly be seen. The Gantt chart can be used in conjunction with a resource histogram, which is discussed later in this chapter, to show the utilization of resources and the schedule simultaneously.

The Gantt chart does not normally show the logical interdependencies between the predecessor and successor activities very well. If that is our interest, it is better served by the network diagram, which shows logic nicely but does not have a time scale axis like the Gantt chart. In the later versions of Microsoft Project, logical arrows have been added to the Gantt chart. This will undoubtedly and perhaps unfortunately force all other producers of software for project management to do the same. These logical connections are useful only for seeing the relationships among a very few activities. When the schedule becomes typical and has several hundred activities, the arrows connecting the activities will be going from page to page and become difficult or impossible to follow. The Gantt chart can be annotated with hundreds of pieces of information about each activity. In Microsoft Project there are over 200 pieces of information that can be attached to any of the activity bars, and the data can be placed in the four positions around the bar as well as inside the bar itself. The bars can also be shown in many colors to indicate various conditions and data. The ends of the bars can be given distinctive shapes to indicate other conditions as well.

Milestones can also be shown on the Gantt chart. A milestone is an activity in the schedule that has a duration of zero. Naturally this would be difficult to show since an activity with a duration of zero has a length of zero and is therefore invisible. Milestones are automatically plotted by a special symbol, usually a diamond shape or a triangle. Milestone charts are discussed later in this chapter.

The Gantt chart (see Figure 5-6) can also show summary activities. These can be represented in a distinctive way so that they are not confused with the scheduled activities. Summary activities are discussed later in this chapter.

In addition to printing the textual information about actual start dates, actual finish dates, remaining duration, or percent complete, progress on an activity can be shown by placing a small bar inside the activity bar with the length of the bar proportional to the percent complete of the activity.

If we want to see the differences between various baseline schedules and the current schedule, they can be plotted according to the same calendar scale, and the various schedule bars for each activity can be shown on the chart. In Microsoft Project as many as four simultaneous schedules can be displayed. Of course the advantages of showing four different schedules might not be worth the difficulty of trying to read the information from them.

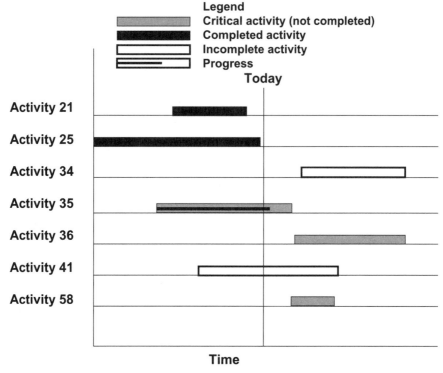

FIGURE 5-6: GANTT CHART

What is the critical path method?

The critical path method or CPM is a management tool that helps the project manager recognize where in the project schedule his management effort should be applied. The critical path method recognizes that the activities in the schedule that have zero float are the activities that cannot be delayed without delaying the completion of the project. These activities are called critical activities and should be identified as activities that require close supervision.

By this definition of critical activities, all the other activities must have some float. This means that those activities containing at least some float can be delayed without affecting the completion of the project and can be managed somewhat less closely than the critical path activities.

Tell me more . . .

The critical path method was developed by the Dupont Corporation in the 1950s at about the same time General Dynamics and the U.S. Navy were developing the program evaluation and review technique, which will be discussed next. The objective of CPM is that it can take projects that have reasonably well known task durations and identify the tasks that should be monitored more closely by management. CPM is therefore a management technique.

The critical path is really somewhat misleading since the critical activities do not necessarily have to fall on a path. The idea of a path comes from a more simple-minded approach to the critical path method where the critical path is determined by finding the longest path through the project network diagram, shown in Figure 5-7.

By using this technique you can find all of the possible ways of getting from the start end to the finish end of the network following the various branches of the interdependencies. This will give you every possible sequence of activities from the start of the project to the finish. When all the paths have been determined, you add up the durations for each possible path. When this is done, you declare that the critical path is the one with the highest total duration.

Obviously this will not simply produce the right answer if you have any kind of relationship in the network diagram other than a finish-start relationship or if you have leads and lags.

The proper method and the method that the computer software for project management uses is to determine the total float of each activity and identify those activities that have zero total float. These activities

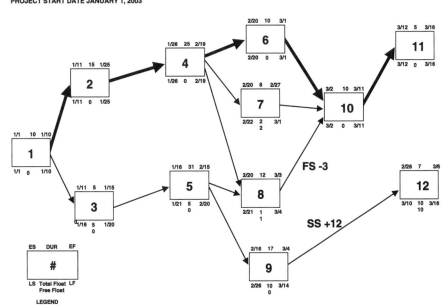

FIGURE 5-7: NETWORK DIAGRAM WITH CRITICAL PATH

may sometimes not form a path through the network. They may even form two paths through the network.

To manage using the critical path, we use the float in each activity as the criterion for managing. Activities that have little or no float are managed much more closely than activities having more float. Since the activities having little or no float will cause project completion delays if they are late, they are obviously the ones upon which we must concentrate our management effort.

Of course, since this is a management tool and we are using it to determine where management effort should be concentrated, we should also consider the activities that have close to zero float since they are nearly critical. In the project management software, the number of days of free float allowed before an activity becomes critical is adjustable so that we can show activities with, say, three days or less of free float. To make this even easier, the software will highlight these activities by showing them in red (or a color of your choice).

What is the PERT method?

The PERT method stands for program evaluation and review technique. It is a statistical approach to project schedules. Actually, it is a statistical way of predicting project completions when there is uncertainty about the project durations.

The PERT method was developed during the Polaris Missile program in the United States in the 1950s. At that time the United States was in the middle of the Cold War and had come up with the idea that ballistic nuclear missiles could be fired under water from a submarine. Of course this was a tremendous advantage in a nuclear war because the submarine could approach the coastline of the Soviet Union and fire the missiles before being detected. It seems no one told the submarine commander that as soon as the rocket took off, the submarine would be spotted and probably blown up. But that takes us a bit off the subject of PERT.

The difficulty for the U.S. Navy and General Dynamics was that they had two separate projects, the missile development project and the submarine development project. Because of the intensity of the Cold War, it would have been difficult to explain to Congress that the missile was ready for deployment when the submarine was not or that the submarine was ready to go on patrol but had no missiles. PERT was created to take project task durations that were uncertain and statistically estimate the amount of time that they would be expected to take and do that with a determined probability and range of values.

Each activity in a PERT analysis must have three different durations estimated for it. These are the optimistic, the pessimistic, and the most likely duration. The activity's expected duration and the activity's standard deviation are calculated from these three values by the following formulas:

Expected Duration = (Optimistic + 4 × Most Likely + Pessimistic) / 6
Expected Standard Deviation = (Pessimistic − Optimistic) / 6

These two values, the expected duration and the expected standard deviation, are approximations that allow us to predict the project completion date and a range of values that will give us the probability that the actual project will be completed within the range of values.

For example, if we predict that the expected value for the project completion is January 10 and that the expected standard deviation is four days, we could say that we have a 95 percent probability that the project will be completed between January 2 and January 18.

Tell me more . . .

The PERT method is used when there is uncertainty in the duration of the activities in a project.

Figure 5-8 shows what would be expected if you were to plot the probability distribution of the expected dates for completing a project. On the left side of the diagram, we have the optimistic completion date for the project. On the right side, we have the pessimistic completion date for the project. The optimistic and pessimistic dates for the project completion are the earliest and latest dates that are reasonable for the

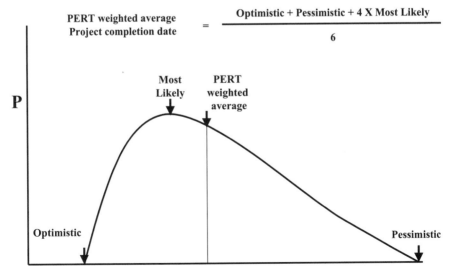

FIGURE 5-8: SKEWED PROBABILITY DISTRIBUTION

project's completion; they should not be dates that are impossibly early or impossibly late.

Notice that the curve of the probability distribution is skewed to the right. This is because it is increasingly unusual for the project to be done earlier and earlier. As most of us have experienced, when things begin to go wrong in terms of project lateness, it seems that they get worse and worse or later and later. So, in this characteristic plot of projects we see more dates later than the most likely date and fewer dates earlier than the most likely date. This causes the PERT weighted average date to shift to a position later than the most likely date. The PERT weighted average is not the most likely date for finishing the project. It is shifted somewhat because the probability distribution is not symmetrical.

Figure 5-9 shows the range of values that is plus or minus two standard deviations from the PERT weighted average value. The standard deviation is always a positive number and is the distance from the expected value. In the case of PERT, it is the distance measured from the PERT weighted average.

The standard deviation of the project completion is the sum of the standard deviations of the durations of the activities that make up the critical path. Since the durations of the activities on the critical path are the only ones that should go into the total that is the project duration, only the critical path items' standard deviations should be used to determine the standard deviation of the project completion.

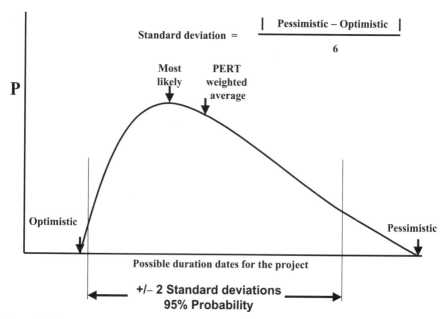

FIGURE 5-9: SKEWED PROBABILITY DISTRIBUTION

To the scheduling example we had been working with earlier, we now add estimated values for optimistic, pessimistic, and most likely. From these we calculate the expected value and the standard deviation (see Figure 5-10).

When we add up the standard deviations of the activities to get the standard deviation of the project, we must first square each one of the standard deviations of each activity, add them up, and then take the square root of the total.

In the example shown in Figure 5-11, the expected value for each activity is calculated by taking four times the most likely value of the duration for each activity and adding this to the optimistic and pessimistic values. The total of the three values is then divided by six. To calculate the standard deviation for each activity, we simply subtract the optimistic duration from the pessimistic duration and divide by six. Strictly speaking we should always take the absolute value of this, but since it is quite unusual for the pessimistic date to be earlier than the optimistic date, it is really not necessary.

To get the project total standard deviation, we add the square of the standard deviation of activities 1, 2, 4, 5, and 8 and then take the square root of the total. Since we are generally interested in a probability of 95 percent, we add and subtract two standard deviations to the expected value of the project duration to get the range of values for project duration that will give us a 95 percent probability of predicting the actual project completion date.

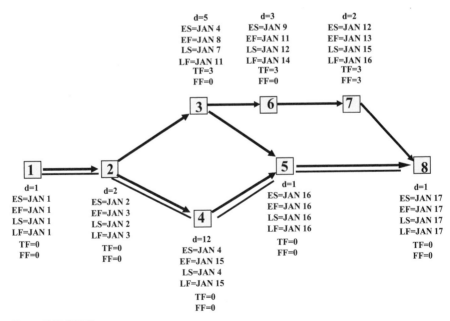

FIGURE 5-10: PERT EXAMPLE

Activity	Optimistic	Pessimistic	Most Likely	Expected Value	Std. Dev.	(Std. Dev)^2
1	1	2	1	1.17	0.17	0.029
2	2	3	2	2.17	0.17	0.029
3	4	7	5	5.17	0.50	0.250
4	10	17	12	12.50	1.17	1.369
5	1	1	1	1.00	0.00	0.000
6	2	4	3	3.00	0.33	0.109
7	2	3	2	2.17	0.17	0.029
8	1	2	1	1.17	0.17	0.029

	Total	18	SD	1.206

95% Probability Range   **20.41–15.59**

FIGURE 5-11: EXAMPLE: PERT CALCULATIONS

Actually, in most projects we are interested in knowing whether the project will finish late or not, and we are not as concerned about whether the project will finish early. In other words we are interested in the project's finishing earlier than the date that is the PERT weighted average plus two standard deviations, and we are not concerned about the date that is the PERT weighted average minus two standard deviations. This raises the probability of the prediction to about 97 percent instead of 95 percent.

One of the problems that many people avoid talking about in PERT analysis is the problem of what happens when the critical path changes during the actual project. When the project is actually done, the tasks will only have one duration each, the actual duration. Since the duration of the task can be any value in the possible range of values for that task, the project could have a combination of durations that would cause the critical path to be different than originally predicted by the expected value durations for each task.

What we mean by this is that when the critical path is calculated in PERT analysis, there is only one critical path and that is determined by using only the expected value of the duration for each activity. Once these durations are found, the critical path is determined, and the project's expected duration is calculated by adding the expected durations of the activities on the critical path. The durations of all the other activities in the project are not added because they are being done in parallel with the critical path activities. The expected value of the duration of the project is then adjusted by adding and subtracting two standard deviations. This results in a range of values for the project. This actual project duration has a 95 percent probability of falling inside of this range.

But what if the durations of the actual project are such that a new critical path forms? To solve this problem we cannot practically solve the equations for all the possible values of all the durations of all the activities in the project. Instead we use computer simulation. This simulation is called Monte Carlo simulation and is discussed later in this chapter.

What is a milestone chart?

A milestone is used to represent groups of activities or significant events or commitments in the project. A milestone chart shows a group of milestones in an organized way similar to a Gantt chart with one milestone per line vertically with a description on the left and the milestone located horizontally along a time scale showing when it occurs. Milestones differ from the bars in a Gantt chart in that they show only a single date and are usually depicted as a triangle instead of a bar (see Figure 5-12). Mile-

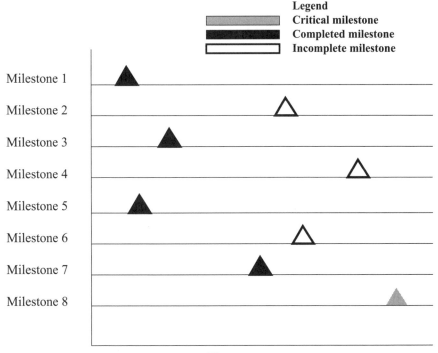

FIGURE 5-12: MILESTONE CHART

stones can be shown in various colors depicting the status of the milestone. Milestones can also appear on Gantt charts; project management software supports the placement of milestones on Gantt charts and other project reports and displays generated by the software.

Tell me more . . .

In the early days of project management, project managers made up Gantt charts for their projects. These Gantt charts could be quite large when projects contained over one hundred activities. It was not practical for the project manager to duplicate the Gantt chart for her manager, and if the supervisor of the project managers had several project managers, it was not practical to display all of the projects' Gantt charts unless there was quite a lot of wall space.

The milestone chart was devised to save space on the project managers' supervisor's walls. Each project manager collected related groups of activities in the project and assigned a milestone to each group. A milestone was placed on the project schedule representing the group. Another milestone was placed on the project managers' supervisor's milestone chart as well.

If there were changes in the schedule that affected the completion date of the milestone, the project manager had to visit the supervisor's office and move the milestone. In all likelihood the project manager gave an explanation of the schedule slide at this time as well. Of course, this kind of explanation was not always the most pleasant sort of meeting.

Milestone schedules can be produced using today's project management software. They are created simply by listing the milestones as activities and giving them a duration of zero. Since they are being created on a Gantt chart, the length of the Gantt schedule bar for the milestone would have a zero length and could not be seen. A triangle or another symbol is put on the chart instead. The symbol can be colored to show various statuses and conditions as needed.

If the milestones are mixed into the normal Gantt chart showing all of the activities involved in the project, the milestone chart can still be produced by simply selecting the activities that have a duration of zero and printing the milestone chart with these activities.

There is one risk in creating these milestone charts. The placement of the milestone on the time scale can be done two ways. One way is to simply assign a date constraint such as "Must Finish On" to the milestone. If any of the activities in the group is rescheduled and the milestone is not changed by hand, it will still show the original date and thus give the wrong information when the milestone chart is produced.

The second way of placing a milestone is to create a finish-start relationship with the activity in the group that has the latest early finish date. In this way the milestone will be rescheduled if this activity is rescheduled. Still, there is risk in this technique as well because it is possible that other activities in the group could be rescheduled without rescheduling the activity the milestone depends on.

If using milestone schedules, the best thing to do is to set up a finish-start relationship between all of the activities that can be delayed past the milestone and the milestone itself. In this way if any of the activities is rescheduled, the milestone will automatically be rescheduled as well.

A better method for summarizing project activities is the summary or hammock activity. This allows more automatic tracking of projects and also gives the start and finish dates for the group of activities.

What is a summary or hammock activity?

A summary or hammock activity, shown in Figure 5-13, is used to represent groups of activities in a project schedule. It is used to summarize the schedule information for a group of activities and to allow the entire project to be summarized as a relatively few summary activities. The summary activity shows the start and finish for a group of activities as one Gantt bar. If the early starts and early finishes are being used for the schedule, the bar will show the earliest early start and the latest early finish for any of the activities in the group.

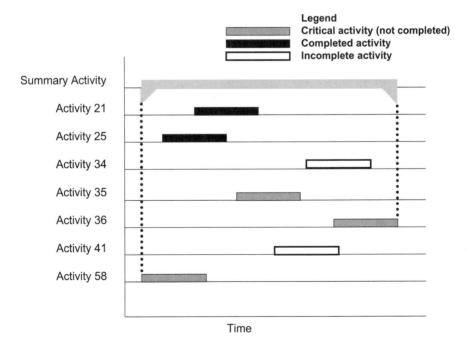

FIGURE 5-13: ACTIVITY CHART

Tell me more . . .

The summary activity has come into use since the development of project management software. The advantage of summary activities over milestones is that it is not necessary to set up elaborate logical relationships to make sure that the milestone is rescheduled when activities in the group represented by the milestone are moved.

The milestone shows only a single date. This can be the start or finish of a group of activities, or it can be some major event or commitment date. The summary activity shows the start and finish for a group of activities. The computer will search through the group of activities and find the earliest early start date and the latest early finish date if the project is being scheduled according to the early schedule. If the project is being scheduled by the late schedule or a combination of the two, the computer will search for the earliest and the latest scheduled dates in the group of activities.

On the Gantt chart the milestones will have a duration of zero and are generally shown as triangles. Summary activities are shown on the Gantt chart as schedule activity bars and usually have a graphic to distinguish them from the normal scheduled activities. In Microsoft Project the summary bars have small triangles below the bar at each end of the bar. The summary activities are created by selecting the activities to be summarized and clicking on the right arrow on the tool bar above them.

The work breakdown structure is entered the same way. The WBS will make a convenient set of summary activities and may be sufficient for your reporting system. If not, other summary activities may be entered as needed.

What is a resource histogram?

A resource histogram is one of the tools given to us by the companies that produce project management software to help the allocation of resources in project plans. Automatic resource leveling does not usually give us the best solution to a resource allocation problem. Until we have good artificial intelligence programs to help us, automatic resource leveling will probably give us very long schedules.

The resource histogram allows us to look at the individual resources in a schedule and the Gantt chart at the same time. By looking at these two displays simultaneously, we can make intelligent decisions regarding the use of the resources. The resource histogram shows the amount of use and availability for the resource, and the Gantt chart shows the activities that the resource is scheduled to be working on.

Tell me more . . .

When project schedules moved from the hands of the draftsmen who were drawing activity on arrow diagrams and Gantt charts by hand to computers, it became much faster to produce results. Unfortunately, many of these results created difficulties. Prior to computerization, resource allocation was difficult to do efficiently. When computerization began and automatic resource leveling was introduced, it was considered a great step forward. It did not take people long to realize that the computerized resource leveling was not terribly intelligent.

The resource leveling algorithm used by most computer software packages examines the project schedule until a conflict arises. A resource conflict occurs when two or more activities require the use of a resource that has less availability than the resources require. Let us say that we have a five-day activity that starts on Tuesday, January 5, and is scheduled to end on Monday, January 11 (no work on weekends), and an eight-day activity that starts on January 7 and is scheduled to finish on January 18. Let us also say that the two activities require the full-time effort of Mary Engineer.

This is a resource conflict; both of the scheduled activities require the resource on January 7, 8, and 11. In this situation the computer's resource-leveling algorithm would schedule the first activity to start on January 5 and reschedule the second activity to start on January 12 when the resource becomes available. This is only one of many possible solutions to the resource conflict, and it may not always be the best solution. There is no consideration for use of total float and free float, length of activity duration, risk, or the number of other activities that depend on the one being rescheduled. In other words it is pretty simple-minded.

Referring to Figure 5-14, we have another example of a resource conflict. Here we will use the resource histogram to help us solve the problem. In weeks one and two the resource, "Engineer 1" is not being

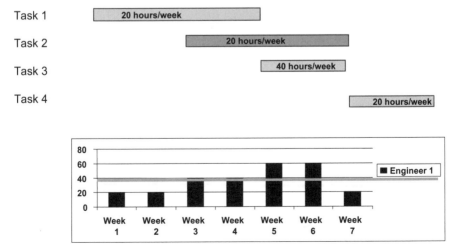

FIGURE 5-14: RESOURCE HISTOGRAM WITH GANTT CHART

fully utilized. "Engineer 1" is used for only twenty hours per week. Task 1 is the only task using our engineer.

During weeks three and four we continue working on task one and also work on task two. Since both of these tasks require our engineer to work twenty hours per week, we can schedule the engineer to work part-time on each of the tasks. This means that she will be used forty hours per week.

Now comes the problem. In week 5 and 6 the project schedule calls for task three to start and for task one to end. The trouble is that task three requires our engineer to work for forty hours on that task alone. If we try to complete the work on task two and start working on task three, we will require sixty hours per week of the engineer's time. Asking our engineer to work twenty hours of overtime may have mixed results from the engineer and her family. We also notice that after week six is completed, we have only twenty hours of work for our engineer again.

There are many ways that this problem could be solved. We could delay the start of task three until task two is completed. We could re-schedule task two to start after task three was completed.

In the solution shown in Figure 5-15, we have chosen to interrupt task two after it has been worked on for two weeks. At this point in the schedule the engineer starts work on task 3 and continues working on it until it is completed. When task three is finished, she starts work on task 4 and continues work on task two. Notice that this solution makes the utilization of our engineer much better. The engineer is now scheduled to be working forty hours each week during weeks 3, 4, 5, 6, and 7.

Using the resource histogram is quite easy. Most software allows you to easily see the scheduled tasks with simple mouse points and

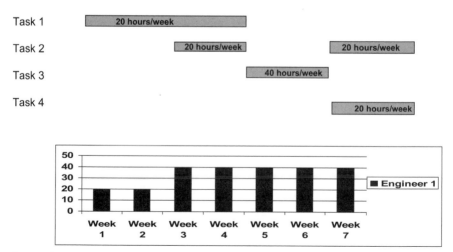

FIGURE 5-15: OVERALLOCATION OF RESOURCE RESOLVED

clicks. The resource histogram will change to reflect the changes made in the schedule, which makes it relatively easy to make an optimum schedule using real people. Although only one resource can be shown at a time, you can scroll through the resources quickly. The Gantt chart can be made to filter out the tasks that do not use the resource.

What is crashing and fast-tracking a schedule?

Crashing and fast-tracking a schedule are ways of reducing the length of a project schedule. Crashing is a general term for reducing project schedules. When we crash a schedule, we spend money or resources to reduce the scheduled time for the project in such a way that we do the things that have the greatest reduction in schedule for the least amount of cost. When we first start to crash a schedule, relatively small amounts of money and resources need to be spent to get rather large reductions in project time. As we continue to reduce schedules, the relative cost increases.

Fast tracking is a special kind of schedule reduction. When we fast-track, we take items that were originally scheduled to be done in sequential order and reschedule them to be done in parallel or partially in parallel. Fast tracking will also increase cost but, more important, it will increase risk. When we have several tasks in a project taking place at the same time and something goes wrong or a problem develops, it may be necessary to disrupt all of the activities in progress.

Tell me more . . .

In an ideal world, all schedules would be optimized in such a way that the time for doing the project and the cost of doing the project would be at a minimum. This is not always the case, and even if it were, we would have managers and stakeholders who would not be satisfied with the predicted date of completion for the project. We will often be asked to reduce the project completion date. Reducing the project completion date means completing the project earlier.

The first thing we should recognize about schedule compression is that there is no value in making any schedule changes to activities that have total float or free float greater than zero. In other words, the only way we can reduce the overall schedule of a project is by reducing the schedule of the tasks that are on the critical path. The critical path determines the overall duration of the project. Items that are not on the critical path have no effect on schedule reduction efforts.

Notice also that as we reduce the schedule by reducing the number of days in the schedule, we are reducing the number of days in the critical path. This also reduces the number of days of total float in the activities that are not on the critical path. Eventually these activities will have their total float reduced to zero, and they will join the critical path as well. As we continue to reduce the schedule length, more and more activities will join the critical path, and it will become more and more difficult and expensive to reduce the schedule. As we can see in Figure 5-16, the cost of reducing the schedule will increase more and more rapidly as we take more and more days from the schedule.

There are many means of crashing a schedule. Reducing the scope of the project will generally reduce the project completion date. If the stakeholders really want to get the project completed early, one of the easiest ways of reducing the schedule is to simply reduce the scope of the project. This can be done by eliminating some of the requirements or delaying them to a later date as in a phased-in approach to project delivery. When this is done, care must be exercised to be sure that what is delivered in the early phases of the project is useful as a stand-alone part of the project and not something that depends on the undelivered part of the project to be usable. It does the customer no good to receive 75 percent of the project if that 75 percent depends on the undelivered 25 percent in order to be used.

Additional resources can be used to shorten the project schedule as well. This can be done by adding resources to the project or by using the resources that are already present on an overtime basis. Adding resources creates a problem for the project team because the additional resources must somehow be absorbed by the project. If we add equip-

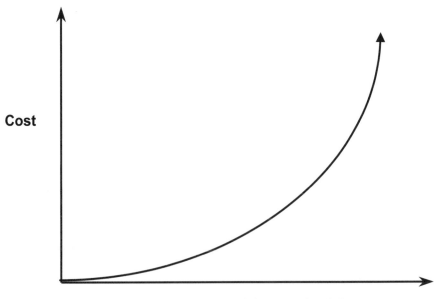

Days removed from schedule

FIGURE 5-16: THE COST OF REDUCING SCHEDULES

ment resources, we must have people to operate the equipment. The additional people required to operate the new equipment must be trained.

If we add human resources to the project, there must be training and familiarization with the project before they can become productive. The new human resources will slow down the already present human resources and cause a further slowdown of the project and a loss of productivity while they are being trained and made familiar with the project tasks.

Creating additional resources by using mandatory overtime is also not without problems. Many companies do not pay an overtime premium for overtime work and some do not pay anything at all for overtime worked. Under the conditions of imposed or forced or mandatory overtime work, there is a noticeable reduction in productivity. This reduction in productivity may reduce the number of productive hours a person works to the point where the actual number of productive hours worked is less than the number of productive hours worked on straight time.

Fast tracking, the special case of crashing, means attempting to do things in parallel that would have normally been scheduled to be done in sequence. Suppose we have a project to install a new gymnasium floor at the university basketball arena. We could begin by removing the old floor, leveling the foundation, installing the new floor, sanding the new floor smooth, and varnishing the new floor.

It can be seen in Figure 5-17 that this project will require thirty-three days to complete. Using this method each step of the new floor installation will be completed before the next step is taken.

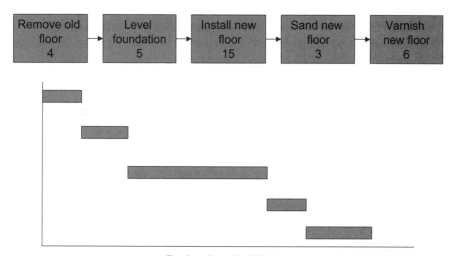

Project length: 33 days

FIGURE 5-17: INSTALLING A NEW FLOOR: ORIGINAL SCHEDULE

In Figure 5-18 an attempt has been made to reduce the schedule. By allowing two days of lead to take place on the second, third, and fourth activities, we can improve the schedule by six days. This is not without problems either. We will begin leveling the foundation while the old floor is still being removed. This may cause some interference problems if the people tearing up the old floor do not have the debris removed as they work. It may also be a problem if parts of the old floor are in place where the foundation leveling people need to work. The new floor installers may also have problems if the areas where they have to work are still being leveled by the foundation levelers. The sanding operations are scheduled to begin two days before the floor installers are complete with their work. If the sanding operations create large amounts of dust, it might slow down or prevent the floor installers from working. There is no overlap on the varnish operation because the dust from the sanding operation would ruin the finish on the varnish.

What is a buffered schedule?

A buffered schedule is one to which free float has deliberately been added. It is when we take negotiated additional schedule time and add it to the schedule as planned delays between the finish of activities and the start of activities that are dependent on them. It does not make sense to buffer any of the activities that are not on the critical path because this would mean that we would just be adding additional free float to activities, and the completion date of the project would still be determined by the critical path activities.

Figure 5-19 shows a project with an early schedule completion date

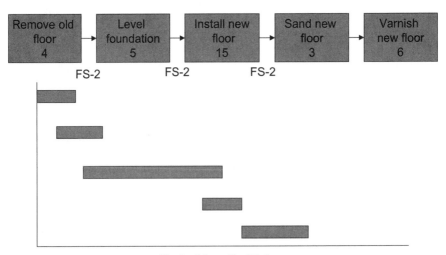

Project length: 27 days

FIGURE 5-18: INSTALLING A NEW FLOOR: FAST-TRACKED SCHEDULE

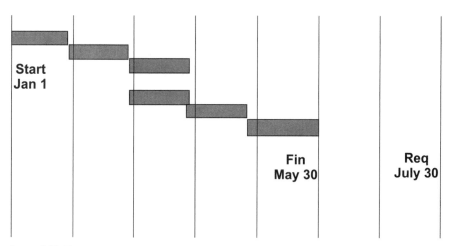

FIGURE 5-19: SCHEDULE WITHOUT CONTINGENCY

of May 30. The project manager gives the stakeholder a promise to complete the project on July 30. Figure 5-20 is the buffered schedule that is created by the project manager.

The amount of time that the schedule is to be buffered is determined by the difference between the promise date that is given to the stakeholders and the late finish date of the project. The late finish of the project is equal to the latest late finish of the last finishing activity of the project.

The buffer time is distributed to the activities according to some scheme. One of the most popular methods of doing this is by using Goldratt's critical chain method, which we will discuss later in this chapter. It can be distributed among the activities of the project according to any scheme that is appropriate for the specific project.

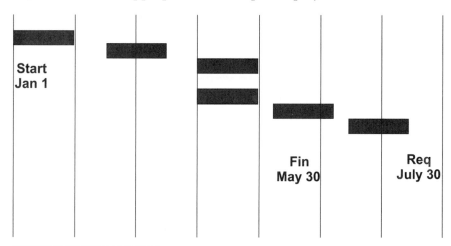

FIGURE 5-20: SCHEDULE WITH BUFFER

Tell me more . . .

Many project schedules are driven by unrealistic mandated completion dates. This has something to do with the psychology of people outside the project. Some stakeholders require projects to be done by mandated completion dates that have little to do with when the project is actually needed. The reason for this is that many of these stakeholders have had disappointingly bad experiences with project managers who did not adhere to schedules. These people request that projects be done as soon as possible because they are certain that there will be delays.

By asking for projects to be completed as early as possible, they feel that the inevitable delay will be added to an earlier promise date, and the actual completion of the project will be earlier. Of course this is also a case of wish fulfillment. If people assume that projects will always be late, projects probably will always be late.

Of course if our stakeholder really has a situation where he wants to crash or fast-track his own project schedule, he wants our project completed as soon as possible and probably wants to take the risk that we will not complete on time in order to take advantage of being able to finish early. In this situation the customer is not likely to agree to the delay we suggest as a means of improving the probability of being able to adhere to the promise date.

Most project schedules have probably had a pretty bad track record and have not met their promise dates. One of the reasons for this is that many project schedules are developed by taking the most likely durations of the activities and using them to predict the most likely project duration and thus the project completion date. We can think of the possible project completion dates as points on a nonsymmetrical probability distribution as shown in Figure 5-21.

We can see that the most likely date has the highest probability of occurring. This date is even earlier than the PERT expected completion date that was developed in our discussion about PERT. If the probability distribution curve were symmetrical, the most likely value of the project completion date would have a 50 percent chance of predicting that the actual project completion date would be earlier (see Figure 5-22).

Of course this means that the project would also have a 50 percent probability of being later than the most likely project completion date. In the case of the nonsymmetrical distribution, the actual project completion date has a greater than 50 percent probability of being later than the most likely date. The question that project managers need to ask themselves is, "Am I willing to promise a stakeholder a project completion date that has a 50 percent probability of being late?"

One of the first things that must be done to buffer a schedule is to convince the stakeholders and sometimes our own management that we

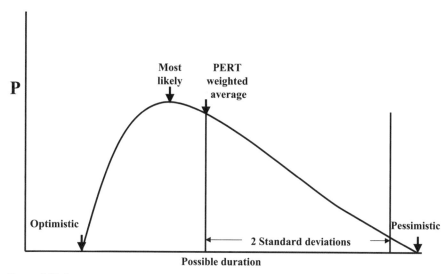

FIGURE 5-21: *PROBABILITY OF PROMISE DATES*

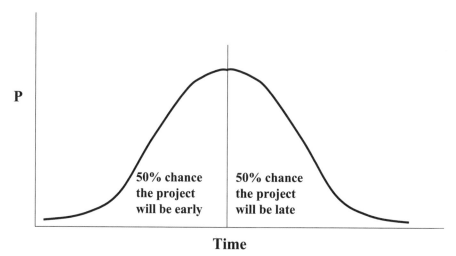

FIGURE 5-22: *WILL THE PROJECT BE LATE?*

will use the schedule change wisely to improve the reliability of the promised completion date. Usually explaining that there is a 50 percent probability that the project will be delivered late will get everyone's attention. Once you have their attention, explain the real meaning of the most likely date for project completion.

Suppose we have a situation in which we are doing a project for a client that depends on our project in order to be able to move forward with a larger project. An example of this might be if our project is to build a machine for a customer that would use the machine to manufacture their product. If we promised the machine to the customer on a specific date, such as 200 days, it is likely that the customer will discontinue the use of its old system to make way for the new machine we are supplying. If we fail to deliver the machine as promised, our customer will have no means of production because the old equipment it had been using has been removed to make way for the new equipment. If we are very late in our delivery, the consequences could be enormous. What we want to do in this case is promise the client a project completion date that has a higher reliability or probability of occurring.

In the symmetrical normal distribution, the range of values that has a 95.5 percent probability of containing the actual value is plus or minus two standard deviations from the expected or average value. In the case of projects we can say that the expected value of the project completion date, plus or minus two standard deviations, will be the range of values that the actual project completion date will fall between. Since we have already discussed the PERT technique, it probably makes sense to use those calculations again.

As a reminder, to predict the expected value of the project completion date by the PERT method:

Expected Value = (Optimistic + 4 × Most Likely + Pessimistic) / 6

To calculate the standard deviation:

Standard Deviation = (|Pessimistic − Optimistic|) / 6

In our example we predicted and promised our customer that we would deliver the machine we were building for them in 200 days. Suppose we want to have a better than 95 percent probability of completing the project on the promise date. We could estimate the optimistic and pessimistic dates for delivery, say 190 and 220 days respectively.

The expected value for delivery would then be:

$$EV = (190 + 4 \times 200 + 220) / 6$$
$$EV = 202 \text{ days}$$

The standard deviation would then be:

$$SD = (220 - 190) / 6$$
$$SD = 5 \text{ days}$$

If we add two standard deviations to the expected value, we will have a promise date that has a better than 95 percent probability of the actual delivery date's being earlier than the promise date.

Promise Date = 202 + 2 × 5 days
Promise Date = 212 days

We have now decided to add ten days to our promised delivery of the machine. The next question we need to answer is, "Where should the ten days of buffer be in the schedule?

The ten days of buffer could be added at the end of the project, but that would mean that every time we need to use some of the buffer we would also have to reschedule the activities between the problem and the end of the project. It would be better to distribute the buffer among the activities of the project. If we do this and if an activity that has buffer is delayed within its buffer, no other activity will have to be rescheduled. This is much like creating free float in an activity.

There is no point in adding buffer to activities that are already off the critical path. These activities already have float and may have free float. We need to buffer the critical path activities first. Once we have buffered the critical path activities, we may want to reschedule some of the non–critical path activities as well.

Selecting the activities to be buffered and the amount to buffer them will be largely done by the project team's best judgment. The critical chain method attempts to put a more formal method of buffer distribution into place, but there is a lot of controversy about its application. See the discussion on critical chains later in this chapter.

Probably the best method of distributing buffer to the activities is to assess their schedule risk. If we have done a reasonable job of risk analysis, we should have a ranked list of risks already identified. Even by subjectively evaluating the schedule risks and looking at their interdependencies we can determine the best place to put our buffer.

Favoring the early part of the project with buffer may allow us to make mistakes that we can avoid later in the project. This method will also allow unused buffer from completed activities to be redistributed to other project activities by starting them earlier than planned. On the other hand, Goldratt argues that early activities with relatively large amounts of float should be scheduled to occur later in the project because we can avoid risks by learning from the successful work that was done early in the project.

Another important consideration in buffer distribution is the criticality of the resource involved. A resource that is rare and scheduled most critically may need to have predecessor activities scheduled with buffer to increase the probability of their being done when the resource becomes available.

What is the Monte Carlo process?

The Monte Carlo process is a simulation technique that is used to statistically predict the duration of a project when there is uncertainty about the duration of the activities of the project. Simulation techniques are used because the number of simultaneous algebraic equations would become quite large even for small projects.

PERT analysis of project schedules allows for there to be uncertainty in the durations of the project activities. In the PERT analysis, however, the critical path is usually held as a constant set of activities. In reality the critical path may actually be different from one set of project activity durations to another.

In the Monte Carlo process a duration is selected from the possible durations for each activity in the schedule. The project schedule and the finish date for the project are calculated. Once the project completion date is calculated and recorded, a new set of dates is picked for the activities in the project, and the next project finish date is calculated and saved. This process is repeated enough times to become stable, usually about 1,000 times, and the statistics are calculated. The most important statistics are the probability of the project's finishing on certain dates.

Tell me more . . .

The Monte Carlo process is used in project schedules to help predict project completion dates when there is uncertainty in the durations of the project activities. The problem with using uncertainty in project durations is the effect these uncertain durations have on the predicted project completion date. Since the completion date of the project is determined by the length of time contained in the critical path, it is important that we know what the critical path is. If there is uncertainty in the durations of the project activities, it simply means that the critical path could be one sequence of activities for one set of durations and a different sequence of activities for another set of durations. It would be incorrect, for example, to predict the completion date of the project by using one set of durations when another set of durations might yield a different critical path and a different project completion date.

The prediction of the critical path for the project when there is uncertainty in the activities' durations can be quite difficult. It would take an impossibly large set of simultaneous equations to analyze the possible critical paths of a project, predict the probability of each occurring, and then calculate the duration of the project. For this reason a simulation method is used instead. This is the Monte Carlo process.

The first things we need to consider in the Monte Carlo process are the durations of the project activities. Since we are considering the use of the Monte Carlo process in the first place, we are recognizing that there is uncertainty in the durations of the project activities. If the durations were known, we would not need a statistical technique at all. But how do the durations vary?

We can think of this variation of durations as a probability distribution. In Figure 5-23 the probability distribution relates a given duration to a probability of its occurring. The even distribution says that the probability of one duration's occurring is the same as the probability of the occurrence of any other duration in the range of possible values. The triangular distribution says that the probability of any duration's occurring increases in a linear way from some minimum value until a value for the most likely duration is reached. At that point the probability decreases linearly until the highest value of duration is reached. The familiar normal distribution says that the relationship between the duration value and the probability is similar to a normal distribution. In any Monte Carlo simulator there will be many choices given for probability distributions.

The distributions given here are only three of many that can be selected for the project activities. Since Monte Carlo simulations must be done on a computer, we will be using software designed to do this process. The software will make available a wide choice of distributions.

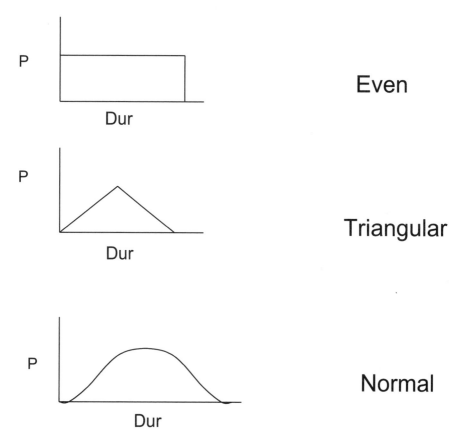

FIGURE 5-23: PROBABILITY DISTRIBUTIONS

Once we have assigned a probability distribution to each of the activities in the project, the computer will do most of the work for us. It will select a duration for each activity in such a way that the combinations of different durations for the different activities is random but they also fit the probability distribution we have specified. Each time a set of durations has been selected, the critical path schedule and the project completion date will be calculated.

Figure 5-24 shows a random number table. In the old days before computers, engineers and mathematicians would use tables like this one to generate random numbers. Random numbers are actually quite difficult to calculate because a truly random number has exactly the same probability of occurring as any other random number. In other words random numbers are the ultimate even distribution. Any number at all has exactly the same likelihood of being the next number in a series of numbers. If we were using two-digit random numbers and started with 56, any number in the range of numbers from 00 to 99 would have exactly the same probability of occurring.

Using a random number table is quite simple. Suppose we want a series of two-digit random numbers. We could pick any row or column in the table as a starting number. In the table in Figure 5-24 let us start with the second column, third row, first two digits, 87. We could then go to the next column and the next column to get successive random numbers. These would be 92 and 60. We could continue with 49 and 50. We could have just as easily continued down the column we were in with 80, 81, 95, and 29. In fact, any scheme for picking numbers is fine.

The random numbers are used to select the durations for the schedule simulation according to the probability distributions that were selected for each of the activities. In Figure 5-25, each of the possible durations for each of the activities is listed with its activity. The probability of each possible duration is listed next to each duration. The probability for each duration is proportional to the number of possible random

04316	01206	08715	77713	20572	13912
78684	28546	06881	66097	53530	42509
65076	87960	92013	60169	49176	50140
20878	80883	26027	29101	58382	17109
66888	81818	52490	54272	24499	74684
44345	95536	81593	21513	17213	95536
49176	29101	90064	57021	27655	46971

FIGURE 5-24: RANDOM NUMBER TABLE

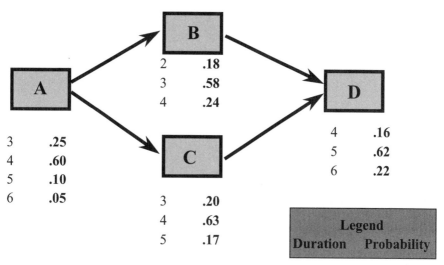

FIGURE 5-25: DURATIONS AND PROBABILITIES

numbers out of 100. In other words, the duration and probability of activity A could be 3, 4, 5, or 6 with respective probability of .25, .60, .10, and .05.

We assign random numbers 00–24 to a duration of 3; random numbers 25–84 to a duration of 4; random numbers 85–94 to a duration of 5 and random numbers 95–99 to a duration of 6. This assignment of random numbers according to their respective probability distributions is done for all of the activities in the project. Of course, if an activity has a certain duration, any random number selected will select the same duration. This is all done automatically by the computer software once we have assigned probability distributions and a range of possible durations to each activity.

Once all of this is done, the computer can begin the simulation. It begins by selecting a random number for the first activity. The random number then selects the duration to be used for the first simulation. A second random number is then selected for the next activity, and a duration is selected for that activity. Once all of the activities in the project have been assigned a duration, the schedule can be calculated normally, the critical path identified, and the project completion date determined.

After the simulation has been run many times, the data are summarized. One popular way of looking at the data is to prepare a histogram for each possible date of the project completion. The height of the histogram bar is proportional to the number of times a particular project completion date has occurred in the simulations. A cumulative probability is also plotted to make reading the data easier. From the cumulative line we can read the probability that the project will finish by a certain date or earlier. In our example (Figure 5-26), we have run the simulation 1,000 times and the predicted calendar weeks that the project could end are shown. There is a 71 percent probability that the project will be completed on February 9 or sooner.

Two other figures that are frequently calculated in Monte Carlo analysis are the criticality index and the critical value. The criticality index is a number between 0 and 1.0 that is equivalent to the percentage of the number of times an activity was found to be on the critical path. The critical value is the criticality index multiplied by the variance of the duration of that activity.

Both of these values are designed to help us manage the project. It is important for us to know the criticality index since this gives us guidance as to which activities in the project we must manage closely. As in the critical path method, we should be more concerned about activities with high criticality indexes since these are the ones that are most likely to cause delays in project completion should they be delayed.

The critical value tells us a bit more. It indicates activities that are likely to be on the critical path and also have large variations in their possible durations.

What is Goldratt's critical chain theory?

In recent years Eliyahu M. Goldratt has developed several interesting ideas about project management. One of the more controversial ideas is his theory of critical chains. This is a method of adjusting schedules to reduce the probability of projects being late.

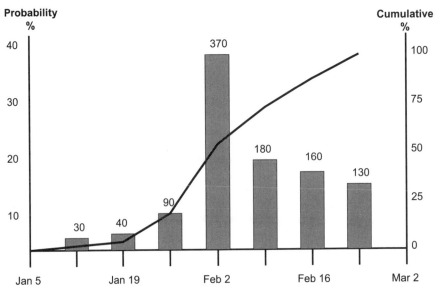

FIGURE 5-26: MONTE CARLO OUTPUT: 1,000 SIMULATIONS

Using the critical chain theory involves delaying activities' schedules until the activities are scheduled close to their late schedule instead of being scheduled to their early schedule as is traditionally done in scheduling projects. Because the late schedule essentially places all of the activities on the critical path, a buffer is placed into the schedule to allow delays in the project activities without delaying past the promised project completion date.

According to Goldratt, delaying the work of the project to more closely follow the late schedule has the advantage of allowing the project team to learn from the experience and knowledge gained in doing other parts of the project.

Tell me more . . .

Traditionally, project schedules have four dates associated with each activity: early start, early finish, late start, and late finish. Most project managers use the early schedule dates to schedule their projects. This means that if all the activity work takes place in the early starts and early finish dates, that work is done as soon as possible. It also means that if anything goes wrong, there will be the maximum amount of time available to do the work needed to recover from the problem.

As we saw in our discussion on buffered schedules earlier in this chapter, scheduling without buffer and using the project activity's most likely durations can have a 50 percent probability of completing the project on the promise date. It made sense to buffer the project completion by two standard deviations and create a promise date that was two standard deviations later than the promise date predicted by the most likely durations.

Goldratt goes one step further in buffering schedules. Most schedules that we see in discussions like this one or in classroom situations are rather simple in comparison to real project schedules. One of the ways they differ is in the magnitude of float. In sample projects, for convenience, examples are given with relatively few activities and short, easy to understand schedules. In reality project schedules are longer and more complicated and frequently have large amounts of float in many activities. In fact, normal projects will have more activities off the critical path than on it. For this reason we need to pay more attention to the activities that are not on the critical path.

To use Goldratt's terminology, a project schedule has critical and noncritical chains of activities. The critical chain of activities is the traditional critical path but includes the effect of resources on the schedule. This means that the critical chain is the list of activities that have no float after any resource conflicts have been resolved. This is really the definition of the critical path as it is normally used. It is somewhat misleading that nearly all of the examples, including ours, calculate the critical path without showing the effect of resource conflicts.

All the activities in the project that are not on the critical chain are, by definition, noncritical activities and have some float associated with them. In real projects these activities tend to group themselves together to form subprojects within the project. These are what Goldratt calls "feeder chains." The characteristic is that the feeder chains are relatively independent of the critical chain until an activity on the critical chain depends on them. In Figure 5-27, feeder chain A, B, C, D has quite a lot of independence until the time activity P on the critical chain depends on it. The same is true of other feeder chains.

The other important point here is that the feeder chains in real projects frequently have large amounts of float as well. As projects grow, it becomes more likely that there will be groups of activities that can be thought of as subprojects. These groupings of activities are not likely to take as long as the activities on the critical chain and will therefore have considerable amounts of float.

If the feeder chains are scheduled to their early schedule dates, early starts, and early finishes, there is a disadvantage. The disadvantage is that if changes in requirements, risks, or other problems occur in the project, much of the work in the feeder chains will already be done and will have to be ripped out. This problem can be at least partially avoided by scheduling the feeder chains more toward their late schedule. Delaying the schedule of the feeder chains will also let us take advantage of lessons learned on the critical chain activities. These can be applied to the feeder chain activities.

Of course, if the feeder chains are scheduled to their late schedule

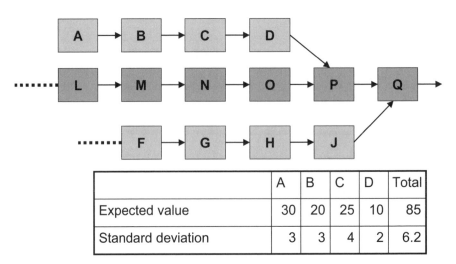

	A	B	C	D	Total
Expected value	30	20	25	10	85
Standard deviation		3	3	4	2	6.2

FIGURE 5-27: FEEDER CHAINS AND CRITICAL CHAINS

dates, this essentially puts all the feeder chain activities onto the critical path. Remembering what critical path really means, the feeder chain activities will cause a delay in the project completion date if they are delayed. We don't want this, so we need to apply buffers as well.

To set our schedule correctly, taking all of these factors into consideration, we need to do the following:

❑ Calculate the critical chain of the project after resolving resource conflicts and all of the resource and other schedule constraints.

❑ Buffer the critical path by calculating a two standard deviation buffer and applying it by starting the project earlier than the early start date or promising the stakeholders a project completion date later than the early finish date of the project.

❑ Group the feeder chain activities into feeder chains.

❑ Calculate the two standard deviation buffer for the feeder chain and schedule the activities in the feeder chain according to their late schedule dates minus their buffer.

By scheduling this way the feeder chains have a 95 percent probability of being completed within their buffered schedule and not affecting the critical chain activities. The critical chain activities are also buffered so that the probability of missing the buffered promise date of the project completion is 95 percent.

6

Human Resources Management

What is leadership?

Leadership is defined as the ability to influence groups of people in order to make them work and achieve prescribed goals.

Leadership, as a type of managerial interrelationship between the leader and the followers, is based on the combination of authority types most efficient for the current situation. Therefore, it is a function of the personalities of the leader, the followers, and the situational characteristics. It is obvious that there could not be one theory describing the whole phenomena of leadership.

The most well-known theories of leadership include:

The trait or "great people" theory of leadership, which considers the need for the best leaders to demonstrate certain personal characteristics allowing them to attract followers.

The behavioral theory of leadership, which relates the leader's efficiency to his or her way of behaving and management style. This includes the ability to produce psychological effects on subordinates in order to coordinate their efforts in achieving goals.

The situational theory of leadership, which is based on the need to combine leadership qualities and certain behavior types depending on a particular situation.

Tell me more . . .

Based on the degree of leadership efficiency and formal support for a leader existing in the organization, four major types of managerial relations can be described:

1. *The nonefficient leadership type,* based on a "master-servant" relationship, where the leader's authority is almost absolute and the degree of a subordinate's participation in the management of the situation and in the ability to reach the stated goals is very low.
2. *The authoritative management type,* based on a classical "boss-subordinate" type of relationship, where the leader's authority is supported by all the administrative documents and where the subordinate's ability to reach the stated goals is quite high, but the participation in the management of the situation is still low.
3. *The democratic management type,* based on an "elected supervisor-subordinate" type of relationship, where the group participates in choosing the leader and therefore participates highly in the management of the situation. Due to the dependency that the leader has on the group, the ability of management and the leader to achieve the stated goals of the company is not the greatest.
4. *The efficient leadership type,* based on the new "leader-follower" type of relationship, where the leader gets the power from the members of the group, recognizing his or her high value for joint work. Given the leader's ability to create an efficient communication system and preserve the group's respect, both the group's chance to reach the stated goals and the degree of participation in the management of the situation is the highest.

In the modern vision of leadership, the concept of leader is changing from being the most competent player in the group and individually influencing people using strong control, to not necessarily being the strongest technical expert and being most focused on team performance using commitment and developing the group's feeling of ownership.

Therefore, the most modern views of leadership correspond to those believed to be successful approaches for good human resource management in projects. However, given the high diversity of people in project teams, a project environment also sets certain additional constraints on a leader's efficiency. These constraints are both technical and psychological. In addition, the lack of formal authority that project managers have as leaders and the need to work with quickly changing temporary groups of people contribute to these constraints.

What is the difference between management and leadership?

In overall management theory, the recent trends consider distinguishing strongly between leadership and managerial qualities. According to this view, managers and leaders have certain major differences in a number of areas, including:

Psychological personality profile: Administrative for a manager and innovative for a leader.

Type of power and approach to making people do things: Administratively supported ordering for a manager and inspiring for a leader; subordinates' respect replaced by admiration.

Approach to task execution: Objective-oriented task fulfillment with lots of detailed planning involved for a manager and overall vision (mission)-oriented movement for a leader; control replaced by trust.

Approach to planning: Acting on the basis of the goals set by others for a manager and fighting for their own goals with a great level of belief and commitment for a leader; professionalism replaced by enthusiasm.

Ways of affecting people: Logical for a manager and emotional for a leader.

Generally: While the manager is the one "doing things right," the position of the leader becomes to "do the right thing."

Tell me more . . .

While all the differences described above might really be of importance in the case of general management, in projects there is a need for both types of behavior, leadership as well as managerial. The leader's behavior is critical in the initial phase of the project when the whole project plan largely sits within the project manager's head and at the moments of major changes and problems. At these times deep emotional commitment and vision of the overall project mission is critical for project success and team members' performance. Meanwhile, managerial characteristics are extremely important during the normal process of project task execution.

The other way of looking at differences between managerial and leadership approaches, as applied to a project management environment, has to do with the different types of project managers. This is determined by the different types of projects carried out and the organizational structure involved. In the case of the managed-by-projects or project-oriented or matrix organization, the project managers carry out certain types of similar projects on a constant basis and demonstrate more management qualities, with the major decisions on project implementation being more or less outside of their competence. In the case of large-scale projects with the project organization formation, the manager of the project is normally much more emotionally involved with the project's overall mission and presents many of the qualities regarded as those of a project leader.

The same situation, strangely enough, could be the case in a weak matrix organization with a project coordinator having very little formal authority but a large level of commitment toward the overall project result.

What are the major theories of behavioral and situational leadership?

The concept of leadership behavior started to be developed before World War II and is still popular because those theories consider the opportunity for leaders to be trained according to special types of programs.

The best-known classical theory of behavioral leadership is Douglas McGregor's Theory X–Theory Y concept of management. McGregor distinguished between those managers who consider people to be lazy and unwilling to work or take responsibility and who use punishment and fear to make them do what they have to (Theory X) and those managers who consider people to naturally be committed to labor if given a correct environment where people are capable of self-education and have the ability to use results-oriented rewards systems to make them more committed (Theory Y).

McGregor's theory reached its purpose of making managers look critically at the style by which they manage people. In McGregor's description, Theory X managers were described as being clearly "evil" and creating the wrong atmosphere for people to be able to work most efficiently. In modern management science and practice, Theory Y managers' approach to managing people is viewed as the best one for most types of jobs, even those that do not necessarily seem to be creative. This was definitely not the case fifty years ago. Needless to say, in a project environment we always strongly recommend Theory Y managers as being the most appropriate for helping people take ownership and increasing involvement and motivation of the project team. Of course these things are normally viewed as one of the key factors of project success.

However, because of its strong ideological orientation, McGregor's approach is too primitive to be sufficient to describe complex situations managers often get into, especially in projects.

Tell me more . . .

The concept that is considered to be more applicable to management situations is the so-called Likkert's leadership styles theory, which shows four styles of leadership behavior: exploitation-authoritative, favorable-authoritative, consultant-democratic, and democratic.

Other theories of leadership behavior basically develop a complicated McGregor's model in order to get it closer to actual situations occurring in groups doing certain types of work. They are normally shown as certain types of matrices describing four to nine types of leaders' behavior. The following theories have been quite popular at certain times:

❑ Leaders' behavior is based on the degree of work coordination and the degree of attention to subordinates.

❑ Leaders' behavior is based on the degree of interest in production and the degree of interest in people.

Theories of situational leadership have allowed further complexity in the process of leadership model development. The major idea of situational leadership is that management behavior has to be different depending on the situation. Thus, another variable is added to the equation models, characterizing the situation where leadership styles are shown. Recognizing the huge amount of management materials on situational leadership that have been written in the last fifty years, we will discuss two theories that, from our perspective, give the overall idea of this approach and also have more relevance to a project environment.

Fred Fiedler's model of situational leadership was developed in the 1960s. The model allows us to predict the efficiency of the work of the group headed by the leader. As in the other models of situational leadership, this one looks at a number of different leadership situations developed by the combination of the leader's characteristics and situational characteristics. The model uses three situational variables: relations between the leader and the members of the group (leader-member relations); the structure of task or the degree of work coordination (task structure); and the official authority (ability to reward and punish). In order to be able to measure the leadership style, Fiedler suggested using a scale of characteristics of the least preferred coworker (LPC).

Following the suggested scale, shown in Figure 6-1, the leaders are to describe the most ideal employee and the least preferred coworker they can work with. Finally, the overall number of scores gained by the leader shows him being oriented toward one of the two styles: relations-oriented (high LPC) or task-oriented (low LPC). The combination of three situational variables and two leadership styles gives eight major types of situations describing Fiedler's model (see Figure 6-2).

Unfriendly	1 2 3 4 5 6 7 8	Friendly

Unpleasant	1 2 3 4 5 6 7 8	Pleasant

Rejecting	1 2 3 4 5 6 7 8	Accepting

Tense	1 2 3 4 5 6 7 8	Relaxed

FIGURE 6-1: FIEDLER'S CHARACTERISTICS SCALE FOR THE LEAST PREFERRED COWORKER

The leaders with low-scoring LPC are more work-oriented and can be more efficient in very favorable situations where they can afford to spend more time developing relations with employees instead of interfering with their work or in very unfavorable situations where they just dictate what the employees do. In a project environment, that corresponds to two types of projects: the very typical project with very low uncertainty, lots of flexibility and reserves, and with team members with lots of experience in implementing projects of this type; or the project that gets into crisis conditions in which the project manager is expected to temporarily break the major rules of HR management and move on to a dictating and authoritative style.

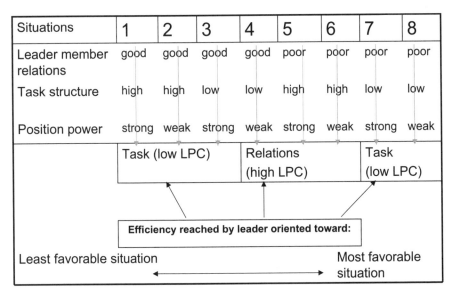

FIGURE 6-2: FIEDLER'S SITUATIONAL LEADERSHIP MODEL

The leaders with high LPC would be more efficient in the moderately favorable situations that are common in the case of projects. The two types of conditions can occur when the tasks are well structured and the relations with the employees are good or when the relations with the leader are good but the tasks are poorly structured. In the last case, the leader is dependent on the employees to have enough desire and creative initiative for task implementation. This is also often the case in projects. However, in this last case the leader has the opportunity to pay more attention to the work itself because the relationship is already well established.

The model allows us to choose a manager related to the situation who has already familiarized himself with the group and organization. It also helps a manager to see ways of changing the situation if changing the manager himself is for some reason undesirable.

However, this model considers the leadership style to be something more or less set for a certain leader. Therefore, for a project environment where the situation can change many times throughout the project, it is more reasonable to pay attention to another model considering the ability of the leader to change his or her behavior during the different project stages.

The situational leadership model of Paul Hersey and Kenneth Blanchard concentrates on something called the followers' maturity level as a key factor that is determined by people who have the ability and wish to fulfill the task set up by the leader. The two components of maturity are:

1. *Professional Maturity:* knowledge, experience, and skills, ability in general. The high level of this component means that the leader will spend less time on directives.

2. *Psychological Maturity:* Readiness to fulfill the task or high motivation of employees. A high level of this component allows the leader to spend less effort on encouraging employees to work because they are already being internally motivated.

There are four stages of maturity described by the model: unwilling and unable; willing but unable; able but unwilling; and able and willing. When people are unwilling and unable to work, they are either incompetent or uncertain. When people are willing but unable to work, they have the motivation but do not have the knowledge and skills. When people are able but unwilling to work, they are not interested in what the leader is suggesting.

As we look at the four levels of maturity described above in the context of a project, it is quite clear that they do not represent different groups of people but rather describe different types of behavior that change as the project moves on. In a classical project, the team members start with high enthusiasm and low competence, then their enthusiasm normally gets lower without changing the competence much as the work develops; further on, the competence level starts to grow as the experience grows with the project; finally, a high degree of professionalism and a high level of motivation are reached as the person starts seeing herself producing really good results.

Based on the Blanchard model, the leader in turn has to balance the attention paid to task implementation with the attention paid to developing relationships with people, the balance being different in different situations, related to the different maturity levels of the followers. There are four styles of leadership a leader can use. The first style, called S1, having to do with the early project stage, has to concentrate more on task direction in order to compensate for a lack of competence among the team members; it is not necessary to pay much attention to people's relationships because of the enthusiasm of the newcomers. Style S2 is used at what is almost the most difficult stage of the project and has to be strong in both respects in order to compensate for the team members' losing their initial enthusiasm. At further stages, as the skill levels grow, style S3, which involves much more delegation and fewer directives, but still high attention to people, becomes more effective. As we move toward the end of the project, style S4 can be used where the efforts on both task implementation and peoples' relationship development decrease and the manager's attention can become less intense.

It is easy to see that none of the leadership theories is complex enough to fully describe the phenomena of leadership. Therefore, in project management we use all the possible approaches and insights that can help us to be flexible enough to be able to move our team members through the different stages of the project with the most efficiency.

What is a project team?

A project team is defined as a small number of people with complementary skills who are committed to a common purpose, performance, goals, and approach. It could also be described as an assembly of people who are directly or indirectly accountable to the project manager.

However, the degree of accountability and the amount of power the project manager has over the team members are largely dependent on the type of organization and the importance and scale of the project. In a projectized organization, the project team involves all the members of the organization, while in a weak matrix or functional organization, the number of people directly and formally reporting to the project manager is relatively low, and therefore the project team is largely a "virtual" structure.

Depending on the nature and type of project, the project team can include other project stakeholders, representatives of other interested departments of the organization, and sometimes even client representatives.

In a balanced matrix organization, the project manager is normally able to colocate the members of the team in one room, which greatly helps the development of team spirit. However, in modern multinational projects it can often happen that not only are the team members located in different divisions of the company, but also that these divisions are situated on different sides of the globe.

However, regardless of the content of the team, the project manager normally uses a large number of team development activities in order to improve performance. Normally, the ability to develop the team and increase its efficiency is considered to be one of the major skills of a project manager. One of the major challenges in this sphere is related to the fact that in a real project environment, different team members are motivated by different things. Therefore, the manager must exercise a large amount of intuition and insight in order to be able to approach the right people with the right motivational factors and allow them to increase the performance and productivity of the team.

Tell me more . . .

Among the most common team development skills, one of the most important is the feeling of ownership by all the team members and the project stakeholders. This is reached by intensifying the participation of the direct and indirect team members in the planning process, which allows a results-oriented type of performance reporting and measurement instead of an objective-oriented type with frequent project team briefings and progress reporting meetings. All this should involve the use of various group techniques and delegating budget and schedule responsibility for certain tasks to relevant team members.

Project team members' collocation is a simple but efficient tool to increase team performance and team members' involvement. The rules developed in the organization concerning the team members' physical location on the project site help to keep and manage the balance between the authority of project managers and functional managers.

Establishment of a just system of rewards can also become a strong tool in the team development process. However, it is important that the project manager choose the approaches to reward system development that are considered honest and fair for all the team members, and also that there is some formal authority supporting his ability to give rewards. It is also important that the reward does not become a "must" in the vision of the person being rewarded; otherwise it loses its positive motivational ability and can become a reason for negative motivation if it is taken away.

In a normal project environment, the project manager should have a certain reserve of project budget that is set up especially to pay for rewards and incentives to project team members. However, even if this budget line were not considered, there are many other types of rewards the project manager can use to increase people's productivity. The ability of the project manager to solve conflict situations and his negotiation skills also play an important role in the overall process of developing a highly efficient and well-performing team.

What are the major team leader skills?

As we discussed in the part of this chapter describing the differences between management and leadership, the project manager is also often required to be able to fulfill the functions of a project leader. As such, he has to be able to:

❑ Set clear goals and make certain that they are followed.

❑ Assist other team members in gaining the overall vision of the project and in maintaining the vision throughout the course of project realization regardless of the problems and confusion.

❑ Create and maintain motivation and a feeling of ownership and involvement in the team.

Among the many tools that the project manager, in the role of a project team leader, has to be able to use well are presentation skills, negotiation skills, and conflict resolution skills.

Tell me more . . .

The project manager often has to be able to use her negotiation skills in the informal negotiations with project stakeholders and the external project environment. Negotiating ability is often critical in the course of staff acquisition for project tasks and in dealing with other project managers and the functional managers of the organization. It is also extremely important to stakeholder and team management during the process of planning the project scope, schedule, and budget as well as in implementing a change management process with new changes of scope, schedule, or budget that are suggested by the client and/or other project stakeholders.

Conflicts are considered to be inevitable in the complex project environment, especially in matrix organizations. Some managers consider it as a sign of organizational health because the large amount of discussion and argument going on in the project often shows a creative approach and a strong involvement of the team members.

However, a long and aggressive conflict atmosphere can strongly inhibit the project team from being productive. Therefore, one of the important skills a project manager has to perform is to be able to track down the sources of conflicts and solve the problems resulting from them.

The best-known practices of conflict resolution involve:

❑ *Forcing.* One of the sides of the conflict forces his or her opinion on the others.

❑ *Smoothing.* A third party makes it seem as if the problems are less then they are.

❑ *Compromise.* All the sides give something up.

❑ *Problem Solving.* Discussion goes on and the conflicting sides try to get additional information to support their position until one of the sides agrees to understand the position of the other side.

❑ *Withdrawal.* One of the conflicting sides just "shuts the door" and removes himself from the conflict.

Withdrawal and smoothing represent temporary approaches to conflict resolution while compromise, forcing, and problem solving provide permanent solutions. Because only problem solving leaves all the sides of the conflict satisfied, it is considered to be the best and most preferable approach to managing conflicts. In forcing, the only party satisfied with the result is the one who forced his opinion on the others. With smoothing, the person who tries to present the conflict as less than it is knows it is a temporary condition and does not satisfy the conflicting parties. In the case of compromise, both sides are slightly dissatisfied because they have to give something up; and finally, in the case of withdrawal, everybody seems to be strongly dissatisfied with the result including the person who withdraws.

What are the concepts of job enrichment and job enlargement?

The concept of job enlargement was developed as a result of the investigations targeted on the improvement of group efficiency and motivation in the early 1960s. The major reason for the investigation was the need for companies to improve the productivity of their employees. The basic concept had to do with the fact that people who deal with boring and simple kinds of job are not motivated enough to perform their jobs well.

The decision therefore was to increase the amount of operations the person performed in order to make the job more attractive to the employee.

The concept proved to be unsuccessful because it tried to simply replace a short boring job with a long boring job without trying to change the content of the job. The further development of this concept led to the second theory of job enrichment, which turned out to be quite successful and has been accepted by many organizations as the correct approach to increasing group productivity. This concept fits very well with the usual project environment and is therefore regarded by project managers as a useful approach to project team development.

Tell me more . . .

The job enrichment concept was developed based on the experiment carried out by the Swedish Volvo company in the 1960s. The management of Volvo decided to try discontinuing one of its assembly lines and instead putting all the people with needed skills in one room with all the tools and equipment needed to carry out the operations. The cost for the process and the length of the process as the result of this organizational change increased; however, the overall life cycle cost of the product, including all the needed repair work, guarantee work, clients' dissatisfaction factors, etc., decreased significantly.

Based on the results of the experiment, it was decided that the increased opportunities for creative work increased the level of responsibility and ownership. The ability to see the final product made the members of the group more motivated and therefore increased their ability to perform good results and check for quality. It was decided that, in order to increase people's productivity, it is critical to give them more opportunities for independent and creative work.

This approach is strongly reflected in modern project management methodology, where the systems of delegation and increased involvement of the team members in all phases of the project are considered to be critical for project success. It is also largely used in other modern management methodologies, such as total quality management. The basic idea is to decrease the cost for quality by decreasing the inspection time and increasing the self-sufficiency of the producers of the products.

What is a team role structure?

The role structure of the team determines the content and distribution of different roles within the team. The knowledge and ability to use the structure of roles within the team is a strong and efficient instrument of human resource management in the project team.

There are three major types of roles we can see in the team: creative roles, communicative roles, and behavioral roles. Normally each member of the team has some of each of the three types.

The *creative role* of a team member characterizes his or her active position in the problem solving process, search for alternatives, and other actions assuming a certain level of creativity. The *communicative role* characterizes the position of a team member in the overall communication structure of the project. The *behavioral role* shows the typical model of a team member's behavior during the course of project development.

Tell me more . . .

Below we present the most typical creative, communication-oriented, and behavior-oriented roles of the team members with their characteristics.

Creative Roles

Idea Generator: A team member who generates principal ideas, sets up key problems, suggests alternative decisions, etc.

Idea Compiler: A team member who develops fundamental ideas into practical solutions that are capable of uniting different ideas.

Erudite: A team member who has knowledge of a wide range of problems in the past and in the present.

Expert: A team member who is capable of evaluating the advisability of the idea and able to give correct advice in the course of a discussion.

Enthusiast: A team member who is capable of inspiring the other members with his or her belief in the success of the project.

Critic: A team member who analyzes the performance and results of team work giving critical, often negative, evaluation of the ideas presented.

Organizer: A team member who organizes work that unites the work of different team members with the final result of achievement.

Communicative Roles

Leader: A team member with high personal and professional authority who influences both the team as a whole and its individual members.

Recorder: A team member who carries out the important routine work of registering ideas, opinions, and decisions and developing final reports.

Liaison: A team member who carries out informal interpersonal linking of conflicting group members by providing external group communications.

Watchman: A team member who distributes and controls the information flow, evaluating the importance of the message and getting it all the way through to the leader.

Coordinator: A team member who carries out the coordination of different team members' activities with the final result of achievement when in contact with the leader.

Guide: A team member who knows the structure of the organization very well and knows how to communicate information about it with the external project environment.

Behavioral Roles

Optimist: A person who is always certain about the success of the project, finds ways to get out of crisis situations, and inspires the other team members.

Nihilist: A person who is always uncertain about the project success, has critical viewpoints that are mostly different from the accepted ones, and seems like a "black sheep."

Conformist: A person who follows the accepted behavioral patterns, passively agrees with group decisions, and represents the "silent majority."

Dogmatist: A person who holds to known norms, holds her own opinion to the end, and does not agree with rational group decisions.

Commentator: A person who comments about the events happening within the project, people's lives, or outside project environment.

Intriguer: A person who collects and spreads rumors that are often untested and false, sees personal offense everywhere, and is ready to write complaints to all the higher levels.

Fighter for Truth: A person who carries and represents social, moral, organizational philosophy and human rights. Can play both progressive and regressive roles.

Public Person: A person who is strongly involved with public work and often dreams of different public "activities" to be carried out during work time. Does not consider his project responsibilities seriously enough.

"Important Person": A person who presents himself as someone who knows a lot.

"Orphan": A person who searches for understanding and sympathy, complaining about his loneliness and his lack of understanding from the other team members and management.

"Ruff": A person who normally is irritated by friends and develops lots of enemies, conflicting with team members and management.

"All for Himself": A person who conducts personal business at work using his work position.

Loafer: A person who shows very little activity at work, does only minor work, and achieves very little.

"Napoleon": A person who is a glorious man with a high feeling of self-importance, who dreams of taking over the leadership position, and who tells stories about his achievement and lack of recognition among management.

Knowing the roles of the team members not only allows the manager to use the human resources of the project efficiently, but also helps to develop the correct environment in various situations, manages discussions and group dynamics, and solves conflict situations.

In order to strongly improve the productivity of the team during the group activities such as meetings and team briefings, it is important to choose a number of typical, most important roles that need to be represented in order for the work of a group to be efficient. Among the roles described above, the key ones may include organizer, idea generator, critic, expert, liaison, and recorder.

The University of California at La Jolla *Handbook for Group Facilitators* also suggests pointing out target achieving roles and supportive roles for leaders, where target achieving roles are directed at setting up major management objectives and provide all the major decision-making procedures. Supportive roles are oriented to the development of a good social-psychological climate and provide for a team's efficient performance.

What is delegation?

The term *delegation* describes the process used by a manager to shift some of the responsibilities for the task implementation to another team member. Delegation is key to improving team members' feelings of involvement and ownership, and the ability to delegate is therefore considered to be an extremely important skill for a project manager.

The ability to delegate responsibility for tasks fully or partially to other people not only gives higher motivation to the team members, but also frees the project manager to be able to carry out other project tasks related more to her area of responsibility, such as planning, management, reporting, and coordination.

Tell me more . . .

The process of delegation requires certain steps. It starts when a new team member joins the project and needs to be given the idea of the nature of the task he is responsible for. Furthermore, the delegation process requires the person to be able to think the task over and reformat it as he thinks appropriate without actually changing the job content. After the newly named task is represented back to the delegator, it's time for an informal or formal—depending on company policies—agreement to be signed. The progress reporting mechanisms are set at the same time. Further work of the delegator will include coaching and monitoring the work implementation process.

Although the process seems to be fully compliant with the major ideology of project human resource management, it does not necessarily mean the process of delegation will always be the same in different situations and with different people involved. The so-called Oncken's levels of delegation include five stages for the process of delegation: "Wait until you are told"; "Ask what to do"; "Recommend, then do it"; "Act, but advise at once"; and finally, "Act on your own, routine reporting." It's easy to see that the first stage requires lots of involvement of the delegator. In stage two, there is at least some initiative allowed for the delegatee. In stage three, the opinion of the delegatee about the issue becomes important to the delegator. Stages four and five are different mostly because of the urgency of reporting about the decision made and the actions undertaken by the delegatee.

Although it seems as if the five stages of delegation describe very well the development of trust and responsibility of team members throughout the course of project development, from early to late stages, this can also depend on other circumstances such as the degree of importance of a certain activity or task. It is also possible that the same person can be in one stage of delegation with one task and in a different stage with another task, and it takes lots of communications and attention from the delegator in order to make it completely clear to the team member so that he is not confused.

What are the major theories of motivation?

The term *motivation* is defined as the process of inducing a person to function actively in order to achieve certain goals. The influence of motivation on people's behavior depends on a number of factors. It is very individual and changeable relative to various stimuli and feedback reactions to people's activities.

By *motive* we normally mean the factor that causes a person to undertake certain activities, as well as her internal and external driving force. Motives determine what has to be done and how it will be done in order to satisfy a person's needs.

Stimulus plays an important role in the process of satisfying needs. Although the usual understanding of the word *stimulus* considers it to be a rewarding mechanism, the initial meaning of the word can be interpreted as either an incentive or a reason for a person's activities. There are four major types of stimuli to be considered: forcing, material incentive, influence, and self-actualization.

Theories of motivation started to be developed in the second part of the twentieth century, after World War II. The question of increasing people's productivity had not previously been of any concern to large companies because social and economic conditions were such that productivity was easily achieved by pure material factors. In other words, the demand for a workforce had been lower than the supply of people willing to find jobs.

In the late 1950s, the need and importance of motivation was first proven by a number of practical experiments. These experiments led to factors that seriously improved the companies' abilities to improve productivity without making large investments. Since then many experiments and investigations have been undertaken in this area. A number of theories of motivation have been developed, and they can be grouped into three major categories: initial theories, content theories, and process theories.

Tell me more . . .

Initial theories of motivation were developed on the basis of the analysis of the historical experience of people's behavior and of the application of simple stimuli of forcing as well as material and nonmaterial incentives. So-called Theory X, Y, and Z is looked upon as a good and simple example of one of the initial theories of motivation. Theory X was fully developed by McGregor, who added his Theory Y, while Theory Z was suggested much later by William Ouchi in his model of personal behavior and motivation. Theories X, Y, and Z represent different models of motivation based on different levels of needs and therefore all three theories should be used by a manager and applied to different members of a group.

Theory X is based on the fact that biological needs are the major factors in people's motives and the fact that some people have a historical and genetically inherited unwillingness to work and can work only under forced conditions and a high level of control. It is clear that people of the type described can be found in any group or society, and therefore a good manager has to be ready to increase the productivity of such people by means of forcing, which is supported by a material incentive.

Theory Y describes the contrary type of people, characterized by a willingness to socialize and to work well, as well as their wish to take responsibility for their work, their readiness and need to use their intellectual and creative potential, and the need for special rewarding factors related to satisfying their wish for self-actualization. These types of employees can be stimulated by opportunities for self-assertion and to a lesser extent by nonmaterial and material incentives. However, the normal percentage of such employees in the group is from 15 to 20 percent; they are most often strong individualists and cannot fully expose their talents in a social group.

Theory Z states that some people have a combination of biological and social needs and prefer working in groups and making group decisions, but they like to have individual responsibility for their results and prefer to be controlled informally on the basis of clear evaluation criteria. According to this theory, a person is the most important part of any enterprise and therefore the attention of the enterprise should be focused on the employee and provide him or her long-term or lifelong employment. This theory describes a good employee who prefers to work in a group and to have stable goals for a long period of time. The major stimuli for these people, in order of importance, include material and moral stimuli, self-assertion, and forcing.

As has already been said, all three theories describe different groups of people and consider different motives and stimuli to be used.

As the investigations in the area of motivation developed, the new theories of motivation added complexity to the initial theories in order to make them more realistic and practical. The two theories we want to look at are the well-known theories of motivation developed by Abraham Maslow and Frederick Herzberg in the United States.

Maslow's theory of needs considers the fact that people constantly have some requirements from the outside world in order to feel satisfied. He tried to group the needs and set them out hierarchically as a pyramid and made a statement that each need, if not satisfied, motivates people to actions that they stop when the need is satisfied. The need is then automatically replaced by the next need. He also considers that the needs that are closer to the bottom of the pyramid have to be satisfied first.

The five groups of needs stated by Maslow are food, shelter, and clothing; security; socialization; recognition; and self-actualization.

Maslow's pyramid of needs, however reasonable it seemed on paper, did not really work out that well in practice when applied on the level of socialization at large companies in the United States. It turned out that there are a number of weak factors in Maslow's theory. Different needs show themselves differently in relation to various situational factors, content of work, status in the organization, age, etc. The needs do not necessarily follow in the order Maslow stated with his pyramid; satisfying higher groups of needs does not necessarily weaken their influence on motivating people. The need for self-actualization and recognition can cause increasing influence on motivation and dampen the physiological needs.

In the second part of the 1950s, Fredrick Herzberg developed a new model of motivation that has a lot in common with Maslow's pyramid but does partially solve its major shortcomings. Based on a major investigation carried out among the high-level managers of a paintwork company to find out the major factors of positive and negative stimuli experienced by these people at their work at different times, Herzberg distinguished between two major categories of factors that he called "maintenance factors" and "motivation factors." The first category was related to external facts and included company policies, working conditions, salary levels, interpersonal relations within a group, and the degree of direct control over work. The second group, motivation factors, had to do with the content of the work and included success, career advancement, recognition, high levels of responsibility, opportunities for creative work, and personal development. Furthermore, Herzberg said that the maintenance factors need to be taken care of to keep people from feeling dissatisfied.

Maintenance factors must be satisfied before people can be affected by the motivation factors. Persons who are motivated will achieve very high levels of performance.

It is easy to see the similarities between Maslow's and Herzberg's theories; generally speaking, the first three levels of Maslow's pyramid correspond to Herzberg's maintenance factors, while the last two levels can easily be related to motivational factors. However, unlike Maslow, Herzberg does not think that the maintenance, or hygiene factors, cause certain patterns of behavior in the employees; it will only prevent them from feeling dissatisfied; meanwhile, in order to get people motivated, a good manager has to use motivational factors, or the higher level needs of Maslow's pyramid.

The content theories of motivation have lots of similarities, but they basically fail to develop an algorithm that will work under any possible circumstance; nor do they explain what is actually underlying the phenomenon of motivation. They pay most attention to the analysis of the factors used for motivation and do not analyze the process of motivation itself. This is done in so-called process theories of motivation, which mainly focus on the way a person distributes his or her efforts to reach various goals and how he or she chooses a certain type of behavior. They also consider the fact that the behavior of a person is a function of his or her expectations and perceptions related to the current situation as well as the possible consequences of the type of behavior chosen.

Victor Vroom's expectancy theory is based on the fact that the active need is not the only necessary condition of motivation for a person to reach stated goals. A person has to also expect that the behavior chosen will allow her to reach satisfaction or get what is being wished for.

According to Vroom, the model of motivation consists of three components:

1. *Expected Results, Ex (Expectancy):* Perceived effort-performance relationship.
2. *Expected Rewards, Ins (Instrumentality):* Perceived performance-reward relationship.
3. *Valence:* Value of a reward for a person.

If the value of any of the three factors Vroom considers critically important for reaching motivation is low, the overall motivation will be weak and the productivity of work will be insufficient.

The combination of these factors can be presented as the following formula:

Motivation Forces (MF) = (Ex) × (Ins) × Valence

The practical application of this approach requires a manager to set up clear relations between the results achieved and the reward given. It is also important to consider that in order to reach the level of results corresponding to the reward, the employees' wish for the reward has to be consistent with their level of authority and professional abilities.

J. Stacey Adams's theory of equity states that people subjectively relate the reward gained to the effort spent and then compare it to the rewards that other people completing similar work are gaining. If the comparison shows inequity, a psychological tension develops. In order to balance the feeling of inequity, people can either change the level of effort spent or try to change the level of rewards obtained. The major conclusion the theory makes is that, until people feel they are getting a fair reward, they are going to decrease the intensity of their work.

Unfortunately, the practical application that many American companies made out of this theory moved them in the wrong direction. Companies set policies to try to hide the salary levels of different employees in the company. Instead of improving the feeling of equity, this action often develops the feeling or suspicion of inequity even where there is none.

Lyman Porter and Edward Lawler developed a complex process theory of motivation that combines the elements of both expectancy and equity theories. Their model has five variables: effort spent, perception, performance achieved, reward, and level of satisfaction. According to this model, the performance achieved is dependent on the efforts expended by the employee, his abilities, and his character, as well as his perception of his role. The level of effort spent is determined by the value of the reward and the confidence that this level of effort will actually result in a certain level of reward. The model acknowledges the relationship between reward and performance because the person satisfies his needs by gaining rewards for performance achieved.

According to the model shown in Figure 6-3, the performance achieved by an employee (6) depends on the effort spent (3), his abilities (4), and his perception of his role (5). The effort spent depends in turn on the value of the reward (1) and how much a person sees the relationship between the effort spent and the reward gained—perceived effort/reward probability (2). The performance achieved (6) can cause intrinsic rewards such as a feeling of achievement (7) as well as extrinsic rewards such as recognition, career advancement, etc. (8). The employee has a feeling of satisfaction (10) if the perceived equity of the reward (9) is present.

There could be a relationship between the performance achieved and extrinsic rewards when these rewards reflect opportunities set by management for this employee. There is also a connection between performance and perceived equity of reward, which brings us back to the equity theory and the fact that people have their own opinion of the level of the equity of the reward. The satisfaction represents the result of intrinsic and extrinsic rewards with the consideration of their equity. Satisfaction is a measure of how valuable the reward really is for a person. This evaluation will influence the person's perception of similar situations in the future.

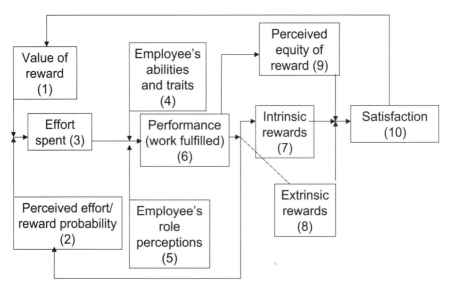

FIGURE 6-3: PORTER-LAWLER PROCESS MODEL OF MOTIVATION

The important conclusion of the theory was that the resulting work leads to satisfaction and not the other way around. Satisfaction leads to higher results, as many managers had thought for a long time.

The theory also had lots of practical applications. For example, based on their model, Porter and Lawler pointed out that an increase in salary leads to increased productivity only in a case where people find salary to be important; they also see a clear relationship between increased performance and productivity and increased salary. Although many managers declare that they are willing and even attempt to relate the salaries of their employees to their work results, they still tend to compensate according to the time spent on doing work and pay off their seniority rather than their ability and effort. Therefore, the model of salary suggested by Lawler consisted of three comparable components, including one of payments for fulfilling certain professional responsibilities, equal for all the people of the same position and professional status in the organization; one that was based on seniority and life cost factors; and one that varied for each employee based on the results achieved by them in past work periods.

What are the main types of power?

In projects, a very important function required of a project manager is influencing the organization—in other words, "making things work." That involves having a good knowledge of both the formal and informal systems of the home organization of the project, as well as the client, subcontractors, and other stakeholders. The ability to influence the organization requires understanding the mechanisms of power and politics.

By power we normally mean the potential ability to influence behavior, change a situation in order to overcome resistance, and make people do things they would have not done otherwise. In general, it involves influencing opinions, decisions, and methods.

Tell me more . . .

There are a number of types of power that can be present in an organization. The list includes:

Legitimate—Formal title or position
Reward—Ability to provide positive consequences
Coercive—Ability to provide negative consequences
Purse String—Budget control
Bureaucratic—Knowledge of the system
Referent—Association with someone else's power
Technical—Knowledge
Charismatic—Personality

It is quite clear that in different situations we are dealing with a different balance of the types of power, In projects, we normally talk about a combination of formal (legitimate) power, power types that have to do with owning resources (rewarding, purse string), and informal powers (charismatic, referent, etc). It is easy to see that the type of power the project manager has in any concrete project depends largely on the type of organization and on internal company policies. For instance, a good matrix organization has a reward budget for the project team as a part of the project budget and thus allows a project manager to use a reward type of power. He or she is not normally responsible for salary payments for team members. Similarly, if a company has a policy of employing project managers with high technical backgrounds in the field, the project manager is able to use the power of the technical expertise with the team members. Unfortunately, this type of power does not really work well in projects because the project team normally brings together people of quite different technical backgrounds. It could well be that a project manager is just not able to be an expert in all those technical areas.

In general, we can combine the presented types of power into two major groups. Position-based powers, or authorities, include formal, legitimate, purse-string, reward, coercive. Person-based powers, or influence, include technical, charismatic, referent. A good project manager in a reasonable project-oriented organizational structure uses both types of power with more accent on influence. In reality, direct formal powers very often do not work with all the project stakeholders. This is especially true with the external project environment of clients and governmental bodies. The third type of power a project manager can use is accountability—power obtained through agreement—in other words, the responsibility of the people on a project team and the other project stakeholders to follow both formal and informal agreements with the project manager. According to good project management practices, the team members are supposed to formulate their accountability in terms of both results and performance indicators. This type of power can be described more or less as the ability of a project manager to make project team members fulfill the work according to their own promises.

What does the staff acquisition process include?

The content of the staff acquisition process in projects is different from the general staff recruiting procedures for the organization. In *The Guide to the Project Management Body of Knowledge,* it is considered to be one of the facilitating processes in the planning process group. In projects, the project manager does not actually recruit personnel for the project from outside of the organization. A clear exception to this is when the project requires some skills and knowledge that are not available inside the company. In this case if the project manager does not make the decision to buy these services from the outside, certain skilled people are recruited for this project only, and this becomes another responsibility of the project manager.

In most cases, however, the staff acquisition process involves a number of activities to select the right types of people and sign them up to certain project tasks.

Tell me more . . .

The major result of the staff acquisition process, according to *The Guide to the Project Management Body of Knowledge,* is to set up the project team with all the needed skills and knowledge important for successful project realization. In order to achieve the stated result, the project manager often has to perform functions not necessarily associated with the normal process of personnel recruitment. For instance, one of the important parts of the responsibilities of the project manager involves good communication skills. These skills allow the project manager to reach a productive understanding with the functional managers and other project managers interested in getting the same types of resources. Needless to say, this process becomes extremely complicated in weak matrix organizations where the project manager does not have enough authority to take people away from the functional departments, and the functional managers are not rewarded for the amount of project work their people are doing.

In many cases the project manager is not clear about which people are best for working on certain tasks in the project at the stage of planning where the decisions are made. It is surely important for a manager to preassign as many people as possible to the specific tasks, especially if a task involves some special skills. The fact that the project manager does not have a clear idea about exactly who would be able to work on the project also negatively affects the estimating process. This is important especially in cases where the company holds the salaries of its employees a total secret from everybody else in the company except the accounting department. In this case, the project managers tend to plan using the average cost for this skill group for their estimates and, what is worse, report performance based on the average figures as well. This creates a strong demand for experienced and expensive employees, leaving the young, inexperienced ones unclaimed.

Generally, all those considerations make it important for the project manager to be able to preplan for certain people to be assigned to certain project tasks at the stage of staff acquisition.

What are the tools and rules for human resource coordination in projects?

As mentioned before, the normal project-oriented environment is often extremely complicated from the viewpoint of the organizational structure. In order to decrease the degree of confusion and argument, the project managers have to undertake every effort possible in order to apply some structure to human resource distribution and coordination between different projects and operational activities of the functional departments.

There are a number of simple but useful instruments used by project managers and a number of rules project managers have to follow in a project-oriented organization in order to make the overall project organization more transparent and satisfactory to various project stakeholders.

Tell me more . . .

Staffing plans are used by functional managers in order to be able to track different employees from project to project. As shown in Figure 6-4, a staffing plan is a simple matrix showing the projects each person is working on at certain periods of time. Functional managers can use the staffing plan in order to see the people available to fulfill certain functional or new project jobs; it also gives the person himself some vision of his coming assignments.

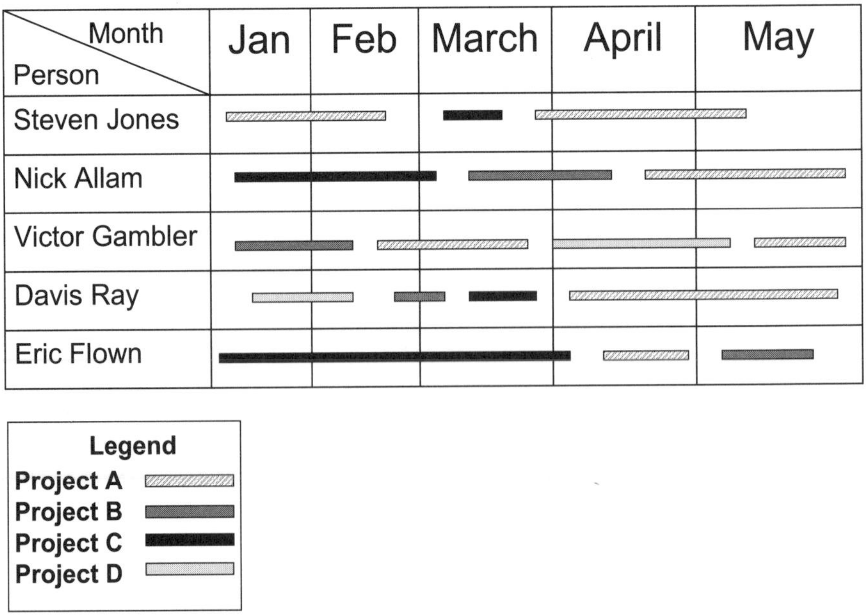

Person \ Month	Jan	Feb	March	April	May
Steven Jones					
Nick Allam					
Victor Gambler					
Davis Ray					
Eric Flown					

Legend
Project A
Project B
Project C
Project D

FIGURE 6-4: STAFFING PLAN

Task / Person	Overall planning	Database development	Survey development	Survey imple-mentation	Result evaluation and reporting
Steven Jones	P	R	P	P	P
Nick Allam	P	P	R	R	P
Victor Gambler	P	P	A	A	P
Davis Ray	R,S	S	S	S	R,S
Eric Flown	A	---	P	---	A

R-Responsible   A-Assists   P-Participates   S-Sign-off

FIGURE 6-5: RESPONSIBILITY-ACCOUNTABILITY MATRIX

The responsibility-accountability matrix in Figure 6-5 is a tool used in some format in projects almost everywhere. Normally it is a matrix table representing a group of people and showing their role and/or responsibility related to certain tasks or groups of tasks. Any types of symbols and signs can be used in order to make the scheme clearest.

In any project, regardless of its size and complexity, it is absolutely essential that an organizational chart be developed for the project showing the names, positions, and responsibilities of the project team members and often other important project stakeholders. The organizational chart can easily correspond to the project WBS where the subproject managers are assigned to certain work groups or subprojects in the structure of the WBS. The organizational chart for the project gives the project stakeholders, as well as the people outside of the project, the opportunity to find the person they need in the overall project structure.

In strong matrix organizations, many people spend months at a time without ever seeing their functional departments, moving from one project to another. In this case, especially considering the fact that it is normally outside of the scope of the project manager's responsibilities to take care of salary levels, career advancements, training needs, etc., of certain team members, it becomes critically important that the communications between the project manager and the functional manager are efficient and reliable. The project manager in this case becomes responsible for relaying information about team members' performance on the project to the functional managers, who are then able to use this information and the information from other projects to make yearly decisions on the employees' career development, salary changes, etc.

7

Building Projects in Organizations

How do I organize for project management?

Projects work best in a balanced matrix type of organization. This is because the resources of the company are permanent and projects are not. We remember that the definition of a project is "... a temporary endeavor. ...." Project teams are formed for the life of a project. This means that we are able to bring the right resources together for a project and use them for the amount of time they are needed. But where do they come from?

As we try to answer this question, we start thinking about the most efficient type of organization for managing projects. To do that, we first have to take a look at the types of organizations developed through history as people learned how to manage their businesses best.

Tell me more . . .

There are really only three ways to organize to accomplish work. Nearly every organization fits one of these types or is a combination of them. These are the pure project organization, the functional organization, and the matrix organization. The pure project organization and the functional organization have been around for hundreds, perhaps thousands, of years; the matrix organization is a rather recent development.

In the pure project organization, shown in Figure 7-1, the project

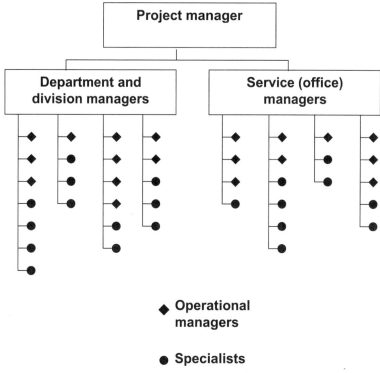

FIGURE 7-1: PROJECT ORGANIZATION

manager is the supreme authority. He or she is the ultimate decision-maker for the project and is not subject to any but the highest level of review. This review is generally at the project level for the budget, schedule, and deliverables. These projects are usually quite large and are done in a remote location. Building dams or remote power plants in Third World countries would be typical applications for the pure project organization. The pyramids at Giza in Egypt were probably built with this kind of organization.

The pure project organization probably developed out of necessity. In a large remote project, communications issues make it necessary to have a single person on site who has the authority to make decisions. This person is the project manager. Even in modern times, it is difficult to communicate about what is really happening in the jungles of Botswana where the project is to build a nuclear power plant.

When the project organization is used, certain common characteristics are generally observed. The organization, though large, has a single focal point that everyone understands. In our example of the power plant project in Botswana, everyone understands that the goal of the project is to generate 900 megawatts of electricity by a certain date. People in the organization are not easily distracted to work on other projects. Because there are clear understandable goals and objectives and because the project manager is on-site and accessible and can make decisions, the project team generally has good morale.

These organizations are inefficient, however, especially when they are not very large. Because of the remote location of such projects, when resources are needed, they have to be obtained exclusively for the use of one project. This means that if a person of a specific skill is needed for the project, she cannot be shared by another project.

An example of this would be if the project needs a metallurgist to analyze the steel used in the reactor vessel. The metallurgist will take twenty hours each week to do the work. What will we do with the metallurgist the rest of the time? It would not be practical to send her back to the United States every week. It would make more sense to keep the metallurgist in Botswana and use her in whatever other skill we could when she is not doing metallurgical work. Of course this means that she will be working outside of her skill for half the week but will still draw the pay of a skilled metallurgist.

The real problem with the pure project organization is what to do with the project team when the project is finished. You can picture the project team in our Botswana project. They are driving to a goal of generating 900 megawatts of power by a certain date. They achieve the goal. The project is on time and on budget, and the customer is satisfied. Everyone celebrates while they are handing out the termination notices.

Thus, although it may seem that the project organization should be the best type of organization for managing projects, in reality it is not. Or to put it differently, it may be good for carrying out a single unique project, but it is not good for a project-oriented organization in which projects are the major part of its long-term activities.

The functional organization, illustrated in Figure 7-2, has been around since long before the industrial revolution and was the preferable type for commercial enterprises in the beginning and middle of the twentieth century. The functional organization is organized on the basis of skills. A typical company sets up departments within the company, and each of these departments will have persons of similar skills within it. In truth this type of organization is not strictly organized by skills. In the mechanical engineering department, for example, there may be a few engineers with different skills such as electrical engineers or computer engineers.

This type of organization is very efficient in its use of people. Since the people in the organization have similar skills, the supervisor of the department is probably a person with those skills as well. As such, that person probably knows what is best for the people in the department as far as salary administration, evaluations, training, and work assignments

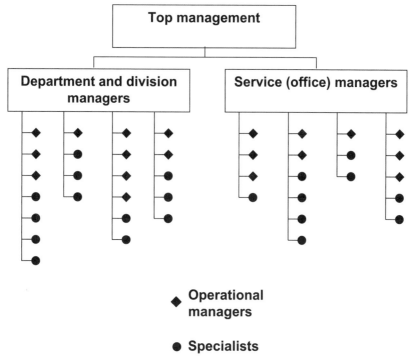

FIGURE 7-2: FUNCTIONAL ORGANIZATION

are concerned. The work assignments can be given to the people who are best at that particular kind of work, and the workload can be distributed efficiently.

The functional organization is also very stable. In fact, that is the problem with it. Let's look at how work is done in a company like this. Typically someone in the sales department finds a customer who needs work done by our company. Senior management decides whether to accept this type of work or not. If a decision is made to do the work, it is portioned out to the departments in the company according to the skills required. The department supervisor decides who in the department should do the work, and the work assignment is made. The people who are best at any particular kind of work are generally given the assignments that properly utilize their skills.

Suppose we have a company that builds products that use motor brackets, which are things you mount a motor on. Suppose further that they have someone in the mechanical engineering department called Sally. Sally is the best motor bracket designer in the company. She has been designing motor brackets for the past ten years, and she is good at it. When the company needs a good motor bracket design, they come to Sally. Sally works on a routine basis. She has an inbox and an outbox.

Requests for motor bracket designs come to her inbox. She works on them and puts finished requests in her outbox. Life goes on in a regular way.

One day the company is trying to get new business, which involves making a motor bracket out of titanium. Sally has designed motor brackets using all kinds of materials but never titanium. It should be noted that Sally's performance appraisal depends on how many good motor bracket designs she does in a given year. She knows that if she takes the time to learn all that she needs to know about designing motor brackets in titanium, it will take her far longer than it would if she did it with mild steel or one of the materials she is familiar with. So she moves the titanium motor bracket design request to the bottom of her inbox.

Eventually she will have to design the motor bracket if she can't pass the design request off to a junior motor bracket designer. When she does, it will already be late, it will become a rush job, and it is likely to be done poorly.

This is the difficulty with a functional organization: It does not work well with new things. As long as the organization continues to do what it does without very much change, it works with great efficiency. When companies try to innovate and create new and different products for new customers, they create problems for a functional organization.

Notice that in this type of organization there is also little concern for the customer. In fact, in our example, Sally did not know who the customer was or where the motor bracket would be installed. Having a weak or nonexistent customer focus is a sure way to deliver products to the customers that are not what they want. In a market environment it means that we will be selling buggy whips when people want to buy cars.

The growing need for organizations to successfully implement projects and to be able to stay responsive to a changing market became one of the main reasons that many functional organizations put more flexibility into their functional structure. Many times this was done through a number of intermediate stages that led to developing a new organizational approach—the matrix organization.

The matrix organization, illustrated in Figure 7-3, is a mixture of the pure project organization and the functional organization. It is the one that will allow project management to work best. In the matrix organization we try to have the best of both organizations without the negative aspects of each. We try to have an organization that has a manager with authority who can be reached easily, an organization with a lot of flexibility, and customer focus. It should be an organization that can quickly bring the proper skills together on a temporary basis for the duration of a project. Resources in this organization are shared.

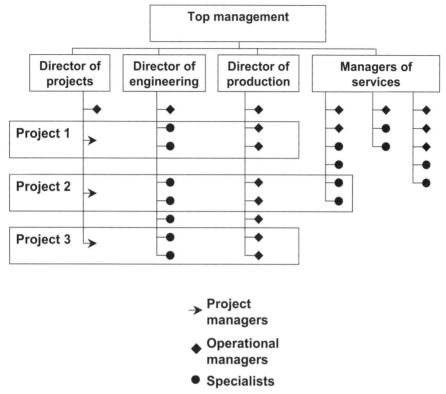

FIGURE 7-3: MATRIX ORGANIZATION

The matrix organization does these things. In the matrix organization we have a group of project managers as well as a group of functional managers. The project managers manage most of the organization's work, which is done in the form of projects. The functional managers are the home office for the people who work on projects.

When a new project begins, the project plans are taken to the functional managers by the project manager. Together they decide which people are most appropriate for the job to be done, and these people are assigned to the project team at the appropriate time. They are assigned to the project only temporarily, and they are permanently assigned to the functional manager based on their skills. The project manager has similar meetings with the other functional managers.

The functional manager has the responsibility of providing appropriate training, salary administration, and other administrative functions to the people in the department. The functional manager is also responsible for the assignment of work that takes place in the functional department.

What is a balanced matrix organization?

Matrix management organizations are difficult to manage properly. One of the difficulties in matrix management is balancing the level of authority between the functional manager and the project manager. If the project manager has too much authority, too many of the people in the functional organization will be taken from that organization and assigned improperly to the projects. If the functional manager has too much authority, the organization essentially stays a functional organization and never becomes a matrix management organization.

Tell me more . . .

If the functional manager is able to dominate the project manager, the organization will remain much as it was when it was a functional organization. The project managers will have to request work from the functional managers, and all the work will be done in the functional organization under the direction of the functional manager. The people will all receive their work assignments from the functional manager, and work will be scheduled and performance will be measured by the functional manager. The project manager will merely advise the functional manager as to what work should be done.

If the project manager is able to become more powerful than the functional manager, the project managers will take control of the functional organization by forcing all work to be done in the projects. This means that the project managers will not allow any of the project work to be done in the functional departments. If no work is being done in the functional areas, the project managers will control all the people doing the work.

In this situation the project managers also become responsible for people's other project assignments. Since the people working are all working for project managers and no one is working in the functional areas, project managers will have to meet with each other to have people assigned to do work on their projects.

Balancing the organization is really less difficult than it might seem. The most effective way is to look at the length of each person's assignments. If a person is going to be assigned to work on a project for the next four weeks, let us say, we move that person to the project team's location, and the person stays there working for the next four weeks. If a person is required to do work that is expected to take less than four weeks, the project manager writes a work authorization to the functional department, and the person works in the functional department.

Some work needs to be done in the functional department so that there is work to do in that department when people are waiting for their next project assignment. If we find that the functional department has very few people working in it, it may be that the project managers are drawing too many people into the project organization. Investigation will likely show that some of the people working on the project in the project team location are being underutilized.

Why would we want to use an unbalanced matrix organization?

During the transition from the functional organization to the matrix organization, it may be necessary to go through several interim organizations. This can be most easily done by first changing to a weak matrix organization where the functional managers retain most of their power and the project managers have very little power. As the project managers gain experience in managing work, they can be given more power. Eventually, as the project managers gain experience, they are given more power, and the functional managers are given less power until a balanced matrix organization is reached.

Some companies will go through this transition fairly quickly while others may go through it very slowly, and others will be satisfied to stop somewhere before a balanced matrix is achieved.

Tell me more . . .

One of the major problems in changing a functional organization into a matrix organization is getting there. Some executives discover matrix management and try to make the transition to it in their companies too quickly.

The problem is that when we have a functional organization, the functional managers not only take care of the administrative and training work of the people in the department they supervise, but they also make the work assignments and manage the results and performance of the people doing the work. When matrix management is used, project managers become responsible for the work assignments and for measuring the performance and progress of the work that is done by the project team.

The functional managers are the company's major assets. Most of them are senior people in the company and have much of the experience and knowledge of the company in their brains. It does not make any sense at all to lose these people for the sake of an organizational change. If we try to change to a matrix organization too quickly, this may happen. The reason is that the senior managers in the functional organization quickly realize that they will have less responsibility in the matrix organization because much of the organization's work will now be done in projects rather than in their home departments.

The transition from functional organization to matrix will take time. The existing functional managers must have time to fit into the organization in such a way that they are promoted instead of demoted. This does not happen overnight. They must not feel threatened by the organizational change or they will resist it. These managers are the major assets of the company and if they choose to resist the change, it will be a formidable resistance.

We can think of these organizations as varying from the functional type of organization to the pure project organization.

Closest to the functional organization is the weak matrix organization. In this style of organization, the project managers are not usually called project managers but something like project coordinators or expeditors, and they probably work only part of the time managing small parts of the project. Even at this low level of project management there are some advantages. There is now some focus on the customer, and there is a person who is concerned with the overall project. In this situation less than 25 percent of the personnel in the company will be assigned full-time to project work.

As we move toward more powerful project managers, we reach the balanced matrix organization that was described previously. Here the project manager manages projects full-time and has the title of project manager. In the balanced matrix organization, between 15 and 60 percent of the personnel in the company are assigned full-time to project work.

In a strong matrix organization, 50 to 90 percent of the company's personnel are assigned to project work full-time, and the project managers become more powerful than the functional managers. Program managers appear in this kind of organization and take on some of the responsibility of the functional managers as well.

What does moving toward matrix management require?

As has already been mentioned, the process of developing a matrix organizational structure in your company takes lots of time and effort in order to be efficient. The overall transition may take a couple of years and may pass through a number of intermediate stages. Different stages of transfer from a functional organization to a balanced matrix organization are known as various types of weak matrices.

Tell me more . . .

Generally speaking, different types of matrices can be distinguished by the level of authority that the project manager and the functional manager have. In a functional organization, the authority of a project manager is equal to zero, and a person who coordinates the project is not normally named a project manager at all. In a project organization, the authority of a project manager is almost absolute. In a balanced matrix organization, the authority of the functional and project managers is relatively equal, and this equity varies to one or the other side in the intermediate types of matrix.

When the organization is first starting to transition toward matrix management, it may employ a so-called project expediter who does not have much authority but whose major responsibility is to focus on the client and the final results of the project, and to put some pressure on the functional managers in the form of advice in order to make the project move in the necessary direction. Certainly, the authority of a project expeditor is much less than the authority of a functional manager and there are no people directly reporting to him.

If the project is of high importance to a company that has not yet moved to a classical matrix structure, the company's top management might raise the authority of a project expeditor by moving her to a level higher in the reporting hierarchy and making her directly responsible to the top managers. In this case, she is recognized as a project coordinator. Although such a change raises the level of a person's informal authority, her formal authority still stays very low and there still are very few people directly reporting to her.

As the organization moves on in its transition, it may start to get some members of a project team to report directly to the project manager and even be physically moved to a room where the project is taking place. Thus, we come to a balanced matrix where major players of a project team are now located at the project site while the rest of the members are still doing their project work in their functional departments under the supervision of their functional manager.

If we go further with this approach, we may come to a strong matrix where there are no people in the functional departments because the authority of project managers has become high enough to take them all away to the project site. That condition may also not be the best for the project because many people do not like being moved around a lot. Therefore, it is important to keep a balance and not allow either of the sides to take over. In fact, if you reach a situation where the functional and project managers of your company are working as partners in assigning people and coordinating and evaluating their work, you may consider yourself to be extremely lucky as a top manager.

Of course, the whole process of moving toward matrix management and then making it work assumes that a number of human factors are taken into consideration. In many cases, especially during the early days of trying to introduce matrix management into organizations, the changes did not actually take place because of the high level of reluctance on behalf of the middle managers. Indeed, being aware that they are going to lose half of their responsibilities to project managers and figuring out that this change in responsibilities may also affect the level of their salaries, these managers do every thing possible in order to keep this change from happening. In this situation, it becomes especially important for top management, which surely does not want to lose the functional managers, to slowly move them on to the higher positions and replace them with more administratively oriented managers. At the same time, the young project managers are given a chance to fulfill a number of projects within the company. By the time the functional managers are either replaced or moved higher, the project managers have enough experience and respect in the organization to start taking over more responsibilities.

It is also important that in a company carrying out matrix management, the project managers put enough effort into evaluation of their project team members and get this information to their functional managers. Other tools the project managers may use include responsibility-accountability matrices, staffing plans, organizational charts, and others we examined in Chapter 6.

How do organizations affect the projects and how does project management influence organizations?

Every project is implemented within a certain type of home organization. This is true even for project organizations that are set up specifically for a certain project. In many cases, the culture and environment of the home organization influence the remote project development.

One of the strongest factors affecting every project implementation is the organizational structure within which it is being realized. We have described the three major types of organization: functional, project, and matrix. Any other organization can be determined more or less to be a derivation of one of these three types.

Tell me more . . .

Of the three types of organizations, the functional and the project represent the extremes in the range of possible variants from the aspect of a lack of or an excess of project orientation. All the organizations that fit in between the two extremes can be determined by a certain type of a matrix organization: from weak through balanced to strong.

There are a number of other organizational factors that influence project implementation. Organizational culture and accepted practices set up standards for a project manager in order to be most successful. Organizational systems, including the way a company is managed and the way the company's services are organized, also have a great influence on projects. Of course, the projects can best be implemented within an organizational system that is project-oriented. When this system is not in place and all the projects have to be carried out within certain general systems, it sometimes requires the project to develop parallel internal systems of expense collection, work hours reporting, and so on.

Of course, the organization that has offices in different countries and is carrying out multinational projects also requires some special structures to be in place. This is especially true in providing communications, choosing communication channels, and creating a workable atmosphere of involvement inside the project team.

As much as projects are being influenced by their organizations, they in turn influence the strategic organizational development and the company's growth. Classical project management grew from construction, defense, and information technology projects and therefore considers project management methodology to be applied mostly to external client-oriented projects of the company. Currently, although the importance of the external project stays high, many organizations are looking at other applications of the project management methodology that have to do with internal changes in the organizations. Indeed, the ability for an organization to change is becoming a critical factor in surviving in the marketplace. This was well demonstrated by Japanese companies when they were breaking into the American automotive, electronics, and other markets. It turns out that project management represents the best methodology for implementing organizational change. Therefore, the ability of the company to introduce and endorse project management methodology is becoming a factor in gaining significant strategic advantages over competitors.

What are the major spheres for change and the problems associated with them?

Any change event can be efficient only if the implementation takes into consideration and keeps a harmonic balance among the three spheres of change:

❏ *Personal Sphere.* Introducing any change will always be related to overcoming the inertia of the old type of thinking and the old way of doing things. This is especially true when change is directly related to restructuring the organization or changing management approaches.

❏ *Organizational Sphere.* Even when the change is not directly related to global structural change, it inevitably results in developing new or getting rid of the old organizational relations and elements. Therefore it is important to provide harmonic interaction and balancing of all the old and new elements both during the change and after it.

❏ *Technical Sphere.* The technological sphere of production and management processes is important because it also changes during the process. We must consider the technical support required by the change itself.

Even if the change is occurring in only one of the three spheres, it always influences the other two.

Tell me more . . .

Any changes normally have to overcome a certain resistance from the organization's personnel.

The major causes for the reluctance of personnel to endorse change include:

- ❑ Fear of the unknown.
- ❑ Traditional thinking—"If something works, don't change it."
- ❑ Lack of understanding of why a change is needed in the first place.
- ❑ Lack of belief in successful change—especially if such efforts have been undertaken and failed in the past.
- ❑ Conscious opposition to change based on the knowledge that it can hurt them.
- ❑ General indifference.

In order to combat the resistance, it is important to remember how difficult it may be to implement the best-planned change event because of the resistance of the personnel involved.

The other important activities that have to be undertaken in order to reduce stress and increase appreciation of change include:

- ❑ *Informing:* Telling everybody what is going to be changed and why it is necessary.
- ❑ *Increasing Interest:* Explaining how the things that will be changed will be better, personally, for each employee.
- ❑ *Comforting:* Explaining that the changes will not hurt—at least not those employees who are really interested in the company's work.
- ❑ *Acting from Inside:* Finding and supporting the change advocates at all levels of the organization.
- ❑ *Providing Support:* Finding and supporting the leaders who are ready for change—formal as well as informal, indicating the leaders who may act against it and neutralizing them by either moving them or blocking their actions.

The change process does not happen at once. It normally has four phases:

1. *Passive Resistance*. When people act as if they are "thunderstruck," it is often seen as no reaction at all to the change event to come and can be wrongly interpreted by management as no resistance. If, due to this misunderstood impression on the part of management, no information nor explanation is communicated to the people, the first phase is quickly changed to the second.
2. *Active Resistance*. When people realize that the changes have started, they enter a stress condition characterized by strong feelings of fear, threat, and anger. This is very often a failure spot for changes; therefore the management reaction should be very careful and include lots of explanations and seem like forcing.
3. *Understanding*. Once the second phase is past, people start entering the third phase of understanding. This is when the employees start understanding the nature of the change, its necessity, and its positive impacts. The level of stress decreases and the stress changes to a less dangerous type. It is important for management to move into explanations of everyone's roles and functions in the change process and the new structure.
4. *Acceptance*. If phase three is carried out correctly, the last phase of acceptance follows. The new process is understood and endorsed with major resisting forces either changing their minds or being removed. It is important to remember that this is the stage at which the new values of an organization are formed and accepted.

Any organizational change is related to the transformation of the company's organizational structure. The scope of this transformation has to be carefully planned in advance regardless of the fact that some details can actually be planned and introduced on the way.

The process of forming the vision of a new organization is called organizational planning.

The goals and objectives of organizational planning are:

❑ To set up the scope of transition in the organizational sphere
❑ To get the organization into a position of primary correspondence to the company's new strategy
❑ To determine responsibilities, accountability, and reporting structure
❑ To provide liaison and efficient coordination between departments/divisions
❑ To formulate new job descriptions

Organizational planning is to be carried out in the following major spheres:

❑ *Structure:* Functions, processes, work groups, hierarchy levels, personnel structure, and accountability

❑ *Decision-Making and Responsibilities:* The processes of making key decisions, governing principles, and responsibilities

❑ *Roles, Assumptions, and Job Functions:* Key organizational roles, distributing responsibilities for implementing groups of work, and determining tasks correspondent to work functions

❑ *Planning Working Groups/Divisions:* Determining related tasks and resources needed for organizational functioning

❑ *Setting Up Result Indicators:* Development of and monitoring success indicators for personnel, groups, divisions, and business as a whole

❑ *Development Mechanisms:* Mechanisms for developing personnel, technical sphere, management systems, etc.

What is organizational change and what are the specific characteristics of project management methodology as applied to change projects?

By a strategic event we normally mean an impact in time and scope change in corporation life that influences the whole corporation or a significant part of it. Very often a strategic event is called a strategic change.

The examples of strategic change may include:

Political changes of the company status: Merging, selling parts of a market, redistribution of ownership between the private and public sector, etc.

Changes in the internal structure of the company: Moving from a functional structure to a balanced matrix or introducing new management approaches such as introducing the methodology of total quality management.

Tell me more . . .

Strategic change can be caused by a number of situations:

In an Ideal Situation: A decision made by top management for a significant improvement or change of business processes or product transitioning of the company to a new level of development.

In a Normal Situation: A decision made by a company's top management under strong external pressure or in order to solve serious problems, such as a significant decrease of profits, a financial deficit, the low efficiency of management systems, etc.

In a Bad Situation: A crisis and/or organizational collapse when further functioning of the organization in its current form becomes impossible.

Unfortunately, in most cases a bad situation leads to organizational destruction. At its best, the collapse decreases the efficiency of strategic changes; at its worst, it denies top management the opportunity to implement strategic actions. Therefore, the strategic change has to be carried out before the organization enters a crisis situation and the inevitability of a change becomes apparent.

It is easy to see that the change event fits all the characteristics of a project.

First of all, in order for a change to be successful, it has to:

❑ *Be compact in time.* If you try to prolong a change process for an unknown number of years, it is going to ruin the company.

❑ *Have clearly formulated goals and clearly stated objectives in its scope.* Any attempt to carry out a change that does not have a well-determined scope will lead to a waste of money and time, and no result will be achieved.

❑ *Be determined in budget.* As a change event always considers expenditures to be made, you have to be careful that it does not lead the company to financial collapse.

❑ *Have well-considered mechanisms of "getting in" and "getting out."* The change process does not just happen; it is a special state of an organization that is characterized by specific management and financial schemes. Before it starts, you ought to have a clear understanding of how you are going to get the organization into this special state and how you are going to get it out of it.

As the change process fits the characteristics of a project, it can be managed with the application of project management methodology. However, this type of project has a number of specific features, including the external environment, the company organization, the project, and the long-term effects of a project on this external environment; the difficulties of applying classical financial justification methods and the need for more qualitative indicators of project success to be considered; the need for a more flexible, changeable chain of relations between the activities and the final results given more opportunities for changing any of the sections of the chain.

The modification of a project management methodology developed for international socioeconomic programs and projects enlarges the opportunities for applying project management to the internal projects of the company oriented toward implementing change. The modification is known under a number of names, including the one we like best— results-based or results-oriented project management methodology. The concept of a methodology is built on the idea of results chains describing project development from inputs to long-term results—sort of a WBS turned 90 degrees to the right where the major long-term results form the top level of the WBS. This is illustrated in Figure 7-4.

The major differences between results-based management and a classical project management approach include:

❑ The orientation on long-term and medium-term project results mainly happening outside of the project scope and outside of the project manager's framework of authority.

❑ The ability to use qualitative result indicators along with quantitative indicators for both justifying the project and using performance management.

❑ The increased flexibility inside the sections of a result chain allowing change on any component of the chain including inputs, activities, outputs, outcomes, impacts, and indicators as the project is developing and its progress is monitored and analyzed using result indicators.

Classical WBS   RBM result chain

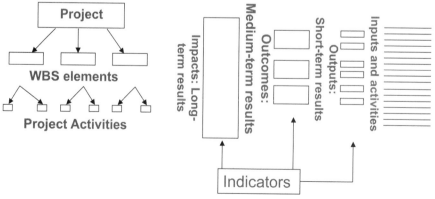

FIGURE 7-4: CLASSICAL WBS COMPARED TO RESULTS-BASED MANAGEMENT

What is a change process and what are its stages?

The change process has two intermediate, somewhat "invisible" phases and three formal change stages. The process starts with the preliminary phase of understanding the need for change. This is illustrated in Figure 7-5.

After that, the change should follow these three stages:

1. Building the foundation for a change
2. Building the concept of change
3. Implementing the change

After the change implementation is over, the final activity of a change process is to bring the company back to normal operation with the results of change being realized and introduced to normal processes.

Tell me more . . .

With the change process, it is important to remember that:

Ignoring the first two stages, building the foundation and building the concept, leads to a change failure. This is the most common managerial mistake.

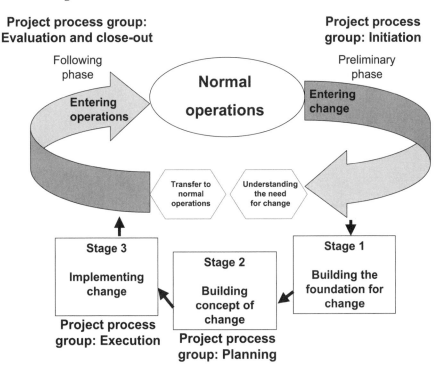

FIGURE 7-5: CHANGE STAGES AND PROJECT PROCESSES

Only the third change stage, implementation, has to do with actual change in project execution and is usually regarded as a whole change project.

The first stage is normally carried out as invisible work that is not seen by personnel and sometimes is not even seen by the company's top management. It has to be carried out by the initiator of the change.

The second stage of change can be carried out within the scope of the normal functional operations of a company or as a separate project, group of projects, or program.

Finally, the last "invisible" process is the transition to normal operations. Although it is not considered as a formal stage of change, it is extremely critical in order for a change to be successful and very often involves major stress on behalf of the change implementation team.

Generally, all three stages for change along with two "invisible" processes are compliant with normal project process groups with the first stage corresponding to project initiation processes; the second stage to project planning processes; and the third stage to project execution processes. The last "invisible" change process is responsible for the organizational transformation into a new state. The results of the change are introduced into normal company operations. This corresponds with normal project evaluation and closeout processes.

Successful change is possible only with eight major factors of transition success being considered (John P. Kotter's eight key change success factors). According to Kotter, in order for change to be efficient, it is important:

1. To form an understanding of the necessity of change and its inevitability.
2. To form a team having enough skills and authority to lead a change.
3. To form a thorough vision of change and the strategy of activities needed for its successful implementation.
4. To pass this vision on to the people, to inform them of the overall strategy of activities, to delegate authority, and to lead by personal example.
5. To eliminate obstacles and support risky undertakings and creativity.

6. To provide small victories; to find and reward successes within a scope of overall strategy and vision of a change.

7. To secure achievements and support continuous movement.

8. To fix changes achieved into the culture and to relate the new behavior with success in people's perception.

8

Risk Management

What is risk management?

A risk is a possible unplanned event. It can be positive or negative. In project management the success of our projects depends on our ability to predict a particular outcome. Since risks are the unpredictable part of the project, it is important for us to be able to control them as much as possible and make them as predictable as possible. A pure risk or threat is a risk that has only a negative possibility as an outcome. A business risk is a normal risk of doing business. It can have a good or bad outcome. An opportunity is a risk that has only good outcomes. These risks can be of two types, known risks and unknown risks. The known risks are those that we can identify, and the unknown risks are those that cannot be anticipated at all.

Risk management is the process of identifying, analyzing, and quantifying risks, responding to them with a risk strategy, and then controlling them.

Tell me more . . .

Risk has uncertainty as its main characteristic. Risks can be thought of as project tasks with the exception that project tasks are work tasks that must be done as part of the project, and risks are work tasks that may or may not have to be done in order to complete the project. The uncertainty associated with any risk relates to the knowledge that we have about it. The greater the knowledge we have about a risk, the less uncertainty there will be about it.

Risk management must be done throughout any project. We must do it at the beginning of the project, at the end of the project, and many times during the project. In the beginning, there is little known about the project, and the uncertainty is at its highest, however small the amount of money that has been put into the project at this point. Care must be exercised not to ignore risks that are identified in the beginning of the project. These risks seem distant and unrealistic in the enthusiasm of starting a new project, but it is truly disheartening to have to deal with a problem on an emergency basis in the middle of the project when it was brought up during the writing of the project charter and forgotten. For example, one of the project team members tells us that the customer has asked for a special salt spray test in the past and we might have to do it again for this new project. He also mentions that our old salt spray test cabinet is no longer usable since it was destroyed when it was dropped off a truck. A little investigation would find that the salt spray test cabinet is custom-made and must be ordered six months before delivery by the only company certified to make the device.

At the end of the project, risks are still important. There are certainly fewer risks at the end of the project than at other times, but there is little time or budget left for them at the end of the project. Even risks that are not all that serious in the beginning and middle portions of the project become serious when time and money to handle them are both short near the end of the project. Two weeks before the project is supposed to have final acceptance with the customer, we find that the requirement for the user manual is not the 30 pages we anticipated but the 300 pages the customer now tells us we must write.

Risks are things that may or may not have to be done. All risks have a probability and an impact. If a risk has a probability of 1.0 it means it is certain to happen; if the risk is 0.0, it is certain not to happen. So, all risks will have a probability that is somewhat less than 1.0 and somewhat greater than 0.0, and all risks have an impact associated with them. If the impact is zero, the risk has no effect and can be ignored.

Of great importance in projects is the question of known and unknown risks. Known risks are pretty obvious. A known risk is a risk that we can identify. The problem is that we can never identify *all* the risks in a project. It would be too expensive to do it and if we tried to do it, we would spend much more money than the risk would cost if it did happen. We are normally satisfied to find an acceptable level of risks. That is, we will identify a practical number of risks. The practical number of risks we identify is a function of our risk tolerance, a topic we will discuss later in this chapter.

Since it will never be practical to find all of the risks in a project, it follows that there will be risks that are not identified. These are the unknown risks. Just because we do not identify particular risks does not mean that we do not have to set money aside for them. The known risks will be budgeted in the contingency budget, and the unknown risks will be budgeted in the management reserve.

It is important to note that the impact cost of the risk is not put into the project's performance or operating budget.

What are the basic steps in risk management?

There are usually four steps considered in managing any risk. This will vary from author to author, so we will stick with the Project Management Institute's *Guide to the Project Management Body of Knowledge*. The PMBOK lists the steps in the risk process as follows:

1. Risk identification
2. Risk quantification
3. Risk response
4. Risk control

Tell me more . . .

Risk identification is the process of identifying the threats and opportunities that could occur during the life of the project along with their associated uncertainties. The life of the project means the complete life cycle of the project, not just the time the project team is in place, the time until the final acceptance by the customer, or even the end of the warranty period. Risks should be considered through the useful life of the product or service that we are providing by doing this project. The risk of corrosion causing a catastrophic product failure during the useful life of a product that we have designed and built should be considered, and corrective action should be taken in accordance with the seriousness of the threat. Risks can be identified in a large number of ways, and all of the productive and economical ways should be employed.

Risk quantification is the process of evaluating the risk as a potential threat or opportunity. We are mainly concerned about two items: risk probability and risk impact. Risk probability tells us the likelihood that the risk will take place, and risk impact is the measure of how much pain or happiness will result if it does take place. Risks that have very high impacts with very low probabilities and risks that have very low impacts with high probabilities are usually of little concern, so we need to consider the combination of these two items before considering how important a risk is. The combination of impact and probability is called severity.

We do not need to worry too much about the risk of a hurricane impacting our construction of an apartment building if the project is taking place in Moscow. Hurricanes seldom occur there so there is a very low probability—even though the impact of a category five hurricane on Moscow would probably be quite significant. We may want to worry about the risk of heavy snowfall, however, which does occur frequently.

We also do not need to worry too much about the risk that one of the construction workers on the project will call in sick one day during the project. Although the probability is very high that this will occur more than once in the life of the project, we are able to anticipate this problem and the impact is relatively small even for skilled workers.

What we do need to concern ourselves about are the risks that have a relatively high impact and a relatively high probability of occurring.

Risk response is the process of doing something about the risk. It is how we respond to risks. In this process we address the best approaches to dealing with a risk that has a high enough severity that consequences of the risk cannot be accepted.

Responding to a risk includes ignoring the risk, letting it happen, and worrying about the consequences at the time. It also includes doing something about the risk before it happens. This might be putting together a work-around plan that can be quickly implemented when the risk occurs. It might include subcontracting the responsibility of the risk to an outside vendor or even an insurance company, or it might include avoiding the risk altogether.

Risk control is the process of controlling the risks. This involves keeping track of the risks that have occurred and can no longer occur, the risks that can still occur, and changes in the probability and impact of such risks. Generally, a reporting system is maintained so that the current picture of the risks is known.

What is risk identification?

The first step in risk management is identifying the risks that we will see in our project. These are the things that threaten to stop us from delivering what we have promised on the schedule we promised for the budget we promised. If we were completely certain about everything in the project and how it was going to turn out, we would not have to worry about risk management. From this lack of knowledge of how the project is going to unfold come the problems that we will have to deal with. These are the risks we want to identify. Every practical means must be used to discover the risks that are associated with the project. Meetings must be held throughout the project to discover new risks that have appeared and to dismiss risks that can no longer take place.

All of the assumptions that have been made to date on the project are potential risks as well and should be listed among the other risks identified.

Tell me more . . .

The first thing we must do in risk identification is recognize the areas of the project where the risks can occur. This means that we will have to investigate the following areas:

Scope. We must look at the work of the project. The work breakdown structure (WBS) will be useful here. The project scope must be clearly defined in terms of both the deliverables and the work that must be done to deliver them. Errors and omissions on the part of the project team and the stakeholders must be minimized. As always, the WBS will be very helpful in doing this.

Time. Estimates for the duration of the project and the duration of the project tasks must be done accurately and reliably. The sequence of work must be identified, and the interrelationships between the tasks must be clearly defined.

Cost. Estimates for tasks must be done accurately and reliably. All associated costs must be considered and reported accurately. Life cycle costs should be considered as well as maintenance, warranty, inflation, and any other costs.

Customer Expectations. Estimates of project success must be considered in terms of customer needs and desires. The ability of the project to be scaled up or manufactured in different quantities or for different uses and sizes must also be considered.

Resources. This involves the quantity, quality, and availability of the resources that will be needed for the project. Skills must be defined in the roles that will be necessary for the project.

Organization. This is the ability to interface with the stakeholder's organization in terms of communications and knowledge.

Many people both inside and outside the project will be necessary for risk identification. This includes input not only from the project team and all of the stakeholders but also from project managers who have managed this type of project before and even consultants who have special expertise about certain kinds of risks. It may be necessary to organize the types of risks into categories so that separate teams of people can be brought together more efficiently.

Many of the risks that will affect the project are risks that have happened in one form or another on other projects of this type. Utilizing the information available in the previous project's lessons-learned documents will be very helpful in identifying risks for this project. An organized review of past projects should be done as part of the risk identification process.

Since much of the risk identification process will involve large numbers of people, formal group dynamics techniques should be used.

Brainstorming Technique. Most people are familiar with this process, and many have had disappointing results. In brainstorming a facilitator briefs the meeting attendees and asks the participants of the meeting to name risks that they think could occur in the project. The facilitator encourages the participants to name any risk they can think of, even ones that seem silly, and makes a list of the risks on a board or flip chart. What happens in brainstorming is that the ideas of one person generate new ideas from another person, and a kind of chain reaction takes place, producing the identification of many ideas about risk.

There are some problems with brainstorming that will affect the success you have with the technique. The main problem is that unless you have an excellent facilitator, there will be minimum participation from the attendees and few risks will be identified. This problem is even worse when there is a large difference in the status of the individuals attending. A person who is the supervisor of some of the participants may intimidate them or dominate the meeting.

Delphi Technique. This technique of group dynamics eliminates the problem of dominance, shyness, or intimidation that sometimes occurs in brainstorming meetings. In the Delphi technique the participants are anonymous to each other. This technique can be conducted with Internet messaging or even by e-mail and has the advantage that people can participate from many different locations.

In this technique the facilitator asks for input from the participants. He takes their ideas and consolidates them into a list that is sent to each participant. The participants then add ideas to those already listed. This circulation of the lists continues until no additional ideas are generated.

The Delphi technique creates a lot of work for the facilitator. All ideas have to be listed by the facilitator, who also usually has to telephone many of the participants in order to get them to participate in each round. The overall time to do the Delphi technique can be weeks depending on how dedicated the participants are.

Nominal Group Technique. This is another type of meeting technique. In nominal group the participants are known to one another as in brainstorming, but the ideas are submitted to the facilitator as written lists. This makes the ideas, if not the participants, anonymous. The facilitator lists the ideas on a flip chart or a board, and the participants add more ideas in another round of written lists until no additional ideas are added.

This technique reduces any status concerns or intimidation that might be present in a brainstorming session but does not eliminate it entirely. There is more work for the facilitator, but the nominal group method can be done in a single meeting, and participation improves over brainstorming even if some enthusiasm may be lost.

Expert Interviews. There might be experts available either inside or outside the company for a new project and a new kind of business. Expert interviews must be handled with care. If the project team is not prepared for the expert interview, much time can be wasted with the expert simply telling stories about his or her past exploits. An effort should be made to develop a list of questions for the expert.

Ishikawa or Fishbone Diagrams. Fishbone diagrams or cause-and-effect diagrams, also called Ishikawa diagrams after their founder, Kaoru Ishikawa, a Japanese quality engineer, are useful in identifying risks.

The diagram, shown in Figure 8-1, is a useful way of organizing and analyzing a process into its subprocesses. The subprocesses can be further broken down into other subprocesses until a level of detail is reached where a small group can look into the subprocess in detail and the risks associated with each can be easily identified. Further use of the diagram will lead to the identification of the causes of the risks as well.

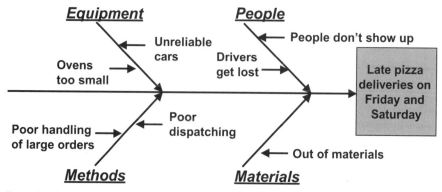

FIGURE 8-1: CAUSE-AND-EFFECT DIAGRAMS

Once the risks have been identified, the same techniques can be used to identify the triggers for the risks. Triggers are the symptoms that indicate that the risk is about to occur.

What is risk quantification?

Risk quantification is the process of evaluating the risks that have been identified and developing the data that will be needed for making decisions as to what should be done about them. Risk management is done from very early in the project until the very end. For this reason qualitative analysis should be used at some points in the project, and quantitative techniques should be used at other times.

The objective of quantification is to establish a way of arranging the risks in the order of importance. In most projects there will not be enough time or money to take action against every risk that is identified.

The severity of the risk is a practical measure for quantifying risks. Severity is a combination of the risk probability and the risk impact. In its simplest form the risks can be ranked as high and low severity or possibly high, medium, and low. At the other extreme, the probability of the risk can be a percentage or a decimal value between zero and one, and the impact can be estimated in dollars. When the impact in dollars and the probability in decimal are multiplied together, the result is the quantitative expected value of the risk.

Various statistical techniques such as PERT (program evaluation and review technique), statistical sampling, sensitivity analysis, decision tree analysis, financial ratios, Monte Carlo, and critical chain can all be used to evaluate and quantify risks.

Tell me more . . .

Qualitative risk analysis is appropriate early in the project and is effective in categorizing which risks should or should not be planned for and what corrective action should be taken for them. Qualitative analysis techniques will not give us the precise values for the risk that we would like to have. They are very effective when we have little time to evaluate risks before they actually happen.

Quantitative values may be applied to risks when using qualitative analysis. Values such as very risky, not so risky; high and low; high, medium, and low; high, high medium, medium, medium low, and low are generally used. Qualitative evaluation might also evaluate the risks on a scale of one to ten. These values can be applied to both the probability and the impact of the risk. The impact and probability can then be combined to give similar descriptions to the severity of the risk.

The table in Figure 8-2 illustrates a method of determining the qualitative value of severity for various values of impact and probability.

Impact

		High	Medium	Low
Probability	**High**	High	High	Low
	Medium	High	Medium	Low
	Low	Medium	Medium	Low

Figure 8-2: Risk Qualitative Evaluation Table

If an evaluation of impact and probability used a scaled evaluation of one to ten, the numbers could be multiplied to get the severity. In this way a probability of 7 with an impact of 9 would give us a severity of 63. This number for severity should give us plenty of information for ranking the risks. Using the high, medium, and low version sometimes creates disagreements about risks that are on the borderline between one value and another. For example, does this risk have an impact of medium or high when it is close to the border between the two values? And what happens when the impact is very high or very low and the probability is the opposite?

If the organization is especially averse to high-impact risks, the resulting severities can be modified to reflect this desire no matter what scale is used. In Figure 8-2, a low probability combined with a high impact results in a medium severity while a high probability with a low impact results in a low severity. It may also be necessary to modify scales to recognize stakeholder risk tolerance relevant to some aspects of the project but not others. Cost risks may be valued much less than schedule risks or the opposite may be true, depending on stakeholder aversion to cost and schedule variances.

While qualitative analysis is less precise than quantitative analysis, evaluating the results is far less expensive in terms of both time and money. The results are good enough to indicate the overall risk of the project and identify the high-priority risks in order to begin taking some corrective action. This kind of information may assist in pricing the project to a client.

Quantitative risk analysis attempts to attach specific numerical values to the risks. The severity can be assessed from these numerical values for impact and probability. Numerical techniques for decision analysis are used for this approach. These techniques include Monte Carlo analysis, PERT, computer simulations, decision tree analysis, critical chain scheduling, statistical estimating techniques, and expected value analysis. Generally we find the use of statistics and probability theory to be useful in quantitative analysis.

Care should always be used in quantitative analysis because using a good quantitative technique with bad data is worse than not using the technique at all. Many people are impressed with statistical models and simulations and never look at the data to see how good they are. It is quite possible to impress people into making the wrong decision based on excellent analysis of bad data. Care should also be exercised in the use of quantitative techniques because the cost of applying the technique and collecting the data can sometimes be more than the cost of the risks the technique helps to quantify.

General statistical techniques

Since risks are associated with probability techniques, it seems natural that we use probability distribution functions to help describe the impact and probability of the various risks in the project.

Figure 8-3 shows a skewed probability distribution. This is typical for project cost and schedule risks. The distribution shows the possible occurrences of cost or schedule completion for a particular task along

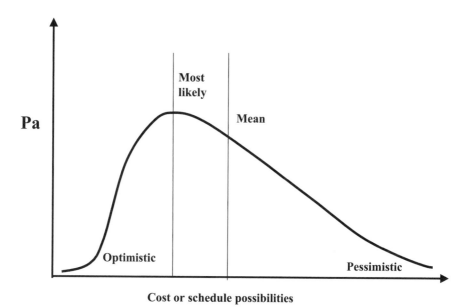

Cost or schedule possibilities

FIGURE 8-3: TYPICAL PROBABILITY DISTRIBUTION FOR COST AND SCHEDULE RISK

the X axis and relates them to the probability of that possibility occurring along the Y axis. The various possibilities are due to the risk associated with the task. For example, a task in a project has a most likely date. This date is plotted along the X axis. The probability associated with this date has the highest probability of any other date and is plotted at the corresponding point on the Y axis.

In a probability distribution the most likely date will always be at the peak of the probability distribution curve. This is not necessarily the average date for the task, which in a skewed distribution can be higher or lower, earlier or later, than the most likely date. Notice that the optimistic and pessimistic dates are the earliest and latest dates on the X axis and correspond to the lowest probability.

There are many distributions that can be applied. They can be symmetrical or skewed. Figure 8-4 shows a few that might be used in risk analysis—triangular, even, normal, and skewed distributions. The triangular distribution shows that probabilities increase uniformly from the optimistic point to a certain point where the highest probability is reached and then decrease uniformly until the pessimistic point is reached.

The even distribution has the characteristic that any value on the X axis has exactly the same probability of occurring. There is no optimistic, pessimistic, average, or most likely point.

The normal distribution is one that most of us have seen many times. It is a convenient distribution because calculations associated with it are simple to make and are generally close enough for most phenom-

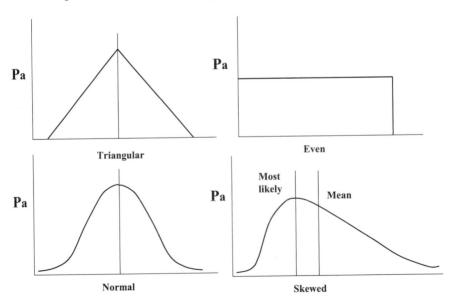

FIGURE 8-4: PROBABILITY DISTRIBUTIONS

ena that we need to estimate. In the normal distribution the mean value and the most likely value are the same because the distribution is symmetrical. A special measurement, the standard deviation, relates specific ranges of values along the X axis with the probability that the actual value will be between the high and low value. This is particularly useful in project management because it allows us to predict a range of values along with a probability that the actual value will occur when we do the project. A skewed distribution is one where the most likely value on the X axis is different from the mean value. The skewed distribution is frequently encountered in cost estimating and schedule estimating for projects.

Computer simulations

Today computer simulations are quite simple and inexpensive to use. Not many years ago simulations were done on analog computers, which made them expensive and not very accurate. The digital computers that most people have on their desks now are able to run simulations quite easily. Simulations use a model to simulate the real phenomena that we are trying to find out something about. There are two reasons to use simulations. One is that solving the problem mathematically is very difficult and expensive or even impossible. The second is that studying the actual phenomena is impossible or impractical in full scale. In either case simulation or modeling can be practical.

The most popular simulation for project management is the Monte Carlo simulation. This technique was discussed in Chapter 5. Monte Carlo analysis is important because it completes the PERT analysis of schedule estimation. In the PERT analysis we predict schedules based on ranges of values and probability for the durations of the project tasks. Since the durations of the tasks can be a range of values, it is possible that the actual duration values will determine a critical path that is not the one that is predicted by the most likely values. The Monte Carlo analysis evaluates these possibilities and gives us statistical guidelines for the project schedule.

Other computer simulations can be used to analyze the risks associated with the engineering, manufacturing, sales, marketing, quality, and reliability of the project deliverables.

Expected value analysis

Expected value analysis is a special way of determining severity in risks. To do this, we must measure the probability of the risk in numbers between 0.0 and 1.0. Of course the numbers 0.0 and 1.0 themselves are not used since these would mean that the risk was either an impossibility or a certainty. If the risk is a certainty, it should be put into the project plan as a required task; if it is an impossibility, it should be ignored.

The values for the impact of the risks are estimated in dollars or some other monetary value. By evaluating the impact and probability this way, we can multiply the two values together and come up with what is called the expected value of the risk. This value for severity has quantitative meaning. The resulting value is the average value of the risk. In other words, if we were to do this project many times, the risk would happen some of the time and not happen some of the time. The full cost of the risk each time it happens is the impact of the risk. Of course, since the probability is less than 1.0, the risk does not occur each time. Adding up the cost of the risk each time it occurred and dividing by the number of times the project was done would give an average value. This is the expected value.

The expected value is extremely useful because it gives us a value that could be spent on the risk to avoid it. If the cost of avoiding a risk is less than its expected value, we should probably spend the money to avoid it. If the cost of the corrective action to avoid a risk is greater than the expected value, the action should not be taken.

The same is true with the other risk strategies. If the difference between the expected value of the unmitigated risk and the mitigated risk is less than the cost of the mitigation, then the mitigation should not be done. If the difference between the expected value of the nontransferred risk and the transferred risk is less than the cost of the transfer or insurance premium, then the transfer should not be done.

The expected value of several risks can be summarized by their expected values into best-case, worst-case, and expected-value scenarios as well. The best-case scenario is the summation of all the good things, but none of the bad things, that can happen in the project or subproject. It assumes that all of the opportunities will occur but that none of the risks will materialize. The worst-case scenario is the situation that assumes that none of the good things will happen but that all of the risks will happen.

The following example illustrates the use of expected value and a best-case, worst-case scenario:

65%	$2,000,000	$1,300,000
15%	$3,000,000	$450,000
20%	($700,000)	($140,000)
Total expected value		$1,610,000

FIGURE 8-5: EXAMPLE EXPECTED VALUE

Suppose a project has a 65 percent chance of being completed successfully and earning $2,000,000. It also has a 15 percent chance of earning an additional $3,000,000 in revenue, and it has a 20 percent chance of an additional cost of $700,000.

It can be seen in Figures 8-5, 8-6, and 8-7 that for this project the total expected value is $1,610,000. The best of all situations that can occur is that the project earns $5,000,000. The worst possible situation is that the project loses $700,000.

Decision tree analysis

Another technique that allows us to make risk management decisions based on evaluating expected values for different possible outcomes of the risk event is called the decision tree. This technique is a way of looking at interdependent multiple risks. It also allows us to evaluate risks with multiple outcomes. For a project environment, this technique becomes extremely useful because one chosen unplanned event can often result in multiple outcomes of various levels of severity depending on the situation and on decisions made by people who are responsible for risk management.

Best

65%	$2,000,000	$2,000,000
15%	$3,000,000	$3,000,000
20%	($700,000)	0
Total best case		$5,000,000

FIGURE 8-6: EXAMPLE BEST CASE

The decision tree can also be useful for us in our further work of developing workarounds in case of active acceptance of risk event (see risk response, later in this chapter).

As shown in Figure 8-8, decision tree diagrams are composed of boxes, which identify decision choices that must be made, and circles, which represent places where probabilistic multiple outcomes are possible. From the boxes, lines are drawn showing each possible decision. The lines lead to other decisions or probabilistic multiple outcomes. On the probabilistic circles, notice

Worst

65%	$2,000,000	0
15%	$3,000,000	0
20%	($700,000)	($700,000)
Total worst case		($700,000)

FIGURE 8-7: EXAMPLE WORST CASE

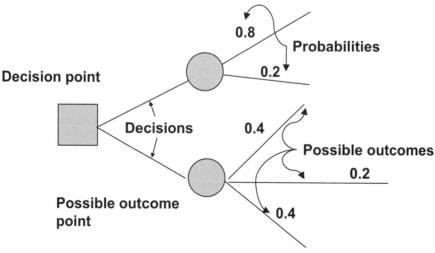

FIGURE 8-8: DECISION TREES

that the sum of the probabilities of all the possible outcomes of this point equals 1.0. This is because all of the possible outcomes are included.

Here is an example of decision tree analysis:

Suppose a farmer must decide what to do with his land for the next growing season. He can choose to plant corn or soybeans or to not plant anything at all. If he plants nothing at all, the government farm subsidy will pay him $30 per acre.

If the farmer decides to plant corn or soybeans on his land, there is some risk involved. The yield per acre depends on the amount of rainfall. Too much rain or too little rain will give poorer results than the right amount of rainfall. There is a 40 percent probability that the rainfall will be low; there is a 40 percent probability that the rainfall will be medium; and there is a 20 percent chance that the rainfall will be high.

If the farmer decides to plant corn, the yield per acre will be $0, $90, and $50, respectively, if the rainfall is low, medium, or high. If the farmer decides to plant soybeans, the yield per acre will be $40, $70, and $20, respectively, for low, medium, and high amounts of rainfall.

As shown in Figure 8-9, the decision to be made is whether the farmer should plant corn, soybeans, or nothing at all. There are three lines coming out of the decision box to indicate the three choices. Each choice leads to a probabilistic occurrence—how much rainfall will occur.

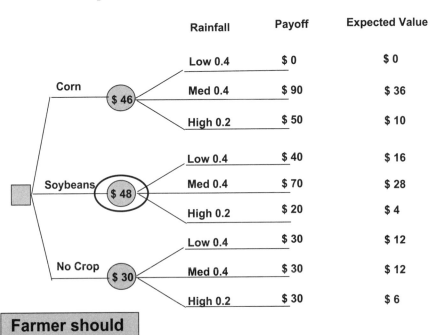

FIGURE 8-9: EXAMPLE: DECISION TREE

Each probabilistic occurrence has three possible outcomes—low, medium, or high amounts of rainfall. For each of these events there is an associated payoff. The payoff amount multiplied by the probability of that event occurring is the expected value of each occurrence.

In order to evaluate the decisions, we must add the expected value of each event associated with each decision to get the expected value for each decision. For corn, low rainfall means that no money will be made from the crop. For medium rainfall there is a 40 percent chance and a $90 yield, giving an expected value of $36. For high rainfall there is not as much yield per acre at $50 and there is a 20 percent probability of that occurring. The expected value for high rainfall is thus $10 per acre. Adding the expected values for the events gives us the expected value for the decision. This is $46 per acre.

Using the same calculation for the soybeans and for not planting at all, we see that of the three decisions, planting soybeans has the greatest yield.

Critical chain scheduling

Critical chain scheduling is a method of improving schedules. Critical chain schedules were discussed in Chapter 5. In a critical chain schedule, buffers are created between the early schedule completion date of the project and the promise date. The activities that have float are first moved to their late schedule dates and then moved back the amount of buffer that they are given from the point where they join the critical path.

One of the important things that critical chain schedules do is to recognize that by delaying the feeder chains toward the late schedule, the risks are reduced. Risks are reduced in the later schedule because knowledge learned in the course of doing the project can be applied to these activities because they have been delayed from their early schedule. Early in the project most of the project team is inexperienced, and mistakes are much more likely to be made. Later in the project experience has been gained by all, which means that risks that might otherwise cause trouble can be avoided.

An important part of the risk quantification process is the ranking of the risks into the order of severity. When quantitative or semi-quantitative analysis is done, this is relatively simple. The expected value of the risk can be used to list the risks. Using the expected value, the risks with the highest expected value are going to be at the top of the list. This is simply because the risks with the highest expected value are the ones that, on average, will cost the project the most.

Even if we are not using expected value analysis to evaluate the risks, we can still rank them. If we are using semi-quantitative techniques, we can multiply the values that we used to qualitatively estimate the impacts and probabilities to get a relative severity. This will be fine as long as the relative scale used for evaluating probability and impact is the same for all of the risks.

In the case of purely qualitative evaluations, judgment can be used to rank the risks. There are several methods for doing this. One of the easiest is to have each person in a meeting rank the risks individually and then combine the rankings of each person into a composite ranking. This will give an overall consensus ranking of the risks.

Another method that can be used either on an individual basis or by groups is the comparison matrix.

In the comparison matrix each risk is numbered from 1 to the highest number of the risks. Numbers assigned to the risks have no particular meaning. In Figure 8-10 the risks are numbered 1 through 7. Above the risk numbers are the comparison boxes. These are organized to ensure that two risks at a time are compared and that every risk is compared to every other risk. Human brains have trouble dealing with seven things simultaneously, but they can easily deal with two things. The comparison matrix allows many items to be ranked by comparing only two items at a time.

In the column above risk 1, the comparisons made, starting at the top of the column, are: 1 to 2, 1 to 3, 1 to 4, 1 to 5, 1 to 6, and 1 to 7. In subsequent columns the numbers of comparisons are smaller since there is no point in repeating comparisons: 1 compared to 2 is the same as 2 compared to 1. In comparing and ranking risks, each time a comparison is made, the more severe risk is noted in the comparison of only those two risks. Each time a risk is considered to be the more severe one, a hash mark is put in the box below that risk. After all comparisons have been made, the risk with the highest number of hash marks is the most severe risk. The one with the next highest number of marks is ranked number two, and so on.

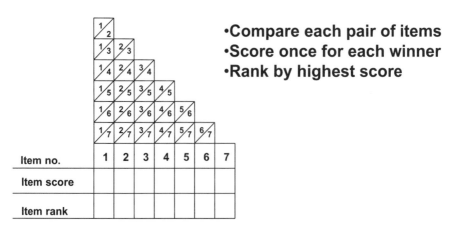

FIGURE 8-10: COMPARISON MATRIX

What is risk tolerance?

Risk tolerance is the willingness of some person or some organization to accept or avoid risk. In any group of people there are gamblers or risk takers and there are nongamblers or risk avoiders. People who have a low willingness to accept risks and the consequences of risks are called risk avoiders. Those people who are willing to take risks are called risk takers.

It is important to know that people and organizations have differing risk tolerances. Some customers do not want to risk the delivery of the project they are paying for by taking a chance on something new. Other customers will welcome the opportunity if the danger is not too great. For example, if we were manufacturing a product like some of the products that are advertised on late-night television, we would probably have a relatively high risk tolerance for the product's failure. This is because the product is priced very low and is not going to put anyone's life in danger. Customers buying very low priced items can expect them to have a shorter useful life than the advertising indicates. If customers want a product that will last longer, they buy an item that is built better and is probably more expensive.

This ability to choose is related to risk tolerance. In the mind of the consumer there is a tolerance for risk, which is expressed in his or her willingness to spend money. A consumer who is interested in having a highly reliable product that will last a long time is willing to pay more to get these features. Another consumer who is not willing to pay more to get a better product will be more accepting of the risk that the product will fail.

Tell me more . . .

If we draw increasing impact and increasing probability on an X and Y axis, we can draw the locus of all points of equal severity as a line on the graph in Figure 8-11.

Acceptable risks are any risks that are below and to the left of this locus of points of equal severity. Unacceptable risks are those risks that have a severity above and to the right of this severity line.

If we shift the severity line up and to the right, as in Figure 8-12, we are describing a person or an organization that is more of a risk taker. That is, the severity of the risks that one is willing to take is higher than before we shifted the line, and the person or organization shown is more of a gambler.

If, on the other hand, we shift the line down and to the left, as in Figure 8-13, we are describing a person or organization that is less of a risk taker. That is to say that the severity of the risks that a person or organization is willing to take is less than before we shifted the line.

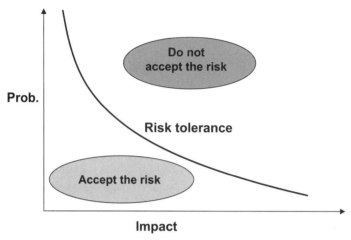

FIGURE 8-11: RISK TOLERANCE

In the classes we teach, we often perform the experiment of telling the students that we are willing to bet money on the roll of a single die, a cube with a number one through six on each side. (That's half of a pair of dice to you nongamblers.) In the bet we say that if the die comes up with a one or a two, we win. If the die comes up with a three, four, five, or six they win. The question is, "Who would be willing to play for a penny?" Nearly everyone stays in the game at this point. Then the stakes are raised to one dollar, and some of the people no longer want to play.

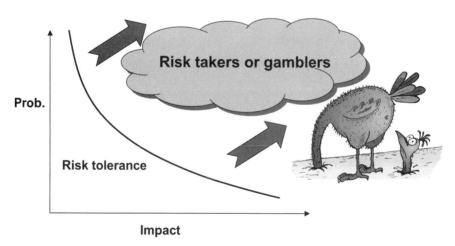

FIGURE 8-12: RISK TOLERANCE: GAMBLERS

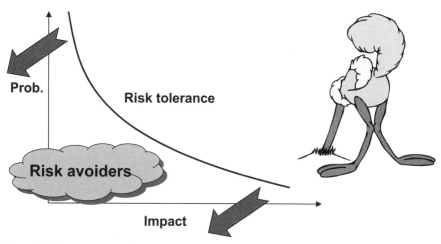

FIGURE 8-13: RISK TOLERANCE: AVOIDERS

As the stakes are raised higher and higher, more people drop out of the game. Eventually, unless there is a really hard-core gambler, everyone drops out of the game because the stakes are too high.

Even though the odds are very favorable, four chances out of six to win, when the bet is high enough, people will not play because the pain of losing is too great even when there are favorable odds. This is a great example of risk tolerance. Individuals and companies do the same thing with threats and opportunities. In risk tolerance we are concerned with people's personal values and views as well as the company's values and views. We may be dealing with a high-flying company that is willing to take many chances, but the individual who is representing the company may not be willing to stake his career on the risk you are suggesting. On the other hand, we do not want to be misled by the salesperson who is optimistic about everything until the sale is made.

Risk tolerance is somewhat describable in monetary terms. Our risk tolerance is how much we are willing to lose if the risk happens. In the case of a product that is sold to a consumer, the cost of the failure of the product might be the cost of the repair or replacement of the product if it fails. In the situation where someone's life is in danger, these decisions become much more important. The tolerance for a risk that is life-threatening is very high indeed. This is because we cannot put a monetary value on human life.

What are risk response strategies?

Risk response strategies are the approaches we can make to dealing with the risks we have identified and quantified. In the section on risk quantification we discussed evaluating the risk in terms of its impact and probability in such a way that we would be able to rank risks in their order of importance. This is what we called severity, the combination of impact and probability.

Risk response strategy is really based on risk tolerance, which has been discussed. Risk tolerance in terms of severity is the point above which a risk is not acceptable and below which the risk is acceptable.

Several strategies are available for dealing with risks. These are avoidance, acceptance, transfer, and mitigation (see Figure 8-14).

Tell me more . . .

There are many reasons for selecting one risk strategy over another, and all of these factors must be considered. Cost and schedule are the most likely reasons for a given risk to have a high severity. Other factors may affect our choice of risk strategy. For example, if a schedule risk is identified for a task in the project, and if this task has many other tasks depending on it, its severity may be calculated as being lower than is apparent, and the severity should be adjusted even though the schedule impact due to the disruption may be difficult to judge. The strategy should be appropriate for the risk it is intended for.

The following four strategies comprise the strategies that are normally used for risk:

1. *Acceptance.* Acceptance of a risk means that the severity of the risk is low enough that we will do nothing about the risk unless it occurs.

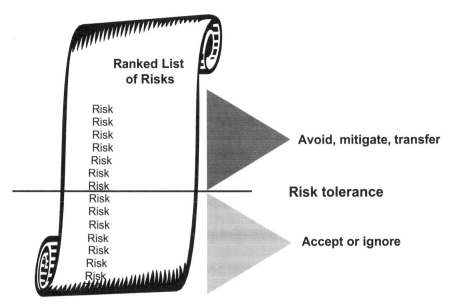

FIGURE 8-14: RISK STRATEGY

Using the acceptance strategy means that the severity of the risk is lower than our risk tolerance level. If this were not the case, it would not make sense to accept the risk. Once the risk occurs, we will fix the problem and move on. The risk is acceptable because the severity of the risk is lower than our risk tolerance. Accepting a risk does not mean that we will not do something about the risk when and if it occurs; it means that we will do something about it *only* if it occurs. Many of the project risks will fall into this category. It is the category where the many insignificant risks are put. Many of these risks cost less to fix when they occur than it would cost to investigate and plan for them.

There are two kinds of acceptance, active and passive. Acceptance is active when a risk is identified as being acceptable but we decide to make a plan for what to do when and if the risk occurs. It is much more effective to have a plan in place when these types of risk occur rather than trying to deal with the risk when there is little time and lots of hysterics. There is also another risk involved: the wrong thing can be done to solve the problem because its solution was not clearly thought out under pressure in the heat of the moment.

Acceptance is passive when nothing at all is done to plan for the risk occurrence. Many of the identified risks in the project will be passively accepted. These risks are simply too small to be of concern. The cost of developing a plan and documenting it can be higher than the cost of dealing with the risk without preparation.

An example of risk acceptance is the risk that off-the-shelf software that was purchased for the project will be defective. There is a probability of 2 percent that this will occur. That is, that the CD the software is delivered on will not work and will have to be replaced with a new CD. This causes a delay of five days to a task that has twenty-five days of free float. Passive acceptance will probably be used in dealing with this risk. It is probably not worth the effort to anticipate the problem and do something about it. It is simpler to wait and see if something is wrong with the CD and take corrective action. Of course, it would be foolish to receive the CD and not test it until it was needed.

2. *Transfer*. The transfer strategy in managing risk is to give responsibility for the risk to someone outside the project. The risk does not go away; the responsibility of the risk is simply given to someone else. This can be done a number of ways. One way is to negotiate the refusal of a project deliverable that has a high risk of causing problems and have that risk contracted to another project. The stakeholder simply agrees that the deliverable is not required as part of the project and finds another project that is willing to do it.

Risks can also be transferred to a contractor working for the project. If this is done with a firm fixed price contract, the vendor will be obligated to deliver the agreed product for a fixed price. In this situation the vendor is responsible for any risks that occur while trying to complete the contract. While this may seem like a good solution to risk management problems, the vendors were not born yesterday afternoon. The vendor's risk strategy may be to increase the selling price to compensate for the risk if it occurs. Of course, if the risk does not occur the vendor will make extra money. If you try to transfer the risk in this way, it may be that you will find that you are paying for the impact of the risk whether it happens or not.

Probably the most common method of transfer is to buy insurance. With insurance you give a relatively small amount of money to an insurance company. This amount of money, called a premium, is usually much smaller than the cost of the risk. If the risk happens, the insurance company pays to have the risk resolved. If the risk does not take place, the insurance company keeps the premium.

It is interesting to note that you can insure against only your own or your company's loss. Buying insurance on someone else's life or property, for example, is not allowed in most places unless that person or property represents a loss to you. If this were not true, there would probably be people hanging around hospitals buying policies on people who looked really sick.

Example. PMI held its annual Seminar Symposium in New Orleans in 1995. Much of the revenue to run the organization is generated through the Seminar Symposium, and if it were called off or canceled, PMI would be hard-pressed to recover from the financial loss.

The Seminar Symposium is usually scheduled in the fall of each year. This is also hurricane season in New Orleans and on most of the Gulf Coast. When PMI met with the hurricane experts and realized the severity of the risk of a hurricane or even the severity of the threat of a hurricane, it decided to buy event insurance for the first time.

3. *Risk Avoidance.* This strategy is used to make the risk cease to be a possibility. Avoidance is a little different from the other strategies we have discussed. In risk avoidance, we completely eliminate the possibility of the risk.

The simplest way to avoid a risk is to remove it from the project deliverables. If the sponsor of the project agrees to allow a risk-filled deliverable to be removed from the project, the risk is removed along with the deliverable. Of course the price the sponsor is paying for the project will probably be reduced to compensate for the reduction in scope. In avoiding risk in this way, we should remember that profits are often related to the risks we take to complete projects that have risks.

Another way to avoid risks is to design around them. This strategy involves changing the design of the product so that the risk cannot occur.

Suppose we have a project to design and manufacture a new kind of barbecue grill. During testing we discover that the screws that hold the bottom of the grill where the ashes collect rust and deteriorate quickly. A failure of the ash collecting bottom could result in hot charcoal being dumped onto a wooden deck and causing a fire. We decide that this is an unacceptable risk and that our strategy is to avoid the risk.

One way to avoid the risk is to not build and sell the barbecue grill at all and abandon the project. We decide that this is an unnecessarily conservative strategy. Another way is to change the material that the screws are made from. Instead of plain steel screws we decide to redesign and use stainless steel screws. The stainless steel screws will not rust, and the potential problem will be eliminated. This completely eliminates the rusting problem of the screws and avoids the risk of a screw failure causing a fire.

4. *Mitigation.* When we discussed risk tolerance, we said that risks that were above the risk tolerance maximum were not acceptable risks and that something had to be done about them. Mitigation is a strategy where some work is done on unacceptable risks to reduce either their probability or their impact to a point where their severity falls below the maximum risk tolerance level.

Using the risk mitigation strategy involves taking some money out of the contingency budget that was the expected value of the risk before mitigation. Some of this money is put into the project's operating budget to carry out the mitigation strategy. Since the probability or impact will be reduced, the expected value of the risk will be reduced as well, and the contingency budget should be reduced accordingly.

Perhaps it would be a good idea to review how the money is allocated for different risk strategies. Risk avoidance is frequently going to cost some money. The money that we spend to redesign the project so that the risk is eliminated is money that will have to be spent regardless of the probability of the risk. The additional work of doing the redesign and adding more expensive parts will be part of the operating budget.

No money needs to be put into the risk reserves if the risk is completely eliminated. If the risk has already been allocated funding in the contingency budget, the increase in the operating budget can be taken from the contingency budget.

Risk acceptance will have money put into the contingency budget if the risk has been identified. If the risk is an unknown risk and has not been identified, the money for it will be roughly estimated and become part of the management reserve. If the risk does happen, the money is taken from the contingency budget or the management reserve and moved into the operating budget when the plan for dealing with the risk is put into place.

Risk mitigation will have money put into the contingency budget to handle the risk if it occurs. There will also have to be money put into the operating budget to take care of the cost of the mitigating activities that are being taken for this risk. The mitigation of the risk will reduce either the probability or the impact of the risk, and the contingency budget should therefore be reduced.

Risk transfer requires money to be put into the operating budget to pay for the additional cost of either subcontracting the risk or buying insurance for it. The money to do the work for the activity affected, not including the risk cost, was put into the operating budget when the task was created. The cost of the transfer, either the additional cost that the supplier will receive or the cost of the insurance premium, must be added to the operating budget. This money can be taken from the contingency budget.

The operating budget of the project, sometimes called the performance budget, is the amount of money needed to do the things that are planned for in the project. This includes all of the work to produce all of the deliverables that were planned for in the project. It is not the total project budget; it includes funding only for the things that are planned for. Subject to limitations in the project policy, this money can be spent freely by the persons responsible for the tasks of the project as long as the expenditures are following the project plan.

The contingency reserve is the money to do the things that may or may not have to be done but that have been identified. This is where the funding for risks that actually take place comes from. When a risk takes place, the project manager authorizes money to be taken from the contingency budget and placed into the operating budget. Generally the project manager must approve money transferred from contingency reserves to operating budgets. In larger projects a subproject manager may approve these funds. The transfer of funds must include any appropriate changes to scope or schedule.

The management reserve is money that is set aside for the risks that have not been identified, the so-called unknown risks. This transfer is made when a risk occurs that has not been identified and money must be spent to solve the effects of the risk. The use of these funds usually has to be approved by a manager one level above the project manager.

What is risk control?

The process of monitoring and controlling and keeping track of the identified and the unidentified risks is risk control. In this process we hope to identify risks that are no longer possible and risks that are coming due, as well as any new risks that may become evident. We will also monitor risk activity to make sure the risk plans have been carried out successfully. Problems that have been found out in the risk plan can help us adjust the plans for future risk activities.

Risk control and monitoring are part of the risk management process and must be started early in the project and continued until the end. As the project progresses, we will find that many of the risks will change, some will no longer be possible, others will happen and be disposed of, and new risks will be identified. In addition we will learn about the project and the risks associated with it and adjust our vision of individual risks.

The level of risk tolerance should be monitored as well. The attitude of the stakeholders will change during the course of the project. Communication with all stakeholders is important since it gives us a means of assessing changes in their risk tolerance.

Tell me more . . .

Risk control may involve changing the way we look at risk. There are several reasons why this might take place. The risk tolerance of the stakeholders may change; the risk tolerance of the project team may change. As the project progresses toward its completion, certain risks that were thought to be very important to the success of the project may become risks that are no longer thought of as being so important.

In the beginning of the space shuttle project, the heat-resistant ceramic tiles were originally thought of as being one of the major risks in the program. If the tiles were lost or their integrity was compromised, the heat of reentry, some 3,000 degrees Fahrenheit, could reach the airframe's aluminum structure and cause breakup of the ship. As time went by and NASA flew over one hundred missions with the space shuttle vehicles and the whole take-off and landing process became routine, the perceived severity of the risk diminished. During this time there were minor failures of the reentry tiles, but these failures proved to be minor repairs, and the shuttle vehicles suffered only minor damage. A program to develop a method of repairing risks in space was discontinued because it was deemed impractical. Part of the impracticality was probably because of the perceived reduction in the probability and impact of heat shield failures.

On February 1, 2003, just three days after the anniversary of the crash of the space shuttle *Challenger, Columbia,* the oldest space shuttle in the fleet, disintegrated on approach to landing. At this writing the investigations have hardly begun, but the heat shielding tiles are once again suspect because there is little that can go wrong on reentry except for a heat shield failure.

We see that during the project, the evaluation of the risk of heat shield failure began as a high risk. As time went on, the risk was revalued lower and lower. After the crash, the valuation of the risk has no doubt been raised higher than its former level.

In all projects, as we gain knowledge and experience about the project and its risks, we will change our attitude toward the risks in the project. This is natural and important. As we learn, we must change the level of effort we spend in certain areas or we will never have the resources, time, or money to complete any project.

A control system for risk is influenced by the organization the project is being managed under as well. In a project that is high in risk, we might have a person who is at a high level and is exclusively responsible for managing risks. On projects that are relatively routine by comparison, the risk manager may be the person responsible for the tasks that are most affected by the occurrence of a risk. These persons are responsible for communicating risk progress to the project manager and other affected stakeholders.

Risk audits can be used to document the effectiveness of the risk plans and the strategies that were used to mitigate, avoid, or transfer risks. A judgment can be made as to whether it was cost-effective to ignore the risks that were ignored.

Deviations in the project performance may indicate the effect of risks on the project. The earned value reporting system is helpful in identifying trends in performance on the project. Generally, schedule slippage and cost overruns are the result of some problems that have occurred. Trends in certain areas may indicate that risks are more severe than was anticipated or that new risks have taken place. One important product of the earned value reporting system is the indication of the cost and completion date at the end of the project. The sooner these slips in schedule or budget overruns can be communicated to the stakeholders, the better it will be for the project. Schedule slides and budget overruns that are severe enough can result in project termination.

A workaround is an unplanned response to a risk that was previously unidentified. These are the unknown risks that were discussed at the beginning of this chapter. They are also the risks that were passively accepted since these were deemed to be risks that would be ignored.

Workarounds are paid for from funds from the contingency reserve or the management reserve, depending on whether the risk was identified and accepted or whether it was unknown until it occurred. In any case, the funding for the workaround comes out of these accounts and is put into the operating budget of the project, and a new baseline is created.

Since contingency plans and workarounds are not part of the project baselines until they occur, they should be initiated and approved by the execution of an official change notification. Remember that changes to the baselines should require an official change notification as the vehicle for showing the change in funding, schedules, and scope resulting in a new and current baseline.

How do risk management approaches correlate with the other parts of project management methodology?

Risk management is, in reality, not a special, separate process that is being carried out somewhere else in a company. In a normal project, risk management is so much interrelated with all the other project management processes that some of the experienced project managers we know in practice do not even want to consider it as a separate process.

Our deep belief is that risk management unites all the rest of project management tools and takes the best of all. This is quite understandable if we consider the major impact risk management may have on a project.

Tell me more . . .

As we have said, most of the tools for risk management come from the other project management processes, and it is therefore easy to show how risk management is related to other areas of project management.

We talked at length about time management and scheduling and particularly the idea of predicting project completion dates in case of uncertain activity durations. It is easy to see that the uncertain duration of a large number of activities in a project is an object for risk management. Indeed, when we develop the multiple duration estimate for an activity, we are looking at the activity with no risk occurring (most likely date) and negative (pessimistic) or positive (optimistic) risk occurring. In all three cases, we are calculating risk impact by given pessimistic and optimistic numbers for activity duration. As we then use these figures to develop a 95 percent probable completion date for the project, we are considering risks and putting them into an operating schedule in the form of schedule buffer. The amount of buffer we are putting into the schedule should be supported by the list of risks we developed with evaluation of its impact in terms of schedule as well as budget. Thus, we see how different parts of project management methodology fit together and support each other. Moreover, it allows us to check accuracy in each calculation by looking at how this calculation corresponds with the other—for instance, how the amount of schedule buffer we put in for a certain activity is supported by the amount and severity of risk we had identified for this task.

We have already shown how risk management correlates with cost management and building overall project budget. Indeed, in the process of budget development, we look at risks the same way we do in schedule management. If, and only if, the budget reserve we calculated on the basis of statistical evaluation of 95 percent probable budget is being supported by risk data gained on certain project tasks, more specifically on concrete project tasks, can we say that the project management processes in our project are consistent.

We can look at all the other parts of project management methodology in order to see the relations between the tools used. To conclude this part of the risk management analysis, we need only to take a look at quality management techniques. Indeed, it is quite clear that most of the techniques we use for quality management are at the same time quite applicable for looking at risks. In reality, what are the quality problems if not risks being identified and taking place in a project? This way, the cause-and-effect diagram allows us not only to look at various causes for a quality problem, but also to identify major risk occurrence areas for a significant risk impact. The control charts may allow us to identify an initially unknown risk event as an assignable cause for certain process changes to happen. A flow chart describing process may be used to identify certain risk occurring points, and so on.

It is also important to mention that many of the practicing project managers are trying to avoid using what we may call "formal risk management" practices. In some application areas, such as information technology and commercial software development, it is hard to quantify both impacts and probabilities for risks without having a chance of being 50 percent wrong. In a case like that, it does not make sense to try and make other people believe we are working with real numbers if in reality we are making quite subjective qualitative evaluations.

That does not however mean that we are NOT doing risk management in such projects. While the normal variability of the process is being considered by ranged estimates for budget and duration, we can look at risks and evaluate them qualitatively as having large or small levels of probability and impact and use it as a basis for developing our risk response strategies.

9

Quality

What are the principles of modern quality management?

Modern quality management approaches relate in many ways to modern project management approaches overall. More and more attention is being paid to the human aspect of the processes, the team approach to quality, and the concept of total quality management. The quality management process is more oriented toward permanent small incremental improvements and multiple inspection points in the processes than it was in the past. In Figure 9-1 it can be seen that one of the major changes in our attitude toward quality is that everyone is responsible for quality. This allows for many more inspection points and allows for

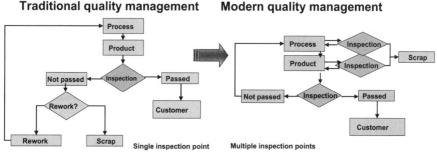

FIGURE 9-1: CHANGES IN MANAGEMENT CONCEPTS

corrections to be made before additional work is done. Scrap and rework cost is significantly reduced.

Tell me more . . .

The history of the total quality management approach is interesting. It was first developed by W. Edwards Deming and a number of Japanese managers on the basis of the Japanese approach to management science. After World War II, Deming and a number of other American consultants were invited to Japan to carry out some consulting work and in particular to develop tools to improve the quality practices of Japanese enterprises. The first finding of Deming and his Japanese colleagues was called the quality circles concept, which gave significant results when applied to Japanese enterprises.

The quality circles approach allowed a gain in quality improvement ideas from the people actually involved in the production process. Deming's next step was to build mechanisms allowing this information to be most effectively communicated to the company decision-makers and to make this process continuous. In Japan, it soon became such a powerful tool that it helped increase productivity in Japanese companies by 10 percent and played an important role in the later ability of Japanese companies to conquer a significant share of American markets. Unfortunately, when Deming came back to the United States and tried to publish his findings and implement them at American enterprises, he was not heard. American enterprises at that time thought the very idea of changing something in the way they operated and, moreover, using the experience of Japanese companies was completely ridiculous. Only twenty years later, after losing a large share of its markets, American business rediscovered the idea of TQM. It became an extremely popular concept after it proved to be one of the major causes for the "Japanese economic miracle." Since then, it has been considered one of the most cost-efficient ways of improving the quality of processes in the organization. However, as in many other good management practices, its usefulness has been largely unappreciated by many cases of misapplication when tried in Western companies.

Later on, some of the Western and Japanese managers understood that the approach of TQM can be applied to all the processes of the organization, not only the quality processes. This is largely how the concept of CPI, or continuous process improvement, was developed. This concept has now become a basic idea underlying most modern standards and thus illustrates the parallels in the development of various streams of management thought.

This last statement is important. As has been mentioned previously, the ideas of TQM had been largely misapplied and misused around the world. However, very few ideas developed by humanity are truly new, and the area of management is no exception. It does not really make much difference if we call this approach TQM, a concept of continuous improvements, or modern quality management practices. The major principle is what stays unchanged, and with that we continue by describing these principles as best we can.

As described by Marshall Sashkin and Kenneth J. Kiser in their 1993 book *Putting Total Quality Management to Work,* TQM is a relatively established entity with accepted components of teamwork, systems thinking, and statistical tools being applied to the areas of "customer, counting, and culture." Major principles of TQM are described by Deming's fourteen points:

1. Maintain constancy of purpose.
2. Adopt a new philosophy.
3. Eliminate need for inspection.
4. Consider only total cost, not price.
5. Improve constantly.
6. Initiate on-the-job training.
7. Initiate leadership.
8. Drive out fear.
9. Break down barriers.
10. Eliminate slogans, targets, and the like.
11. Eliminate management by standards and quotas.
12. Remove barriers to pride of workmanship.
13. Institute education and self-improvement.
14. Get everyone involved.

A strong orientation toward getting all the participants of the process involved in implementation makes this approach similar to the modern project management approach of basing project efficiency on team members' high level of involvement and responsibility in project activities. Modern quality management practices generally require the implementation of the whole new concept of personnel management, "human resource development," or even the latest concepts representing some of the Japanese human resource ideas as applied to Western ground, "human being management." Briefly, all of these modern concepts suggest a high level of people's responsibility and involvement. This in turn develops a feeling of ownership within the company as well as a global company philosophy. The result of this type of thinking is enriched job assignments introducing elements of creativity and challenging tasks to be fulfilled. We have discussed this topic further in Chapter 6, "Human Resources Management."

The other important component of modern quality management is its orientation to the client or customer, the ultimate user of the product or service produced by the project. In the context of the customer, we are interested in a product or service from the point of view of its "fitness for use"—the guarantee that the customer receives the goods or services that justify what was paid for them—and customer satisfaction—the customer's feeling after receiving the product or service.

Another important feature of modern quality management is that it considers small incremental improvements as the best approach to improving quality. The TQM approach has a number of formalized practices for introducing step-by-step, small change processes in the normal operational cycle of the organization. Moreover, there are special systems set up that allow all the participants in any process to suggest their changes for improving the quality of processes and products. In the case of projects, these people are the project team members.

The quality circle is Deming's idea that people having a low position in the organization, the actual producers of the product, be involved in the decision-making process, introducing small changes to the production cycle. The idea was to allow special time during the working day for these people to get together and talk about possible quality improvements. In order to make it more efficient, each quality circle had a person from middle management assigned to it whose responsibilities included providing overall methodological support to these people as well as making sure that their ideas reach the organization's decision-makers. For introducing small incremental improvements to the processes, Deming suggests a so-called PDCA, or Plan-Do-Check-Act cycle.

In the planning phase, Deming suggests that you select the problem, describe it and the process and all potential causes for the problem, and then develop a solution. In the do phase, you put a solution into a process—in other words, you carry out a pilot process with the solution implemented. In the check phase, you see how the solution worked and, if it did, you act, moving on to operate this process with the solution.

The steps of Deming's cycle correspond very well to what is later suggested as the four steps for process improvement in CPI, as shown in Figure 9-2.

What are the quality management processes?

The quality management function of the project can be described as:

❑ Assuring conformance to mutually agreed to expectations.
❑ Assuring conformance to requirements and specifications.

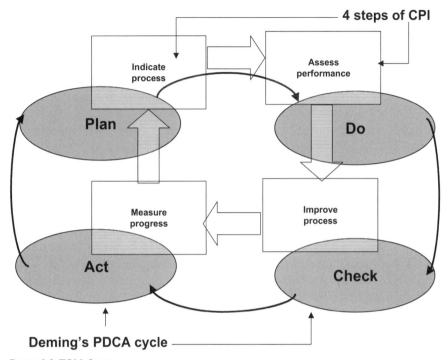

FIGURE 9-2: TQM: STEPS

❑ Assuring conformance to ALL the characteristics that allow it to satisfy the function intended.

The transfer of initially assumed needs to planned ones is the critical aspect of quality management in the project context. According to the Project Management Institute's *Guide to the Project Management Body of Knowledge* (PMBOK), project quality management considers three major processes: quality planning, quality assurance, and quality control.

Tell me more . . .

At this stage of quality planning our major goal is to find the regulations and specifications suitable for the current project and to find ways for implementing and introducing these standards into our project cycle. It is important to remember that we should concentrate on the quality standards for processes as well as the final products. Generally, modern tendencies of quality management make us shift our attention more and more from checking the quality of the final product (inspection) to predicting changes of quality in the processes (prevention).

In order to carry out our quality planning process, we have to get all the documents describing the standards and regulations we are going to use (the quality policy of our company, standard descriptions, etc.) as well as the documentation describing the requirements to the project product (scope statement) and then use the quality tools (flowchart, cost-benefit analysis, simulations) that allow us to visualize and predict the results of applying the standards and regulations to our project scope.

The quality assurance processes are carried out in order to assure that our project product complies with accepted standards and regulations. Quality assurance should be carried out throughout the project both internally (for the company, project team, etc.) and externally (for the customer). In many cases, the quality assurance function can, but not necessarily should, be carried out by a special quality assurance department of the company.

Quality control processes monitor the final results of the project—both management results and product results—in order to see how much they correspond to the standards planned and what can be done to improve the results to meet the standards. Quality control processes include both inspection and prevention, but as we said above, the tendency in modern quality management is shifting toward prevention in order to reduce the overall cost of quality. The quality control function can be carried out by a special quality control department, but this is not a rule in modern quality management practices. It is becoming more a function of the producing units of the company, the idea of "being your own inspector."

In quality control, the rest of the quality management tools such as Pareto diagrams, cause-and-effect diagrams, statistical sampling, and control charts are used.

What are the major principles of economics of quality?

As in most of the decision-making processes in project management, when we consider the opportunity to improve our management functions we normally look first at what is called the cost-benefit analysis. In other words, when we are thinking about quality improvement for our product, our first concern is to see if this is cost-efficient for our product. Normally we try to work only with the level of quality that is optimal from the point of view of the quality benefit we gain for each new dollar invested.

Although it is generally considered that improving quality will result in increasing cost, this is not necessarily the case in modern quality management. In the past it was generally believed that high quality would come only with high cost. Today, with the concept of total quality management, we have learned that high quality actually reduces overall cost.

Tell me more . . .

Some of the statistics developed for the cost of quality for major companies show that the overall cost of quality makes up to 12 to 20 percent of sales, with the major part of expenses formed by internal costs and costs of appraisal. It has been proven that by spending a higher percentage of cost on quality prevention, up to 70 percent, we can decrease our overall cost for quality to 3 to 5 percent of sales. The 70 percent cost of prevention should not startle us because we are talking about 70 percent of a much smaller figure but still a larger figure than we are used to.

The reason for such a huge change is that there are three major components of quality cost: the cost of production, the cost of acceptance, and the cost of unsatisfactory products.

What is known as production costs will actually increase in the case of increased quality because it will consider using better and more expensive materials as well as improving tools and equipment and increasing labor cost.

Acceptance costs include cost for inspection as well as costs for quality management in each of its three parts—quality planning, quality control, and quality assurance. This part of the overall quality cost can actually go down with the introduction of new quality management concepts because it may allow a significant decrease in the number of formal inspections needed.

However, the largest class of expenses saved with the introduction of new quality practices has to do with unsatisfactory costs. This includes the cost of the replacement of defectives, repair of defects cost, customer goodwill, and even such an important cost line for the company as the cost of liabilities. It is easy to see that some of the aspects of these costs have huge influences on the company, especially those having to do with customer goodwill and follow-up on orders. In general, this way of looking at overall costs of quality improvement has a lot in common with the life cycle cost approach to project cost management as discussed in Chapter 3. It becomes especially important to recognize these large cost savings in the justification of various quality improvement projects.

The other very important issue that needs to be considered when making decisions concerning the cost of quality for your project has to do with any cases in which people's lives or health is at stake. In these cases, normal cost-benefit analysis becomes useless and even dangerous. A number of companies throughout the world, including some of the "giants" of production, have proved by their negative experience that the attempt to evaluate financially the cost of improving the quality of products can lead to some potentially serious injuries to people that result from poor quality characteristics and can ultimately bring the company some really serious financial losses.

What are the Seven Tools for Quality Management?

The so-called Seven Tools for Quality Management form a basis for over-all TQM methodology. In general, all the tools are based on two major approaches: statistics and team involvement. We can formulate their major goal as a set of instruments to unite the team around some of the quality issues for discussion, prediction, and preventive actions concerning potential project or product quality problems.

The major tools are the flowchart, the cause-and-effect (fishbone or Ishikawa) diagram, the Pareto diagram, the check sheet, the scatter diagram, the histogram, and the control chart.

Flowcharts and cause-and-effect diagrams are used in quality planning and quality assurance processes; the remainder, control charts, check sheets, etc., are used as instruments of quality control.

Tell me more . . .

A flowchart is a quality management tool that allows the team to look more closely at certain processes, to identify the events and steps in the processes, and to show places for data collection and possible interdependency and points of complexity. Everybody who has studied computer science in school knows how to do flowcharts. In order to do it, you need to get the group of people interested in getting more information about the process together; then, after some brainstorming, you finally determine the steps for the process and their sequence. Now the only thing to be done is to draft the chart on a sheet of paper.

In the example shown in Figure 9-3, we are looking at a Russian roulette game as a process with a number of necessary steps and decisions on how to carry on with a process. The example given is the Russian version, which is a much tougher version of the game than Americans are used to.

The cause-and-effect diagram was developed by a Japanese manager by the name of Kaoru Ishikawa as a means of allowing the project team to accumulate all the knowledge it has about some potential causes of a problem and then graphically display it in a useful way. The diagram allows us to concentrate the attention of the group on the problem

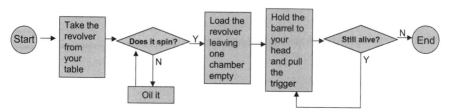

FIGURE 9-3: SEVEN TOOLS FOR QUALITY MANAGEMENT. FLOWCHART: "RUSSIAN ROULETTE"

itself, not its symptoms. It really does look like a skeleton of a fish with the head as a problem discussed and the bones showing all the potential causes that came to mind.

In order to do the cause-and-effect diagram properly, the team needs to select the problem, brainstorm it in order to get all the potential causes from the group members, rank the reasons and place them on the diagram in ranked order, and then explore any branch of the diagram more deeply if someone feels one branch is more important than the others.

In Figure 9-4, we show an example of building a cause-and-effect diagram for a car wreck with the major sources of the problem being the weather, the state of a driver himself, something happening with parts of the car, other drivers, and so on.

A Pareto chart, or diagram, shown in Figure 9-5, is used in order to select the most important problem areas of the project that can cause the most pain. It is based on the well-known 80-20 rule, which says that 20 percent of the problems are responsible for 80 percent of the total cost of the project's problems. The diagram thus explores all the potential problem areas of the project according to the number of their occurrences. The problem areas are ranked according to that number and then plotted on the diagram as in a frequency diagram. The upper part of the diagram shows cumulative cost for the problems measured in the percentage of the total cost of whatever it is being measured against.

We are looking for all the possible problems with an organizational change happening in corporation A. It is easy to see that the first and second problems are the most significant considering their contribution to the overall result.

The check sheet is an instrument for collecting data on some pro-

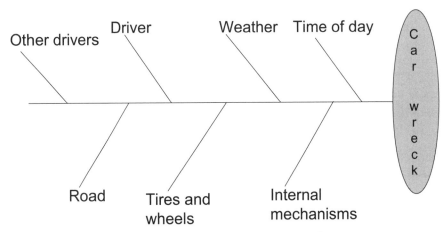

FIGURE 9-4: SEVEN TOOLS FOR QUALITY MANAGEMENT. FISHBONE DIAGRAM: CAR WRECK

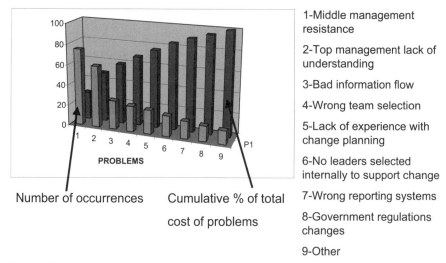

1-Middle management resistance

2-Top management lack of understanding

3-Bad information flow

4-Wrong team selection

5-Lack of experience with change planning

6-No leaders selected internally to support change

7-Wrong reporting systems

8-Government regulations changes

9-Other

Figure 9-5: Seven Tools for Quality Management. Pareto chart: Organizational transfer in Company A

cess or, more often, on certain problems happening within the process. The check sheet is actually a sheet of paper on which all the potential problems of the process are listed. The person carrying out the facilitator function looks at the process at random times and records the results on the sheet. This method allows us to see if there are some problems occurring repeatedly in the process. As these problems are identified, we look deeper for the causes and potential tendencies using either a cause-and-effect diagram or some of the statistical tools we will talk about later.

1	Meat missed	✓✓✓
2	Mayonnaise forgotten	
3	Salad items forgotten	✓✓
4	Meat overcooked	✓✓✓✓
5	Meat undercooked	
6	Served cold	✓
7	Served too hot	✓

Figure 9-6: Seven Tools for Quality Management. Check sheet: Bad hamburgers

In Figure 9-6 we show an example of various problems associated with serving a hamburger at a fast-food restaurant.

The scatter diagram is used when we need to analyze two characteristics of a process and see if there is any interdependency between them. In this case, the observed data must be collected on both characteristics. It is important that the pairs of data being collected are random with no time or other dependency present. The overall pool of data is then represented as a group of points set up on a plot of two variables. After the plot is developed, by looking at the pattern of the points, you can make general conclusions if the two parameters correlate and if this is a positive versus negative as well as a strong versus weak correlation.

In Figure 9-7 we look at various types of correlation between the two parameters of a production process—temperature and humidity.

The last two of the seven tools—a histogram and control chart—are the most statistically oriented of all the quality tools. A histogram is used when we are dealing with a need to analyze large sets of data. It gives the observer an opportunity to see the frequency of occurrence of each value; more important, it shows the centering and dominance of values as well as the level of data and correspondingly the process dispersion.

In order to build a histogram (shown in Figure 9-8), you first need to collect enough data on the parameter of the process you are interested in measuring and viewing. While doing this, you have to make sure there are no outside influences that might bias the data. The number of

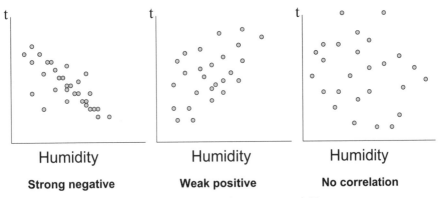

Humidity	Humidity	Humidity
Strong negative	**Weak positive**	**No correlation**

FIGURE 9-7: SEVEN TOOLS FOR QUALITY MANAGEMENT. SCATTER DIAGRAMS: HUMIDITY VS. TEMPERATURE

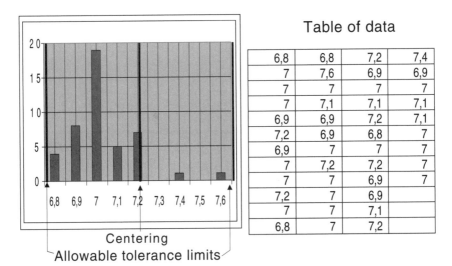

Table of data

6,8	6,8	7,2	7,4
7	7,6	6,9	6,9
7	7	7	7
7	7,1	7,1	7,1
6,9	6,9	7,2	7,1
7,2	6,9	6,8	7
6,9	7	7	7
7	7,2	7,2	7
7	7	6,9	7
7,2	7	6,9	
7	7	7,1	
6,8	7	7,2	

FIGURE 9-8: SEVEN TOOLS FOR QUALITY MANAGEMENT. HISTOGRAM: HISTOGRAM WITH SHIFTED CENTERING. CERTAIN ASSIGNABLE CAUSES FOR PROCESS NONSTABILITY TO BE EXPLORED

data points is normally not less than a hundred. Then you have to determine the range of values, the number of classes, and the size of intervals and plot the data as a set of bars, each of which corresponds to the frequency of occurrence of certain values of the parameter observed.

After the histogram is built, you can look at various characteristics of the chart and see if this parameter stays within the limits you set up for it. The comparison of the overall range of values for the parameter to the normal limits set up for this process will show you how much the process is out of control, in other words, whether the variability is in, closely in, or out of the allowable tolerance. The shifts of data centering also show you if the data are out of control and if some special causes are present that influence the process and must be attended to.

To explain the last statement, as well as to better understand the last of the seven tools, the control chart, we have to define a special or assignable cause and the difference between it and a common cause. In any process, both in management and in production, there is some normal variance that results from the nature of the process. This variance creates an acceptable error in the final product that is being considered by engineering tolerance. The causes for such variances are called common causes. These causes normally do not attract our attention and do not show that the process is getting out of control. Among possible common causes in the production process we can name:

❑ Temperature controlled by thermostat
❑ Part diameter within specification
❑ Tolerance of electrical resistance, capacitance
❑ Operator differences
❑ Different vendor for materials
❑ Machinery looseness

The special or assignable causes show some external interference or internal error in the process that could finally lead to producing a product defect. The occurrence of a special cause is a signal for us to check the process. The list of assignable causes may involve:

❑ Machine tool worn
❑ Lack of training
❑ Mistake
❑ Operator error
❑ Breakdown (of anything)
❑ Bad material

Now that we understand the nature of a special cause and how important it is to control these causes for overall process quality control, we can move to reviewing the last of the seven tools. The control chart actually develops the idea of controlling the process onto a new level where we want to prevent and predict potential problems and scrap long before they are ever produced. In doing control charts, it is important to understand that we can use them only when the control limits we set up for our process are well within the acceptable tolerance level for this measurement. In other words, when our process is initially pretty well controlled and the mechanisms and tools we use are relevant. It is also important to remember all through the process of developing the control chart that we are looking at the process during a time when it is actually under control and not producing defects. In order to do this, we have to start with a 100 percent sample of a lot of parts in order to determine that the lot is 100 percent good. When this is done, we take a number of samples from the "good" lot. Twenty to twenty-five samples of four or five parts each that are randomly selected will generally be adequate. We then measure each of the parts selected. For each sample, then calculate the average (X) and the difference between the highest and lowest value (R) of the measurement. This is the range. After this, we can calculate the average of the samples' averages (X bar) and average of the samples' ranges of values (R bar).

In order to calculate upper and lower control limits (UCL and LCL) for the chart that we are going to use to control our process, we will need to determine the standard deviation and set the upper and lower control limits at the points plus and minus three standard deviations. We could calculate the standard deviation but quality assurance engineers seldom, if ever, do this. Instead they use standard formulas and tables that can be found in most quality manuals.

After calculating the UCL and LCL, the next step is to build up the two parts of the control chart, one for average (X), the X bar chart, and the variance (R), the R chart of the measurement that is being controlled as it is shown in Figure 9-9.

After the upper and lower control levels are set up on the charts, you start taking samples from a normal production lot of parts you want to control. Of course it is important to remember to take the samples on a random basis. Measure the measurements you are viewing, calculate the average and the range of values for each sample, and plot it on the chart. Generally, as long as the points are within the UCL and LCL you may be confident that your process is working well and no special causes are influencing it. However, there are a number of other ways of looking at data that show quality control people that there is some tendency in the process that may represent the need to be further explored (see Figure 9-10).

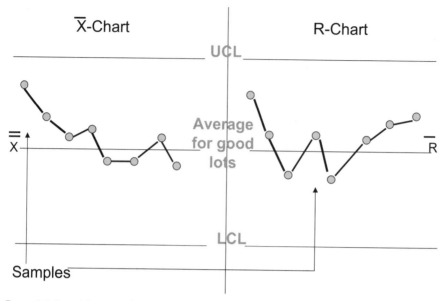

FIGURE 9-9: SEVEN TOOLS FOR QUALITY MANAGEMENT. CONTROL CHARTS: BUILDING A CONTROL CHART

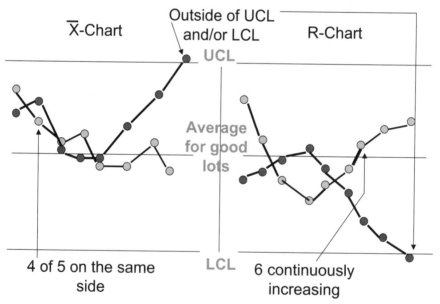

FIGURE 9-10: SEVEN TOOLS FOR QUALITY MANAGEMENT. CONTROL CHARTS: SOME PATTERNS INDICATING NONSTABLE PROCESS

The last thing that needs to be said about the control chart is that although it looks very production-oriented, it can not only be used for production processes, but can also be applied to some of the management processes and thus becomes an important tool for managing projects as well. Of course, as we have already said, we can apply this technique to the process only in cases where the process is initially clearly described and well controlled and where the instruments used are relevant and well developed; in other words, from the management processes we need to choose those with the least uncertainty and best developed mechanisms, like the earned value reporting or estimating system.

To conclude the observation of the tools, it is important to once again point out that although these tools seem strongly mathematical and statistically based, we are using them primarily with the aim of centering our team on some problems and determining some zones for our special managerial attention as project managers. In other words, we use these tools as management tools, not as tools of statistical analysis. That's why in real projects we need to pay more attention to the actual application of the tools for working with people and less attention to the scientific background.

10

Earned Value Reporting

What is an earned value report?

An earned value report is the preferred method for measuring progress in projects. It has the advantage of showing on one piece of paper the pertinent performance criteria for a project. From the earned value report the time-phased, planned expenditures for the project can be seen along with the actual cost of the project work that was accomplished and the amount of work that was actually completed. From this report the cost variance and schedule variance can be calculated.

Tell me more . . .

There are several factors in the earned value report that we must know in order to use it effectively. These factors are the budgeted cost of work scheduled (BCWS), the budgeted cost of work performed (BCWP), and the actual cost of work performed (ACWP). These three elements form the basis for the earned value reporting system.

PMI has seen fit to change this almost universally accepted alphabet soup. It remains to be seen whether PMI will be able to persuade the entire project management community to make the change or whether PMI will have to change back to the more widely accepted way of calling things. There are certainly going to be some difficulties since most managers use PV to mean present value and EV to mean expected value. We shall see. In the year 2000 version of the *Guide to the Project Management Body of Knowledge* (PMBOK), PMI refers to these as follows:

budgeted cost of work scheduled (BCWS) = planned value (PV)
actual cost of work performed (ACWP) = actual cost (AC)
budgeted cost of work performed (BCWP) = earned value (EV)

We will keep the traditional terms, which are still commonly accepted.

The first one of these factors is the BCWS or PV. This stands for the budgeted cost of work scheduled or the planned value. Once you catch on, you will say that it is just what it says it is. It is a plot of the budgeted cost of the project activities on a cumulative basis over a horizontal axis of time. All project tasks have a task cost that was derived from the estimated cost of each activity and a schedule that says when the activity will take place. The BCWS is simply a plot of these values according to when in time the expenditures are expected to take place. So, this is pretty simple to see, as it is just the project plan plotted out in terms of dollars of budget showing when those dollars are expected to be spent.

This is a method of showing the project plan in an easy-to-see way on a single piece of paper. By showing it in a cumulative way we can see the total expenditures to date for the project as well as the total cost of the project all on the same piece of paper. Notice in Figure 10-1 that the shape of the curve is similar to the letter *S*. Nearly all of the planned value curves for projects will have this shape because projects generally start out spending money slowly and then increase the rate of expendi-

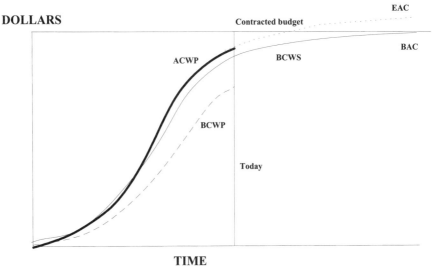

FIGURE 10-1: EARNED VALUE REPORTS

ture, reach a peak where money is being expended at its greatest rate, and then reduce the expenditure rate until the project is ended.

Sometimes in very large projects there is a problem with representing the project plan and the other earned value factors on a cumulative basis. When the project budget is very large, the vertical scale of the report is so small that minor but important variations cannot be seen well. In this situation a variance reporting method can be used.

To plot the earned values on a variance chart as shown in Figure 10-2, we simply plot a horizontal line and label it zero. Now, instead of plotting the actual values of the BCWS, BCWP, and ACWP we plot the differences between the BCWS and the other two earned value reporting factors. When we do this, the vertical scale that we need is greatly reduced in size since we are concerned only with plotting the difference between the earned value factors and not the entire budget of the project.

The next one, the ACWP or AC, is pretty simple too. This stands for the actual cost of work performed. Like the BCWS it is a plot over time of expenditures. This time, instead of plotting the project's planned expenditures we are plotting the project's real expenditures over time. At the end of each reporting period, we take the total amount of money that was spent on the project during that period and plot it as an addition to the total amount of money that had been spent as of the last reporting period.

It is important that every expenditure that is made on the project be collected and be collected in a timely way. The timing of the collection of the actual cost of work performed must match the anticipated timing of the expenditures that were planned and plotted as the BCWS. This is terribly important since, if expenditures are collected early or late in the project in relation to the project plan, the earned value report will show a positive or negative variance when there may really be none.

The ACWP plot is a cumulative plot as well. If the project expenditures are actually what they were planned to be, then the ACWP and the BCWS lines will plot one on top of the other. If the lines do not coincide, there is something different from the plan taking place in the project. We

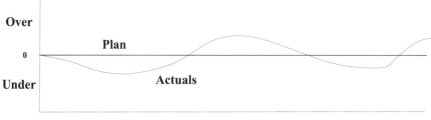

FIGURE 10-2: CUMULATIVE VARIANCE REPORTS

are either spending too much or too fast or we are not spending enough or fast enough to meet our plan.

The next factor is the BCWP or EV. This is the only one that is a little tricky. BCWP stands for the budgeted cost of work performed. It is sometimes called the earned value as well. This is where we get the name of the earned value report. Like the BCWS and the ACWP, the BCWP is a plot of money over time. If you recall, we said earlier that each of the project tasks has a budget and schedule associated with it. The BCWP is a plot of the work that was actually accomplished. If we complete a task that had a budget of $1,000, then the BCWP for that task when it is completed is $1,000. We plot this on a cumulative basis as well. It does not matter whether we spend $1,000 or $2,000 or any other amount to accomplish this task, we earn and plot only the budgeted amount in the BCWP.

Like the ACWP, the BCWP should plot right on top of the BCWS line. If the plot of the BCWP is above or below the BCWS line, it means that the number of tasks that are being completed is greater than or less than the plan. This tells us that we are ahead of or behind schedule. If we have done all of the tasks that were supposed to be done at this point in time, the cumulative value of the BCWP will be precisely equal to the BCWS.

When we put all three of these plots together, we have the earned value report. The plots should plot right on top of one another if the project is being done on time and in accord with the budgeted amount that was in the project plan.

Example. Suppose a project is in progress and as of today the planned expenditures for the project were to have been $500,000. Suppose also that there were five tasks and the tasks had budgets of $30,000, $100,000, $250,000, $100,000, and $20,000, respectively. The actual cost of each of the tasks that were worked on was $11,000, $120,000, $230,000, $105,000, and $20,000. Tasks 1, 2, 3, and 4 are complete.

What are the BCWS, ACWP, and BCWP (PV, AC, and EV)?
BCWS is $500,000.
ACWP is $486,000.
BCWP is $480,000.

From these figures we can see that the accomplishments of the project as of today are somewhat less than what was planned for. This is the difference between the earned value and the planned value to date. The planned value is the BCWS and the earned value is the BCWP. This means that we are $20,000 behind schedule.

We can also see that the actual cost is $14,000 less than the planned expenditures to date. This means that we are somewhat under budget. Unfortunately we are $14,000 under budget but also $20,000 behind schedule. If we add the $20,000 of work that should have been completed but was not, we find ourselves projecting a $6,000 over budget condition. It could be that things are actually worse than they appear at first glance. If the performance to date continues, the amount over budget will probably be even higher at the end of the project. This is usually considered a bad situation.

What is the budget at completion?

The budget at completion (BAC) is the total operating budget allocated for the project. In the earned value reporting system, the BAC is a point that is at the end of the BCWS or PV line on the chart (see Figure 10-3). Since the BCWS line is a plot of the budget for each task in the project over time, the point at the end of the line is over the point in time when the project is scheduled to be complete and the point on the vertical axis corresponding to the end of the line is the total project budget.

Note that the BAC does not include the allowance for the contingency budget and the management reserve. As the contingency and

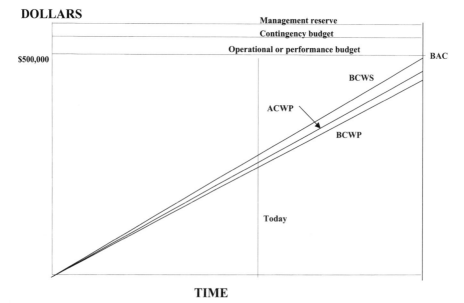

FIGURE 10-3: EARNED VALUE REPORT

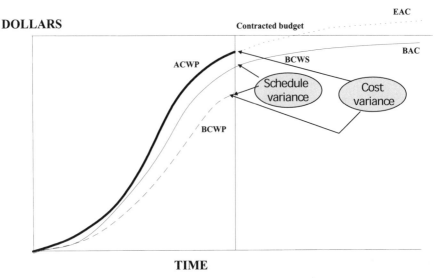

FIGURE 10-4: EARNED VALUE REPORT

management reserves are used, they will be removed from the reserves and added to the operating budget as needed and approved.

What is cost variance?

Cost variance (CV) is the amount of money that was actually spent on a project or a part of a project compared to the amount of work that was actually accomplished. Cost variance is the budgeted cost of work performed minus the actual cost of work performed.

$$CV = BCWP - ACWP \text{ and } CV = EV - AC$$

Tell me more . . .

In the earned value reporting system for projects, we are concerned with knowing how our project is doing with respect to the amount of money being spent and the accomplishments being achieved. The measure for this comparison is the cost variance.

To compute the cost variance, we compare the work that was actually completed to the actual amount spent to accomplish it. This means that we will be comparing the budgeted cost of work performed, the BCWP, with the actual cost of work performed, the ACWP (see Figure 10-4).

People always have trouble remembering these things. They get them mixed up and end up having a positive variance when they are really having a negative variance. It is good to remember that bad variances are always negative and good variances are always positive. If we consider that completed project tasks have an actual cost that is less than what was planned for, we could say that this is a good variance and it should have a positive value. If, on the other hand, we have spent more to accomplish our tasks than the plan allowed for, we could say that this is a bad condition and our variance will be a negative number. Of course "good" and "bad" must be qualified. Just because we have a positive cost variance does not always mean something good. If our cost variance is positive and we have left out some of the required work it would not be such a good thing. A good rule of thumb is that any variances, whether positive or negative, should be investigated.

The cost variance is an important figure to the project manager and the other managers of the company because it is an indicator of how well the project is doing in terms of spending its budget. It can be used to predict or forecast how much money it will cost to finish the project.

Example: Suppose a project is in progress and that as of today the ACWP is $190,000, the BCWP is $210,000 and the BCWS is $200,000. What is the cost variance?

Cost variance is the difference between the work that was really accomplished, the BCWP, and the cost of doing the work, the ACWP.

$$CV = BCWP - ACWP$$
$$CV = \$210,000 - \$190,000 = \$20,000$$

What is schedule variance?

Schedule variance is the comparison of the amount of money that was planned to be spent on a project or part of a project to the amount of work that was actually accomplished.

Tell me more . . .

In the earned value reporting system for projects, we are concerned with knowing how our project is doing with respect to the actual work that was done, the BCWP, and the amount of work that was expected to be completed, the BCWS. The measure for this comparison is the schedule variance.

It may seem a bit odd that we would be measuring schedule variance in terms of dollars since most of us are used to hearing that the project is ahead or behind schedule by so many days or weeks or months. Measuring schedule variance in dollars is actually a more indicative way of showing this. If, as is often the case, we say that we are ahead of or behind schedule by three weeks, it might not be serious if there is only one person working part-time on one task over the three weeks. On the other hand, it might be quite serious if there are one hundred people working on twenty tasks and they are all behind three weeks. If a person's time is worth $1,000 per week, the earned value report's schedule variance for the first condition might say that the schedule variance is $1,500. The second condition would have a schedule variance of $300,000. This is quite a noticeable difference in two situations where the project is three weeks behind schedule. So, it really makes a lot of sense to consider project schedules as being ahead or behind in terms of dollars rather than weeks or months.

To compute the schedule variance, we compare the work that was actually completed to the work that was planned to be accomplished. This means that we will be comparing the budgeted cost of work performed, the BCWP or the EV to the budgeted cost of work scheduled, the BCWS or the PV.

$$SV = BCWP - BCWS$$
$$SV = EV - PV$$

As with the cost variance, people often have trouble remembering this calculation. They get them mixed up and end up having a positive variance when they are really having a negative variance. It is good to remember that bad variances are always negative and good variances are always positive. If we consider that completed project tasks are greater than what was planned, we could say that this is a good variance and it should have a positive value. If on the other hand we have accomplished fewer tasks than the plan allowed for, we could say that this is a bad condition and our variance will be a negative number.

The schedule variance is an important figure for the project manager and the other managers of the company because it is an indicator of how well the project is doing in terms of following the project schedule. It can be used to predict or forecast how much time it will take to finish the project.

Example: Suppose a project is in progress and that as of today the ACWP is $190,000, the BCWP is $210,000, and the BCWS is $200,000.

Schedule variance is the difference between the work that was really accomplished, the BCWP, and the planned work that was supposed to be accomplished, the BCWS.

$$SV = BCWP - BCWS$$
$$SV = \$210,000 - \$200,000 = \$10,000$$

What is the cost performance index?

The cost performance index or CPI is a measure of how well the project is doing in terms of spending the project budget. It is a comparison of the actual expenditures to the work that was accomplished. The index is a value that allows projects of different sizes to be compared.

Tell me more . . .

The cost performance index is like the cost variance discussed previously with one important difference. When we calculated the cost variance, the result was a figure in dollars. If the dollars were a negative number, the variance was considered bad, and if the dollars were positive, the variance was considered good. The problem with this method is that it is difficult to compare projects of different sizes to one another. It would be better to have a measure that gave the health of the project regardless of its size. For this purpose we will use indexes.

Instead of subtracting the actual cost of work performed from the budgeted cost of work performed as we did when we calculated the cost variance, we will divide the same two numbers.

$$CPI = BCWP / ACWP$$
$$CPI = EV / AC$$

We can see that if the project is following its plan, the amount of work accomplished and the amount of money spent to accomplish it are the same, and the resulting value will be one. So, an index of one means that the project is following its project plan.

If the actual cost is greater than what is being accomplished, the denominator in the fraction will be larger than the numerator, and the resulting value will be less than one. This is generally considered to be a bad condition. If the actual cost is less than what is being accomplished, the resulting number will be greater than one and this is considered to be good. Of course any deviation from the project plan is bad even if the deviation is considered favorable. We should investigate to determine why this condition exists.

Example: Two projects have their cost performance index calculated. Both projects are 10 percent over budget at the time of the calculation. Project One has a budget of $1,000,000, and Project Two has a budget of $10,000. These budget figures are the amounts that should have been spent as of today's date. We will assume that the project is on schedule at this point in time. What is the cost performance index for each?

Project One is over budget by 10 percent of its budget or $100,000.

Project Two is also over budget by 10 percent of its budget or $1,000.

$$CPI = BCWP / ACWP$$

The BCWP is $1,000,000 for Project One.

The ACWP is $1,100,000 for Project One ($1,000,000 + $100,000).

The BCWP is $10,000 for Project Two.

The ACWP is $11,000 for Project Two ($10,000 + $1,000).

$$CV = BCWP - ACWP$$

The cost variance for Project One is $1,000,000 − $1,100,000 or −$100,000.

The cost variance for Project Two is $10,000 − $11,000 or −$1,000.

The CPI for Project One is $1,000,000 / $1,100,000 or 0.909.

The CPI for Project Two is $10,000 / $11,000 or 0.909.

Notice that the size of the project does not make any difference in the calculation of the index. Projects that are each behind 10 percent have the same value for their cost performance index. This makes assessing the health or sickness of projects of different sizes much easier.

What is the schedule performance index?

The schedule performance index is a measure of how well the project is doing in terms of following the project schedule. It is a comparison of the project tasks that were planned to be accomplished to the work that was really accomplished. The index is a value that allows projects of different sizes to be compared.

Tell me more . . .

The schedule performance index is like the schedule variance discussed previously with one important difference. When we calculated the schedule variance, the result was a figure in dollars. If the dollars were negative, the variance was considered bad, and if the dollars were positive, the variance was considered good. The problem with this method is that it is difficult to compare projects of different size to one another. It would be better to have a measure that gives the health of the project regardless of its size. For this purpose we will use indexes.

Instead of subtracting the budgeted cost of work scheduled from the budgeted cost of work performed, as we did when we calculated the schedule variance, we will divide the same two numbers.

$$SPI = BCWP / BCWS$$
$$SPI = EV / PV$$

We can see that if the project is following its plan, the amount of work accomplished and the amount of money spent to accomplish it are the same, and the resulting value will be one. So, an index of one means that the project is following its plan.

If the budgeted cost of work scheduled is greater than what is being accomplished, the denominator in the fraction will be larger than the numerator, and the resulting value will be less than one. This is a bad condition. If the budgeted cost of work scheduled is less than what is being accomplished, the resulting number will be greater than one and this is considered good.

Example: A project is two weeks behind schedule at the time of the calculation. The project has fifteen people working full-time. Assume that each person costs $1,000 per week. BCWS at this point in the project is $500,000. What is the schedule performance index?

The project is two weeks behind schedule and there are fifteen people working full-time on the project. This results in being behind schedule by thirty person-weeks or $30,000.

$$SPI = BCWP / BCWS$$

The BCWP is $500,000 − $30,000 = $470,000.
The BCWS is $500,000.

$$SV = BCWP − BCWS = −\$30,000$$
$$SPI = BCWP / BCWS = \$470,000 / \$500,000 = 0.940$$

Notice that a smaller project such as one that had a BCWS of $50,000 and a BCWP of $47,000 would also have a schedule performance index of 0.940. Again, this helps the project manager who is managing different parts of a project in which the sizes of the parts are different. The schedule performance index, like the cost performance index, indicates the health of the project regardless of its size.

What is the estimate at completion?

The estimate at completion, frequently shown as the EAC, is the forecast value of the project when the project is complete. It should be noted that the EAC can be calculated in a number of different ways and is only an indicator of what the project's cost will be at the end of the project.

Tell me more . . .

The estimate at completion is a value that can get project managers in trouble. In its most commonly used form it is the budget at completion divided by the cost performance index.

$$\text{EAC} = \text{BAC} / \text{CPI or EAC} = (\text{BAC} \times \text{ACWP}) / \text{BCWP}$$

This is a rather pessimistic estimate of the amount of money that will be spent at project completion. It says that the things that have gone wrong in the project until now will continue to go wrong, and we will not learn how to improve them between now and the end of the project. There are many reasons why this is true. There could be bias in our estimates. If the early items in the project were underestimated, it is likely that the later items in the project will be underestimated as well. If there is a chronic problem that has been evident in the early part of the project and the same people and equipment will be used on the later project activities, then the EAC will probably be accurate by this method. On the other hand, if different estimators and team members or different pieces of equipment are being used later in the project, the EAC may not indicate the project's true estimated cost at the end.

Unfortunately, as we will see, much of the research that has been done in this area indicates that projects that are over budget when they are 25 percent complete are very likely to finish over budget. Not only that, but these projects are likely to finish with a worse cost performance index than they had when they were 25 percent complete.

Are there other ways of calculating the EAC?

Yes there are, but they are not used as widely as the calculation described above, EAC = BAC / CPI.

Tell me more . . .

Taking the actual cost of work performed and adding it to the remaining work to be done can describe a somewhat more optimistic view of the EAC. This says that the project's estimate at completion will be the sum of the remaining work to be done at the originally estimated budgets for that work plus the actual accumulated cost of the work already completed. The actual cost of the work already completed is nothing more than the ACWP, and the cost of the remaining work to be done, based on original estimates, is just the difference between the budget at completion and the work that is already completed.

$$EAC = ACWP + (BAC - BCWP)$$

Of course, the most optimistic calculation of the EAC is the one that is usually imposed on project managers. It says that in spite of the problems that have occurred on this project to date, the project is not only going to complete all the remaining tasks according to the original plans and estimates but is going to recover the budget overruns already spent. The calculation of EAC is quite simple.

$$EAC = BAC$$

While it may seem pessimistic to calculate the EAC by dividing the BAC by the CPI, it turns out that there have been a number of studies that have been done in this area.

Quentin Fleming states: "The cumulative CPI is a particularly reliable index to watch because it has been proven to be an accurate and reliable forecasting device. The cumulative CPI has been shown to be stable from as early as 15 to 20 percent in the project's percentage complete point."[1]

From David Christensen: "Researchers found that the cumulative CPI does not change by more than ten percent once a contract is twenty percent complete; in most cases, the cumulative CPI only worsens as a contract proceeds to completion."[2]

What this is telling us is that the project managers who report that although bad things have happened early in the project, they expect to recover and finish the project within the originally planned budget are not very realistic. Unless they have good reason to defend this position, it should be accepted very reluctantly. The more probable outcome of the project is that the CPI will remain the same or get worse as the project progresses.

It is even rational to think this way. If a project cannot follow the project plan early in the project when the tasks planned were relatively close to the time the planning was done, then how likely is it that the tasks that were planned further in the future will have been estimated more accurately?

What is the to complete cost performance index?

The to complete cost performance index, TCCPI, tells us the required cost performance that is necessary to complete the project for the original budget based on the performance of the project as of today.

Tell me more . . .

The to complete cost performance index is a seldom-used indicator, and there are some difficulties in its use. The TCCPI is calculated by dividing the work remaining by the money remaining in the budget to do it. The remaining work in a project is simply the difference between the work already accomplished, the BCWP, and the total work of the project, the BAC. You will recall that when the project is completed, the BCWP must exactly equal the BAC. Mathematically it is impossible for this not to happen since the BAC is equal to the sum of the BCWP and is also equal to the sum of the BCWS. The remaining budget for the project is simply the difference between the total budget for the project, again the BAC, and the amount of money that has been spent to date, the ACWP.

$$TCCPI = (BAC - BCWP) / (BAC - ACWP)$$

It can be seen that as a project's cost performance index moves below one, the TCCPI will increase and become greater than 1. Although called an "index," this is not really accurate since all indexes indicate something bad when they fall below one and this index indicates something bad when it is greater than one.

The TCCPI gives us a rough estimate of the performance that is required for the remaining portion of the project in order for the project to be completed for the original budget. A TCCPI of 1.33 indicates that the project team must perform with a CPI of 1.33 from now until the project is completed in order for the project to be completed at the original budget.

There is a mathematical difficulty with this term as well. If a project is over budget toward the end of the project, it is possible for the BAC and the ACWP to be equal. This produces a division by zero and a point of discontinuity.

Under normal conditions it results in a value that indicates the required performance that the project must have from now until the end of the project.

Example: Suppose a project is somewhere near 50 percent complete:

$$BCWS = \$100,000$$
$$BCWP = \$95,000$$
$$ACWP = \$97,000$$
$$BAC = \$200,000$$
$$CV = BCWP - ACWP$$
$$CV = \$-2,000$$

What is the TCCPI?

$$TCCPI = (BAC - BCWP) / (BAC - ACWP)$$
$$TCCPI = (200,000 - 95,000) / (200,000 - 97,000)$$
$$TCCPI = 1.02$$

In this example the project would be required to do all of the remaining work at a 2 percent higher cost performance than was originally planned. This may be particularly difficult since the cost performance index to date is only 98 percent. We will be asking the project team to improve their cost performance by some 4 percent.

Notice that if the cost variance remains the same as the end of the project approaches, the TCCPI increases rapidly. Suppose we have the following when the project is approximately 95 percent complete:

$$BCWS = \$195,000$$
$$BCWP = \$190,000$$
$$ACWP = \$192,000$$
$$BAC = \$200,000$$
$$CV = BCWP - ACWP$$
$$CV = -\$2,000$$

What is the TCCPI?

$$TCCPI = (BAC - BCWP) / (BAC - ACWP)$$
$$TCCPI = (200,000 - 190,000) / (200,000 - 192,000)$$
$$TCCPI = 1.25$$

As we approach the end of the project, the cost variance has not changed, but the TCCPI has changed from 1.02 to 1.25. This is an indicator that the cost variance will be much more difficult to recover now than it was earlier in the project.

Is there a similar measure to the TCCPI for schedules?

Yes, there is a calculation called the to complete schedule performance index, the TCSPI. It is similar to the TCCPI except that it calculates a required schedule performance index that will be necessary to meet the project schedule. This measure is rarely used. It is included here for completeness. It has the same problems as the TCCPI and is even more abstract and difficult for people to understand.

Tell me more . . .

The calculation for the TCSPI is done by dividing the work remaining by the remaining schedule.

$$TCSPI = (BAC - BCWP) / (BAC - BCWS)$$

It can be seen that as a project's schedule performance index moves below one, the TCSPI will increase and become greater than one. Although called an "index," this is not really accurate since all indexes indicate something bad when they fall below one and this index indicates something bad when it is greater than one.

There is a mathematical difficulty with this term as well. If a project is over budget toward the end, it is possible for the BAC and the BCWS to be equal. This produces a division by zero and a point of discontinuity.

Under normal conditions it results in a value that indicates the required performance that the project must have from now until the end of the project.

Example: Suppose a project is somewhere near 50 percent complete:

$$BCWS = \$100,000$$
$$BCWP = \$95,000$$
$$ACWP = \$97,000$$
$$BAC = \$200,000$$
$$SV = BCWP - BCWS$$
$$SV = -\$5,000$$

What is the TCSPI?

$$TCSPI = (BAC - BCWP) / (BAC - BCWS)$$
$$TCSPI = (200,000 - 95,000) / (200,000 - 100,000)$$
$$TCSPI = 1.05$$

Notice that if the schedule variance remains the same as the end of the project approaches, the TCSPI increases rapidly. Suppose we have the following when the project is approximately 95 percent complete:

$$BCWS = \$195,000$$
$$BCWP = \$190,000$$
$$ACWP = \$192,000$$
$$BAC = \$200,000$$
$$SV = BCWP - BCWS$$
$$SV = -\$5,000$$

What is the TCSPI?

$$TCSPI = (BAC - BCWP) / (BAC - BCWS)$$
$$TCSPI = (200,000 - 190,000) / (200,000 - 195,000)$$
$$TCSPI = 2.00$$

As we approach the end of the project, the schedule variance has not changed, but the TCSPI has changed from 1.05 to 2.00. This means that the work that must be accomplished from now to the end of the project must take place at a rate that is twice as fast as was originally planned.

What is the estimate to completion?

The estimate to completion or the ETC is an estimate of the additional money that will be necessary to complete the project. It is calculated from the estimate at completion that we discussed previously.

$$ETC = EAC - ACWP$$

Can you get into trouble with estimates at completion? You bet you can. As we have seen in the discussion of the EAC, there are many ways that this estimate can be made. The most common form is the budget at completion divided by the cost performance index. This is only a rough estimate of what the project will cost when it is completed.

Tell me more . . .

Using the estimate at completion predicts that the project will overrun or underrun its budget at the end of the project. While it is a good thing to keep the stakeholders and the managers of your company informed that projects are in trouble, it is a weak support for asking that the project be given additional budget. A good project manager who wants to keep his job will take the EAC and use it as additional supporting information to show that the project budget was originally over- or understated. In addition to the EAC, the project manager should have much supporting information as to why the project is in the condition that it is in.

What is the percent complete?

Percent complete is a simple calculation. It is simply the amount of work that has been completed divided by the budget at completion.

$$\% \text{ complete } = \text{ BCWP } / \text{ BAC}$$

Notice that the percent complete can never be greater than 100. This is because the BAC is the sum of the budget in the project. The individual values of the budgets in each of the project's activities, the BCWS, are the same as the individual BCWP for each activity. Since the only difference between the BCWS and The BCWP for an activity is whether or not the activity has been completed, at the end of the project the sum of all of the budgets must equal the sum of all the BCWP. If an activity has not claimed its BCWP, the project is not yet completed. As soon as all of the activities in the project have claimed their BCWP, the project is said to be completed.

What is the percent spent?

Percent spent is another simple calculation. It is the amount of the budget that has been spent. It is calculated by dividing the actual cost of work performed by the budget at completion.

$$\% \text{ spent } = \text{ ACWP } / \text{ BAC}$$

Notes

1. Quentin Fleming and Joel Koppelman, *Earned Value Project Management* (Newtown Square, Pa.: Project Management Institute, 1996), p. 106.
2. Ibid.

11

Communications

What is communications?

Communications is the art of transmitting an idea from the mind of one person to the mind of another, with understanding. *Understanding* is the key word.

A classical communications model, shown in Figure 11-1, consists of a sender who is developing, coding, and transferring information through certain message channels to a receiver. When the receiver is reached, the message is decoded, filtered, and then studied. The receiver usually sends his feedback to the sender through a feedback channel. The overall model is called the loop of understanding.

Tell me more . . .

Good communications skills are considered to be the most important ability the project manager must have in order to manage projects successfully. In a well-planned project the major responsibilities of the project manager past the planning phase involve providing efficient communications and informing the project stakeholders of the progress achieved and thus coordinating the team effort with maximum success. It is therefore very important that the project manager have a well-planned structure of internal project communications as well as a good

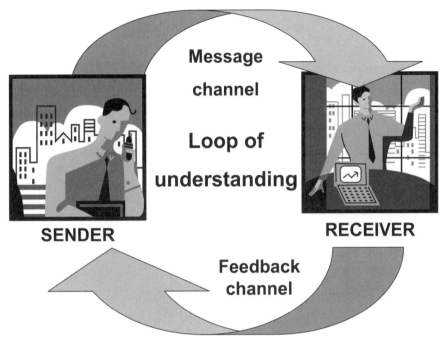

FIGURE 11-1: CLASSICAL COMMUNICATION MODEL

knowledge and the ability to use the most efficient communications approaches.

The major functions of the project manager in building the communications infrastructure of her project involve activities related to planning communications, distributing information, reporting progress, and administrative closeout. Communications planning involves a thorough analysis of the project stakeholders and their needs as well as knowledge of the communication technologies that are gong to be used in the project. The organizational structure and the process of organizational planning for the project will determine some major communication requirements.

Information distribution is a process that involves the development of systems for gathering and distributing information and the major communication skills that we are going to review in the rest of this chapter, which include:

- ❑ The ability to transfer information correctly and provide a clear understanding of the message transferred, which involves good listening and talking skills

- ❑ The understanding of different types of communications (written, oral, formal, informal, etc.) and knowing when to use which

❏ Presentation skills and meeting management techniques
❏ Knowledge and utilization of the personality types present in-side and outside of your project team and the ability to correct your approach according to personality type

What are the major types of communications?

Communications between persons are carried out verbally and non-verbally. Verbal communications are in the form of oral and written messages. Oral communications can be carried out through dialogues, meetings, negotiations, presentations, or telephone conversations where the main part of the information is transmitted through vocal signals. Written communications can be realized through documents in the form of letters, instructions and orders, and regulations and statutes when one person transfers signals to another person in written form.

Tell me more . . .

Nonverbal communications occur through body language and the mod-ulation and coloring of speech. Body language is a main component of nonverbal communications influencing the other participant in the com-munication process. It includes dress, gestures, pose, facial expression, eye contact, and even the space between the people who are communi-cating.

Examples of the most known conscious body signs include:

❏ Clenched fist in front of someone's face means threat.
❏ A finger put up to someone's mouth means: "Keep silent."
❏ An open hand put to an ear means: "Speak up, I can't hear you."
❏ A raised hand or finger means a person wants to say something, etc.

The examples of unconscious body expressions may include:

❏ Enlarged eye pupils in the case of increased interest.
❏ Lifted shoulders in the case of tension.
❏ Mouth corners dropped in the case of person who is tired, un-happy, or angry.
❏ A hand closing the nose and lips if the person is uncertain.
❏ A head bent to the side in the case of a listener being interested, etc.

The position of the shoulders and the head can give lots of information about whether a person is opened or closed, in control of the situation or not, tensed or relaxed. Normally a person lifts the shoulders when he or she is tense and drops them when relaxed. The head dropped and shoulders lifted may also mean a feeling of losing, dissatisfaction, fear, uncertainty.

If you need to make a presentation in front of a group of people, you can predict how the audience feels about you by watching the pose of the shoulders and heads of people; the more tense and aggressive the audience is, the more lifted shoulders and dropped heads and month corners there will be.

Head lifted and shoulders dropped may mean openness, interest, orientation towards success, feeling in control.

The pose of the body is important for the analysis of how a person feels. You need to remember it may have one meaning or multiple meanings. When a person is saying what he thinks, his pose sends out single-meaning signs. If it is mostly erect, without much curve, the head and feet on the same line, this is a pose of a person controlling a situation, satisfied with what he is doing and having no hidden intentions.

A person who is trying to dictate and make people obey takes a pose that is somewhat leaning forward. It may also mean uncertainty when the person is not sure that he wants to do something.

When the body is bent back, it normally means resistance, defensive feelings, dissatisfaction, a willingness to have the least possible contact with the interlocutor. All of these are the single-meaning poses, but it is also important to remember the pose can have multiple meanings; a leaning forward and at the same time "looking from above" pose can mean the person is willing to dictate, but in reality feels his fault and wants to be excused for it.

It is important to understand, particularly for communications in a project environment, which can often involve representatives of different cultures, that body language can depend on a person's nationality. Different nationalities have different specifics and characteristics of body language. First of all, there is conscious body language. A person who wants to talk raises a hand or a finger, a person who wants other people to keep silent puts a finger to his lips, etc. However, there is also unconscious body language, which, if interpreted properly, gives much important information about people's intentions and attitude.

In order to understand body language correctly, it is not enough to look at one detail and come to a conclusion; body signs have to be considered integrally and correlated with the whole situation.

Important unconscious body language includes the position of the shoulders and the head, pose (position of a body), facial expressions including the position of the mouth, the eyebrows, and the eyes, and the size of the eye's pupils.

In order to reach harmony with your counterpart and increase the efficiency of communications, it is important to help him or her to open up. This can be done by imitating or mirroring the poses of a closed person and slowly making changes to the pose in order to encourage the other person to a higher level of openness. This technique not only helps you move the person into a more open state, but also helps you understand the person's attitudes, and it distracts your attention from your own problems or lack of confidence.

Communications are made much more efficient if the listener demonstrates an open, active, and polite listening style to the person communicating using body language.

Speech parameters form a second important component of verbal communications. A great percentage of communicated information is transmitted this way. It includes intonation, voice timbre, speed of speech, choice of words, volume of the voice, pronunciation of words, etc.

The ways of providing communications are well known to most people and include listening, speaking, reading, and writing. Listening is a one-sided process when one person is talking and another perceives information without interrupting. Listening is the most important skill of interpersonal communications. The major types of listening include:

❑ Information gathering (neutral)
❑ Defensive listening (with a skeptical attitude toward the speaker)
❑ Aggressive listening (with an effort to "catch" the speaker)
❑ Polite listening (pausing between statements)
❑ Selective listening (hearing what one wants to hear)
❑ Active listening (understanding the listener and encouraging communications during the dialogue)

Speaking represents a dialogue between two persons and makes up a major part of communications during meetings, negotiations, and presentations. It is the second most important skill of interpersonal communications after listening.

Reading is the process of perceiving written information. It is especially important for people who are intellectual types who prefer formal logic to a more emotional perception of the world.

Writing, which has played an important role in providing communications during the last thousand years, is losing its importance in the twenty-first century. By writing we mean actual written communication with handwriting or printing on paper. E-mail, which has emerged as a new communications technology, is actually a new kind of communication somewhere between written and verbal.

How can we increase accuracy in communications?

It is a well-known fact that 80 percent of a manager's time is spent communicating. It is a somewhat less-known fact that the normal efficiency of communicating is pretty low: right after the information is heard by a person, he can remember only 50 percent of it, and after a month the retention falls to 25 percent. Thus, it seems reasonable for a project manager, for whom communication skills make up one of the major tools for managing project results and stakeholders' expectations, to be able to increase the accuracy of communications and thus the efficiency of information transfer to the people involved with the project.

Tell me more . . .

There are a number of important considerations in increasing the accuracy of information transfer between two people. Some of these are listed briefly below:

❑ *Avoid negative evaluation.* In order to increase understanding, you have to avoid expressions that belittle the personality of a partner. If such evaluations are being used by your partner, it is reasonable to balance them with social etiquette and politeness.

❑ *Avoid ignoring what your partner is saying.* The efficiency of a dialogue is strongly decreased by statements resulting from your own thoughts or feelings that have little to do with the thoughts or feelings expressed by your partner.

❑ *Avoid inquiring too much.* Asking one question after another, clearly trying to find something out without explaining your goals, inhibits communication. It is also important to make a difference between open and closed questions. A very narrow targeted or closed question can strongly interfere with the thinking process of the person talking and is therefore a mistake on the part of the listener.

❑ *Try to minimize inserting observations in the course of a conversation.* Various types of observations like "let's get closer to the theme" can inhibit the speaker and therefore decrease the efficiency of communications.

❑ *Practice active listening.* It is good to accompany your partner's words by signs of understanding and perceiving information, such as "I see," "Indeed?" etc. When choosing the types of words to be said, it is important to consider the personality type and the mood of your partner so that you don't give the impression you are doubting what is being said.

❑ *Ask for clarification.* Asking a person who is speaking to repeat or clarify something that was not understood or that seems arguable might help increase your understanding of what was said.

❑ *Paraphrase.* It is useful to repeat what was said by your partner in a shorter form using your own words at certain times during the conversation.

❑ *Develop thoughts further.* A technique that can increase the efficiency of communications includes further developing what was said by your partner. Be careful to do this only within the logical framework set up by the person who is talking; otherwise it might be regarded as ignoring what is being said. In order to develop a thought of a partner, you can do several things:

> Add to what the partner is going to say but has not yet said without interrupting.
>
> Add the logical consequence of the words being said.
>
> Add your assumption of what your partner meant or what is underlying his words.

❑ *Describe your emotional state.* It is useful to tell a person about your emotional reaction to what had been said; this is especially efficient if combined with paraphrasing.

❑ *Periodically summarize what has been said.*

Summing up all the principles described above, we can understand that the major rules of listening to a person include the following:

❑ Pay respect to the person talking, valuing his wish to tell you something.

❑ Try to establish your sincerity at the beginning of the conversation.

❑ Look at the person who is talking.

❑ Try not to interrupt your communications partner.

❑ Don't draw conclusions in advance.

A significant factor in increasing efficiency of communications involves getting rid of aggressiveness toward your partner. For that, it is important to remember to:

❑ Try not to dominate during a conversation.

❑ Not give way to emotions.

❑ Not object to what is being said right away.

❑ Not put yourself into a defensive pose.

❑ Find a place for a pause in your conversation.

It is also important to get rid of passiveness. You can achieve this by:

❑ Not keeping complete silence.

❑ Holding in your thoughts and emotions only to a reasonable level.

❑ Not showing yourself to be "the most clever one."

❑ Not allowing your relaxation to transform into frivolity.

❑ Apologizing when you are tired.

What are the major barriers to communications?

When certain information is being transmitted to the receiver, it has to pass through a process of decoding and filtering. Only then can it be received and interpreted by the receiver. Unfortunately, there are a number of factors that create problems in the decoding and filtering process. These are known collectively as communication barriers.

A short list of problems that may negatively affect the decoding of a message transmitted includes past experience, intelligence, personality, expectations, language, culture, semantics, reputation, and situation.

There are many other factors. It is clear that we have to pay attention to breaking down the barriers in order to be sure the information is being transferred and perceived accurately.

Tell me more . . .

Among the communication barriers, we should first of all pay attention to individual ones. We mentioned some of them before, including different assumptions, emotions, semantics, cultural background, etc. Unfortunately, these barriers are not the only ones that we have to face in order to increase the efficiency of our communications. Organizational structure also puts its own restrictions on an open exchange of information and efficient communications. As we have already mentioned, communications are built in a very different manner in the three major types of organizations. The project organization could be regarded as best for efficient communications because there is a single authority and a single goal, and good horizontal linkages are developed among the members of the organization.

In a functional organization, the communications can be set pretty efficiently within one department because of the similarity in technical and educational backgrounds and goals and attitudes among the people in the department. However, the interdepartmental horizontal communications as well as vertical communications through a number of management levels can create a real problem in understanding. Investigations show that the information distributed at the top level of management of the company loses 80 percent of its content as it filters down to the worker.

A matrix organization is probably the most difficult environment for communications. Although the people participating in each project are united around the same major goals and objectives for this project, the differences in their professional and technical backgrounds often create problems in communicating. To that you may also add the difference in goals between "vertical" (functional) and "horizontal" (project) management, the fact that a number of projects involving the same people can be going on simultaneously, and the temporary position of people on the project, which sometimes does not allow enough time to set up good relationships, etc. All that emphasizes the fact that it is extremely important to a project manager to manage well both the interpersonal skills of improving communications efficiency and the skills needed for setting up an efficient communication infrastructure in the project (communications management plans, staffing plans, a responsibility-accountability matrix, organizational charts, etc).

What are the major personality types?

The knowledge of the personality types of the members of a group of people who are communicating plays an important role in providing efficient communications. Determining personality type is a widely used technique, and there are a number of classifications used. Needless to say, this technique becomes extremely important in an environment where many people of different cultural, technical, and educational backgrounds and different levels of authority have to work together in order to achieve a common result—which closely matches our definition of a project environment.

Tell me more . . .

One of the most popular classifications of personality types is called a Myers-Briggs classification; this approach has a serious scientific background and has been proved by many years of scientific investigations in Europe and North America.

The classification results in types based on different combinations of four preference scales characterizing how a person restores his energy

Energy recovery	**Extrovert**	**Introvert**
	Prefers to gain energy from outside (people, activities, etc.).	Prefers to gain energy from internal world (thoughts, emotions, impressions).
Information gathering	**Person of sensor type**	**Person of intuitive type**
	Prefers gaining information through five senses. Pays attention first to the real.	Prefers to gain information through "sixth sense" and pays attention to opportunities.
Decision making	**Person of thinking type**	**Person of feeling type**
	Makes decisions with "head" based on logic and objective considerations.	Makes decisions with "heart" based on personal beliefs and subjective values.
Lifestyle	**Person of decisive type**	**Person of perceptive type**
	Prefers well-ordered and planned lifestyle.	Prefers spontaneous and flexible lifestyle ignoring planning and order.

FIGURE 11-2: MYERS-BRIGGS' CHARACTERISTICS: SCALES OF PEOPLE'S PREFERENCES

level, gathers information, and makes decisions and what lifestyle a person prefers (see Figure 11-2).

The classification is based on four major assumptions:

1. Each person is unique.
2. There are common features in the behavior of different people.
3. None of the personality types can be considered to be "bad."
4. In life we see all types of prejudices.

If you have identified the personality type of your counterpart, you can build and adapt your suggestion based on this knowledge, so that it is perceived by the other person in the best possible way. This technique is not an absolute guarantee of success but it may give you an opportunity to reach it.

Mode indicator characterizes the ways of perceiving and transferring information and forms an important element of so-called neurolinguistic programming technology (NLP), which was developed in the United States in the late 1970s. This technology can be simply defined as a system of tools for understanding and changing people's behavior. It is based on the assumption that different people perceive, think, and remember information in different ways. These internal processes happen in three different modes related to three major spheres of sensory experience:

1. *Visual Mode.* External and internal information is perceived as complex visual images.
2. *Audible Mode.* Information is perceived as a complex of sounds.
3. *Kinesthetic Mode.* Information is perceived as a complex of sensations: taste, sense of smell, sense of touch, etc.

There are a number of mode indicators that can help you understand what mode type a certain person has. The first indicator considers the expressions a person is using:

Visual Expressions. You see? Wonderful! Look! It seems . . . etc.—for visual mode.

Audible Expressions. Listen! Logical, etc.—for audible mode.

Sensory Expressions. Don't you feel . . . touching, comfortable, etc.—for kinesthetic mode.

The second mode indicator, as seen in Figure 11-3, looks at eye signals that demonstrate the internal thinking of a partner. The field of vision of a partner in communications can be divided into nine zones, with the upper three zones corresponding to visual mode, the middle three zones corresponding to audible mode and the lower three zones to kinesthetic mode.

By knowing the mode of a person you are communicating with and by using the right approaches (words used to attract attention, hands, and eye positions, etc.) corresponding to a certain mode, you transmit

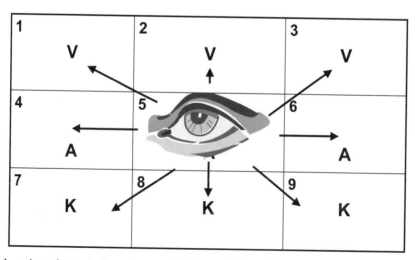

V – visual modality; A – audible modality; K – kinesthetic modality

FIGURE 11-3: SCHEME OF EYE SIGNALS

your wish and your readiness to have equal and open communications. This gets your counterpart into a more comfortable state, which increases the efficiency of your communications.

What are the major communication skills a project manager needs to know in order to manage projects successfully?

As we've talked for some time about various communication schemes, ways for improving communications, communication barriers, and personality types, we can summarize the major aspects of what a good project manager has to know in order to be efficient communicating with the team.

First of all, it is important to remember that communication skills are either given at birth or are the result of long, hard work. Probably they are the hardest of all the skills a good project manager has to be able to develop in him- or herself. Don't let yourself be misled by the fact that this part of our book does not include many statistical and other scientific-based tools and techniques. It is rather unfortunate that it does not since it makes the process of learning the needed skills much more difficult. In the area of psychology there are no set rules that work in any given situation, no formulas, and no strict instructions. All of them are dependent on the situation, the type of manager, the people involved with a project team, etc.

The primary skills of a project manager with regard to communications involve:

Talking and presentation skills. Knowing how to get your idea or a task through to a person or group of people in order for the information to be perceived most accurately.

Listening skills. Being able to gain information from a person even if the person does not really want to give you the information or has problems opening up. This skill has another very important aspect: giving your team members a chance to be adequately heard. You increase people's self-esteem and their willingness and ability to involve themselves fully with the project work.

The ability to choose the right communication channel. Since any project has many external and internal stakeholders, all of which need to be able to deliver different types of information in different ways, it is important to realize that you can plan and use various communication channels depending on the situation, the type of information transferred, the type of person receiving information, and the type of feedback you need. It is also good if you are able to use

Winners	Losers
The more winners work, the more time they have available.	Losers never have time to do something important.
Winners get deeply inside the problem.	Losers try to "work around" the problem but are always running against it.
Winners take responsibilities.	Losers give promises.
Winners know where to fight and where to step back.	Losers step back when they need to fight and fight when it does not make sense.
Winners feel strong enough to be friendly with other people.	Losers rarely feel friendly toward other people. They either feel their weaknesses or behave as small tyrants.
Winners can listen to others.	Losers do not listen, they wait when their turn to talk comes.
Winners respect people who are more able than they are and try to learn from them.	Losers do not recognize that other people can have abilities; losers always look for others' weaknesses.
Winners are convincing and explain.	Losers make excuses.
Winners feel responsibility not only for their part of the work but for the whole task.	Losers say: I am a small person, I do not matter.
Winners set up their own speed of work.	Losers have only two speeds: hysterical and apathetic.
Winners use time in order to improve themselves.	Losers waste time in order to avoid criticism.
Winners are not afraid to make mistakes when trying to reach a result.	Losers refuse to do anything. They are afraid to make mistakes or be criticized by others.
Winners concentrate on opportunities.	Losers concentrate on problems.
Winners look for answers.	Losers look for excuses.

TABLE 11-1

many of the informal channels existing in the organization in case you need them.

The ability to distinguish among different personality types and address them properly in various situations.

The ability to open up closed personalities and discipline the ones who behave too informally. In other words, you need to be able to manage people's behavior based on the knowledge of their personalities.

The ability to manage meetings. As lots of a manager's time is normally spent in meetings and many important project functions are carried out through meetings, it is very important that the project manager can manage meetings professionally and increase their efficiency by being able to set people's attention on the theme to be discussed and get the people who need to be involved to speak out.

In Chapter 6, "Human Resources Management," we discussed the fact that project managers often have to use informal types of power in order to manage people on their project team. This is an important reason for you to always remember that you are being watched by your people day and night, and it is your responsibility that the project team members retain the vision of the overall goals of the project and believe in its successful results even in times of major problems. It is therefore important that you show a special attitude that can distinguish a loser from a winner, as shown in Table 11-1 on the preceding page.

Even if you are NOT a winner, you have to make it look as if you are and lead your team with a certainty that they may lack from time to time.

To summarize, it is not necessary for you to be a good natural-born communicator. In some types of projects, especially internal ones such as organizational change, it is preferable to choose such a person for a project manager, but if you spend time and effort developing such skills in yourself, both using your own experience and insight and looking for it outside by observing other project managers, you can be successful.

INDEX

accelerated depreciation, 78, 80–82
acceptance costs, 209
acceptance of risk, 191–193, 194–195, 198
accountability, 150, 153
accounting equation, 72–75
  balance and, 74–75
  defined, 72–73
  illustration of use, 73–75
  importance of, 73–74
accounts
  asset, 73
  liability, 73
accounts payable, 74
accounts receivable, 74
active acceptance of risk, 195
active listening, 241–242
activity on arrow network diagrams, 83–85
activity on node network diagrams, 83, 85–86
actual cash flows, 65–69
actual cost of work performed (ACWP), 218, 220–221
Adams, J. Stacey, 147
advanced payments, 18
analogous estimating methods, 44–45
annual interest rate, 70
Apollo Project, 27
assembly lines, 58, 139
assets
  accounts, 73
  defined, 73
  depreciation of capital, 78–82

  weighted average cost of, 74–75
audible mode, 246
authoritative management type, 129
authority, 150
availability, in estimating process, 46
avoidance of risk, 191–193, 196–198

BAC (budget at completion), 63, 222–223
backward pass, 92–93
balanced matrix organization, 154, 160–161, 162–163
baselines
  cost, 10, 11, 60–62
  project, 10–11
  scope, 10, 11, 39–41, 60
  time, 10, 11, 60
BCWP (budgeted cost of work performed), 218, 221–222
BCWS (budgeted cost of work scheduled), 62–63, 218, 219–222
behavioral leadership, 131
behavioral role of team members, 140, 141–142
behavioral theory of leadership, 128
Berg, Cindy, 32
best-case scenario, 186
Blanchard, Kenneth, 134–135
body language, 238–240
bottom-up estimates, 44, 60–62
brainstorming technique, 179, 211
break-even point, 18–20, 21–22
budget
  contingency, 10, 63–64, 198, 201, 222–223

ABOUT THE AUTHORS

Michael Newell is a certified Project Management Professional (PMP) who has been managing projects for the past thirty-five years. In that time he has managed such diverse projects as those involving many manufacturing systems, electronics assembly, foundry operations, rubber molding, robotics, aerospace manufacturing, and automation of manufacturing process and control. More recently, Mike has been involved in the management of projects for developing and implementing computer systems.

Mike has been teaching project management professionally for the past fifteen years and has taught in many countries throughout the world. He has recently established a branch of his firm, PSM Consulting, in Moscow, Russia, to teach and consult in project management.

He is Vice President of Operations for PSM Consulting. He has authored several courses in project management. Mike's courses are approved by the Project Management Institute for recertification as a Project Management Professional and as part of the PMI Professional Development Program. PSM Consulting is a Charter Member of the Registered Education Providers of the Project Management Institute.

Marina Grashina is currently the manager of PSM Consulting, Moscow. Marina holds a PMP certification from the Project Management Institute and has extensive experience in managing international projects. She holds a masters degree in bio-chemistry from Moscow University.

Marina has been a manager for PSM Consulting Services for the past seven years. In this role she has managed many projects for the Canadian government in Moscow. These projects involve the training and education of Russian entrepreneurs in Canadian business practices and the development of small business in Russia. Marina has traveled extensively in Russia and the world working with developing business. She has presented several papers for the International Project Management Association and the Project Management Institute.

Marina has worked extensively in presenting and developing many courses in project management for Russian businesspeople in the areas of project management for both commercial and government projects. She has been the director of the Yeltzin Democracy Fellowship Program.

Marina also has a strong interest in traditional Russian culture and has successfully executed several grants in Russian cultural development and study.